LOGOLOUNGE 9

LOGOLOUNGE 9
2,000 INTERNATIONAL IDENTITIES BY LEADING DESIGNERS

BILL GARDNER AND EMILY POTTS

Cincinnati, Ohio
www.howdesign.com

 Published by HOW Books, an imprint of F+W, A Content + eCommerce Company, 10151 Carver Road, Suite 200, Cincinnati, Ohio 45242. (800) 289-0963. First edition.

For more excellent books and resources for designers, visit www.howdesign.com.

19 18 17 16 15 5 4 3 2 1

978-1-4403-4053-6

Distributed in Canada by Fraser Direct100 Armstrong Avenue
Georgetown, Ontario, Canada L7G 5S4
Tel: (905) 877-4411

Distributed in the U.K. and Europe by F&W Media International, LTD
Brunel House, Forde Close, Newton Abbot, TQ12 4PU, UK
Tel: (+44) 1626 323200, Fax: (+44) 1626 323319

Email: enquiries@fwmedia.com

Distributed in Australia by Capicorn Link
P.O. Box 704, Windsor, NSW 2756 Australia
Tel: (02) 4560-1600

Art Directed by Bridgid Agricola, Claudean Wheeler
Design: Brian Miller/Gardner Design, Michelle Thompson, Hanna Firestone
Production Coordinator: Lauren Osoba/Gardner Design, Greg Nock
Cover Image: Brian Miller/Gardner Design
Edited by Emily Potts, Amy Owen and Callie Budrick

CONTENTS

CASE STUDIES

COLLECTIONS

INTRODUCTION & JURORS

INTRODUCTION

Connecting with consumers is more than the holy grail of the craft: It's an imperative. Learning to tug the right heartstrings and subtly convey a concept in a simple iconic logo is perhaps the most challenging and rewarding feat for a designer. Logo designers have to know when to pull a great visual idea back from the edge just enough for the public to finish the thought—and seal their loyalty with an *a-ha* moment.

LogoLounge.com is the most comprehensive professional resource of logos from around the world, featuring 230,000 logos. This LogoLounge volume is a curated collection of more than two thousand freshly designed logos, selected by an international panel of renowned identity designers who reviewed more than twenty-five thousand logo submissions.

LogoLounge 9 is organized in twenty-one visual content categories to provide context, clarity and immediate inspiration. Logos within each category can be compared and contrasted, giving designers the opportunity to understand the critical nuances that define very different solutions to addressing a single audience.

Peeking behind the curtains at the backstory of dozens of exceptional logo designs allows a designer to better understand what does and doesn't work. Viewing the near-misses and the bull's-eye solutions confirms for even the most jaded professional that our process is never perfect. But the creative experience of others provides a rich foundation on which to bolster our own technique.

Every logo has a story, and in this edition of LogoLounge, we share some of the best with you. For instance, when designer Matt Stevens found that a Dunkin' Donuts' logo he had designed for an April Fools' Day parody was being used by an actual donut shop, he turned what could have been a bad situation into an opportunity. It turns out, the shop owner didn't know it was a copy, but after chatting for a bit, she asked Stevens if he would design her a new logo and mascot, and he did. It was a win-win.

When Tether was contacted to design the brand identity for a caffeinated chocolate start-up called Awake, they exchanged their services for equity in the company. Tether principal Stanley Hainsworth even appeared on Canada's *Dragons' Den* with the Awake founders to pitch the product to a panel of investors, which resulted in a bidding war. Not surprisingly, Awake is the top selling chocolate on university campuses, and its mascot, Nevil the owl, has his own Twitter following.

And then there are times when a logo isn't loved at all, at first. Such was the case with the logo and team name for El Paso's minor league baseball team, designed by Brandiose. When the name *Chihuahuas* was introduced, fans hated it. However, over time, they have embraced this fierce little icon wholeheartedly, and the franchise is breaking merchandising records. Sometimes a logo has to earn consumer loyalty. It isn't always a hit right off the bat.

Consumers don't live in a vacuum and neither will the exceptional designer. Through much research and trial and error, brand identity designers must learn the ins and outs of the products and services they are designing for in order to understand the intricacies and nuances that define it in its category. They also have to earn the trust and respect from their clients to push through the challenges. Logo design is an art form like no other because so much of a brand's personality has to be captured in a single iconic mark. Not an easy task. Good logo designers see what the public responds to—and better yet, they know why it works.

—Bill Gardner

JURORS

KENDRICK KIDD
SHEPHERD

Kendrick Kidd has been designing professionally for the past fifteen years. He is currently working as an associate creative director at Shepherd, an agency in Jacksonville, Florida, and he also owns a small design and screen-printing business that operates during his off time. His recent work focuses heavily on branding, packaging and illustration for craft breweries, action sports companies and editorial publications. Some of his clients include Nike, Billabong, REAL Skateboards, Modus Bearings, Bold City Brewery, *ESPN The Magazine* and *GQ*. Kidd's work has been featured in *Print* magazine, *Communication Arts*, *Los Logos*, *The Dieline* and *Grain Edit*.

ECOJET BY KARL DESIGN

I've never heard of EcoJet before, but at a glance the leaf-jet mark gave me a clear impression of their company. The idea is simple, and it communicates a lot in a quick and clever way. From the color choices to the subtle rounding of corners, the thought, design and mechanics of this logo are all lining up. Everything about this feels right.

SEBASTIAN PADILLA
ANAGRAMA

Sebastian Padilla was born in Monterrey, an industrial city in northeast Mexico. After studying graphic design in college and working at an agency, Padilla went out on his own doing freelance design projects. In 2009, he and two other partners (and later a third) formed the multidisciplinary agency Anagrama, which offers a wide range of services including graphic design, architectural and interior design, and software development. The studio's work has been widely recognized for its unique branding and build-out of boutique shops in and around Mexico City and Monterrey where Anagrama has studios, as well as an international cast of clients. Padilla travels and lectures extensively on branding and design, and Anagrama's work has been featured by several international publications including *Print*, *HOW*, *Etapes*, *Communication Arts* and many others.

REDFOX BY IVAN BOBROV

I chose this logo because of its quick iconic appeal, its colorful dynamic quality and its spotless execution. The quick read of the sleek red fox is appealing and the aesthetic is timeless.

TRACY SABIN
SABINGRAFIK

Tracy Sabin has been an illustrator for more than forty years, crafting over five hundred logos in that time. His skills include animation, package design, paper engineering and mosaic design for public spaces. He has illustrated a number of children's books, including the *New York Times* bestseller *Castle*. Sabin's work has been featured in *Graphis*, *Print*, *Communication Arts*, the Society of Illustrators and in books and articles about contemporary graphic design and illustration. His ebook *Pictorial Logos* examines the process of inventing the iconic part of a trademark, from early conceptual thinking and pencil explorations, to comprehensive workups and final realization.

OPTIMISTIC BEVERAGES BY HELMS WORKSHOP

I love it when a designer uses a cliché image in a logo design but portrays it in such a way that it becomes something new. The icon for Optimistic Beverages does this by rendering the "glass is half full" motif but floating the liquid (looks like beer in this case) in the upper half of the glass. What better way to represent an optimist's half full glass! Everything about this logo is working for me, from the simple, deadpan rendering of the glass and liquid, to the carefully matched weights of line work and typography, to the clever use of humor. It all works to make this a memorable logo.

PLANE GUARD BY JOHN FAIRLEY

A logo with a hidden message has always struck a cord with me—that moment of surprise when you notice that the FedEx logo contains an arrow or discover the hidden bear in the Toblerone logo. Designing a logo of this type subtly is no easy task, but it gives viewers a sense of ownership and a real connection with the brand when it's well executed. When I initially came across this design for Plane Guard, a company that clears snow from planes, I had that same moment of surprise. Initially, I saw only the snowflake, but upon realizing the design also cleverly displays a series of planes coming together to form the shape, it stuck with me as one of my favorite designs. It's clever, yet very simple and well executed.

IAN PAGET
LOGO GEEK

Ian Paget has worked as a graphic designer and illustrator since 2003. In his day job he works as creative director for an ecommerce agency, where he designs for both web and print for companies that have included Lucozade Sport, GlaxoSmithKline, Yakult and Kuehne + Nagel. He also runs Logo Geek, where he designs logos for small- to medium-sized businesses around the world. Paget a popular blogger and has a thriving social media following through Facebook and Twitter, sharing, reporting and discussing the latest logo design news, trends and resources with the design community.

Plane Guard by John Fairley

Ultimately a logo must be memorable and embody the spirit of the brand it represents in an efficient and precise way. The best logos often work at multiple levels, combining related ideas into new concepts and often revealing deeper meanings the more they are studied. The Plane Guard logo did all of these things and pulled it off effortlessly. At first look it appears to be a simple snowflake, simple and well executed. Upon further examination the concept is revealed of multiple planes all arranged to form this mark and to express the nature of the business it represents. This a-ha moment is what makes this logo unforgettable, and the bold and graphic execution makes it my "Judge's Choice."

MATT STEVENS DESIGN OFFICE OF MATT STEVENS

Matt Stevens is a designer and illustrator living and working in North Carolina. He has spent the majority of his career in small to midsized brand shops and agencies as a designer and creative director. In early 2012, he opened the Design Office of Matt Stevens to pursue his own clients and incorporate more illustration into his daily practice. He currently works on a mix of brand identity and illustration projects. Stevens's background in multiple disciplines helps him consider a client's problem from all sides and to produce work that is driven by strong ideas and that presents a unique point of view. Select clients include Nike, Evernote, *Esquire*, Facebook, Pinterest, Google, Asana, JJ's Red Hots, *New York* magazine, TBWA London, Leo Burnett, the Salvation Army, the WWE, *Money* magazine, Sony Music and *Wired*.

CHRISTOPHER SIMMONS MINE

Christopher Simmons is a Canadian-born, San Francisco-based designer, writer, design advocate and educator. As principal/creative director of the San Francisco design office MINE, Simmons designs and directs brand and communication design projects for clients ranging from Facebook and Microsoft to the Edible Schoolyard Project and Obama for America. His work has been exhibited internationally at institutions ranging from the Hiroshima City Museum of Contemporary Art to the Smithsonian Institution. Simmons is the author of four books and writes the hamburger/design blog *The Message Is Medium Rare*. From 2004 to 2006 he served as president of the San Francisco chapter of AIGA and founded San Francisco Design Week—prompting then mayor Gavin Newsom to issue an official proclamation declaring San Francisco to be a city where "Design Makes a Difference." He is currently a director on AIGA's national board.

The Color Condition by Steven Schroeder

This logo was untitled and didn't even indicate what company or product or category it was for. Absent this context it's difficult to say with any authority whether it is successful or even appropriate. But a logo's function isn't only to give us a symbolic entryway to an idea; logos connect with us on emotional, visceral and intellectual levels as well. This furry little creature is delightful. He is happy and lighthearted and generally brings me joy. It is so absurdly different from almost everything else we encounter that he stands out as unique and self-assured. It's hard to say whether or not it is even well crafted, but even craft is secondary here. I just want to stretch out my arms to accept its warm, shaggy hug.

ALINA WHEELER

Alina Wheeler works with global teams to achieve a competitive advantage for their brands. A brand consultant and coach, she describes her work as "strategic imagination." Her passion is brand identity, and she has had a lifelong fascination with how companies and individuals express who they are and what they stand for. Over her career, she has worked with large enterprises, entrepreneurial ventures and nonprofits. She is an AIGA Fellow, a former AIGA national board member and chapter president. Wheeler is the author of *Designing Brand Identity*, a leading global resource for the whole branding team—from the leaders to marketing and design.

FRED HUTCHINSON CANCER RESEARCH CENTER BY HORNALL ANDERSON

I believe that the symbol for the Fred Hutchinson Cancer Research Center will fuel recognition, amplify differentiation, and help build trust with its stakeholders. It triggers associations with science and research through a well-drawn translation of cells as if viewed through a microscope. The cells feel like they are moving in a positive direction, adding a feeling of optimism. The mark and its color palette strike an appropriate balance between friendly and academic, and the integration of the *H* is an important and distinctive element. This mark will be easy to apply consistently across digital, print and environmental channels—and will work well at different scales. It feels timeless and I believe it will serve this organization well.

EXTINCT FOR GALLO BY GLITSCHKA STUDIOS

I kept coming back to this logo. I love how the birds are illustrated. They have a nice vintage feel that's loose but also geometrical, like something you'd see on an old book cover. They fit together perfectly to create the hidden image of a wine glass, which takes the logo to another level. It's clever, interesting, has great balance and is well thought out. I'd buy the wine based solely on this logo.

MATT MCCRACKEN DOUBLENAUT

Matt McCracken began designing under the name Doublenaut in 2004 with his twin brother Andrew. The Toronto-based studio specializes in screen-printed posters and all forms of print design. Heavily influenced by midcentury modern design, their work features simple illustration, bold color schemes and strong typography. They have worked with a wide range of clients such as Bellwoods Brewery, Polaris Music Prize, Facebook, Jack Daniel's and Arts & Crafts Productions. Doublenaut's work has been featured in *The Globe and Mail*, *Communication Arts*, *Applied Arts*, and numerous publications from Gestalten.

CASE STUDIES & COLLECTIONS

DESIGN /// HORNALL ANDERSON

CLIENT /// FRED HUTCHINSON CANCER RESEARCH CENTER

CATEGORY /// INITIALS

The Fred Hutchinson Cancer Research Center in Seattle, Washington, is a world-renowned cancer research organization. Its scientists and researchers have developed life-changing breakthroughs like HPV vaccines and bone marrow transplants. However, much of this work is done with little fanfare. Most people don't understand the significance of what the center does and how its research potentially impacts the lives of people who have cancer.

Hornall Anderson was charged with rebranding the institution from top to bottom—not an easy task, considering the obstacles the center has faced. The new brand needed to resonate with "Hutch" employees, many of whom were wary of coming across as inauthentic, and it needed to clearly and quickly communicate the organization's role to potential donors. "The fight for federal research grants and private money is getting more competitive. Institutions are becoming much more sophisticated in communicating what they do. Over the years, Fred Hutch faced an increased challenge in getting the attention they needed," says Andy Kribbs, design director at Hornall Anderson.

"The Fred Hutch team is quite sophisticated and experienced, so we had really good conversations with them in the early stages to get a clear understanding of what the organization stood for and what they believed in," Kribbs notes. They then held a series of town hall meetings, inviting everyone on campus to come and participate in the brand discussion. "This effort couldn't just be plopped in the lap of all these researchers. They have to know where it came from and what it means," he says. "You can have the most beautiful and well intentioned mark, but it means nothing if you don't bring them along in the process."

The design team really got a sense of what goes on day-to-day at Fred Hutch by listening to the organization's members. They also got the

The original identity for the Fred Hutchinson Cancer Research Center lacked character and said nothing about the research center.

Andy Kribbs and his design team interviewed employees and hosted town hall events in order to develop the brand platform. Through this process it became clear that the logo needed to communicate that Fred Hutch does the scientific research and development that leads to cures. He says, "This opened up vast creative opportunities within scientific and research territories for us to explore."

> "They needed to clearly communicate what they do and their role in the fight against cancer externally and equally energize the institution itself."
> —Andy Kribbs

tagline, "Cures start here," from one of the employees during a town hall gathering. That line embodies the essence of Fred Hutch, and it created new meaning for the design team, taking them out of the competitive mentality to one of a supporter for an overall cause. Kribbs explains, "We rallied around, 'A win is a win for all' mentality. There was now a platform that really got us running to develop copy and visuals."

The logo design initially explored many visual territories using DNA and genetic codes as design cues. As it progressed, the team explored the idea of cells dividing. "Essentially a cancer researcher looks for something different—that moment of change. Cancer cells look different from regular cells, and that's what we were trying to get through in the logo design," Kribbs says.

Color was another major factor in the design. Blues and greens are dominant in the scientific world, and they are also subtle references to the Seattle landscape. Other color palettes were explored, including warm colors like reds and oranges, but Kribbs notes, "You start to see blood and other related imagery, and it feels too real."

The final logo and identity was really well received by employees, and Fred Hutch is experiencing a new level of exposure locally and nationally as banners roll out citywide and ads pop up in publications like *Wired*, *Forbes*, *The New Yorker*, and *Entrepreneur* magazines.

"The reception has been wonderful. Everyone was understandably a little nervous about how it would be received, but the Fred Hutch employees identify with the new brand identity and embrace it as their own," Kribbs says.

"We ultimately presented three marks that represented very different takes on research. Each had a compelling narrative linked directly to the strategy," Kribbs explains. "Having this conceptual foundation in place helps our clients talk about the logo beyond aesthetics and gives any nonvisual stakeholders information to respond to. The logo that became the front-runner appears as if you were observing a cell culture through a microscope. The dots and dashes can also read as data and a modern approach to research. Some also saw a globe, cueing the global impact that Fred Hutch has on the world."

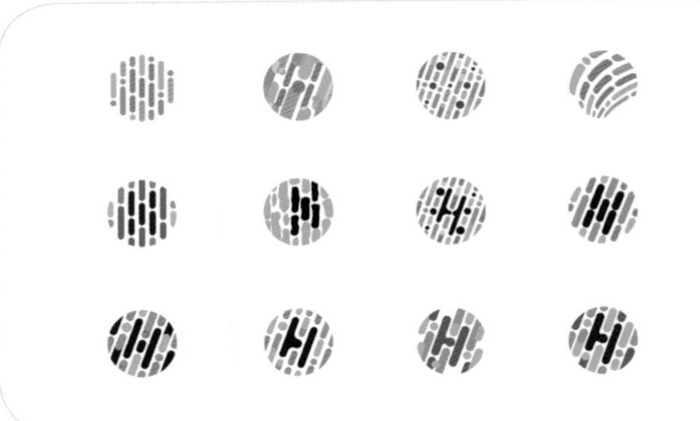

"For the next round, we tried to sharpen the visual language of the mark by refining details and exploring rendering techniques such as textures, realism and incorporating the *H* as a way to integrate *Hutch*. One of the researchers from our interviews had mentioned that looking for cancer is looking for a moment of change—when cells begin to behave differently than they should," Kribbs notes. "Since we had conducted lots of creative exploration already, this was the key that made it all click together. The joiner between the two stems of the H became the catalyst moment that ultimately brought the mark to its final state."

This sequence shows how the logo progressed from the initial concept to its final state.

Final logo design.

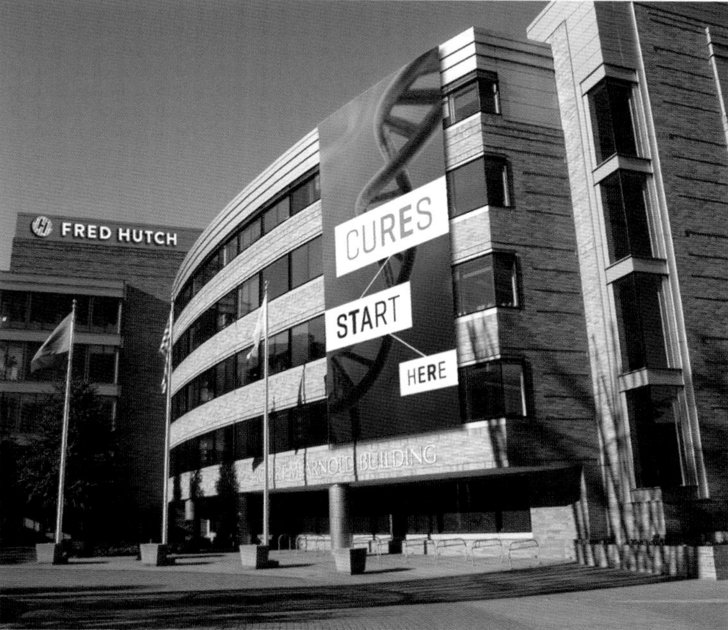

The Hutch logo is prominently displayed throughout the research center's campus on buildings, banners and wayfinding signage.

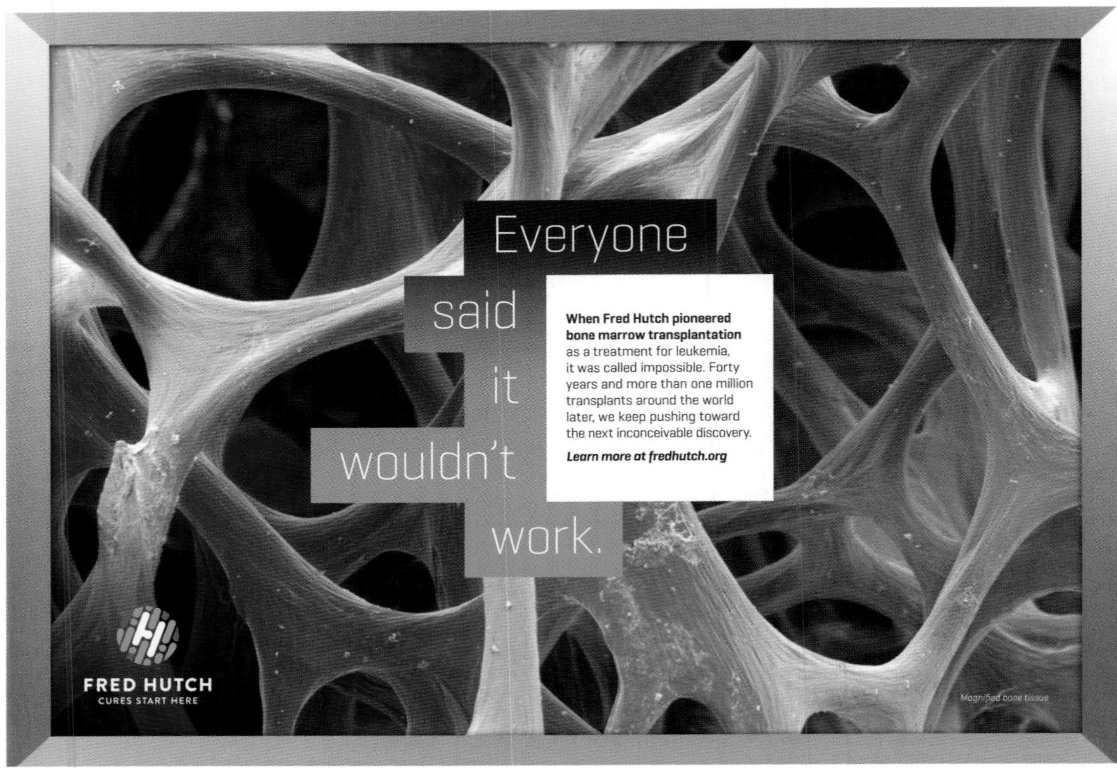

Everyone
said
it
wouldn't
work.
When Fred Hutch pioneered bone marrow transplantation as a treatment for leukemia, it was called impossible. Forty years and more than one million transplants around the world later, we keep pushing toward the next inconceivable discovery.
Learn more at fredhutch.org
FRED HUTCH
CURES START HERE
Magnified bone tissue

FRED HUTCH
CURES START HERE
Cancer ends here.
Once – and for all.
RAPIDRIDE
Until cancer is gone,
we'll keep going.
FRED HUTCH
CURES START HERE

The logo was displayed prominently throughout the Seattle area on billboards, buses and in advertisements. Consistent use of the brand colors and messaging tied the campaign together visually.

	A	B	C	D
1				
2				
3				
4			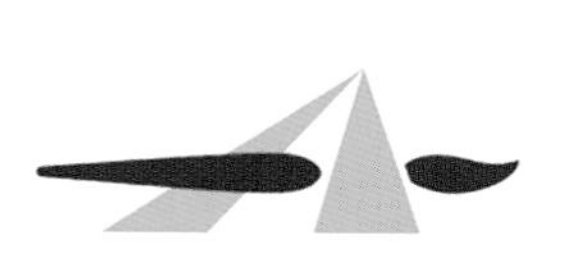	
5				

1C D C The russian pension administrator **1D** D Paul Tynes Design C Aperture
2A D Swanson Russell C FMC **2B** D PhD-mtl C Aubut & Fils **2C** D Dmitry Zelinskiy C Amulet tea **2D** D Kreativbuero Jonas Soeder C ARCA Records
3A D Hayes Image C Accuras **3B** D Double A Creative C Adam Anderson **3C** D Pavel Saksin C N/A **3D** D Dmitry Zelinskiy C N/A
4A D Brittany Phillips Design C Growthwise Group for Adexus **4B** D Independent graphic designer C Atmospheir **4C** D Just Creative Design C Artistic Highways **4D** D JonathanHowell.com C AD Destinations
5A D Barker C Metrô News **5B** D Lippincott C Allegion PLC **5C** D Alphabet Arm Design C Promoboxx **5D** D Design Sense C Advocaat Van Hecke

	A	B	C	D
1				
2		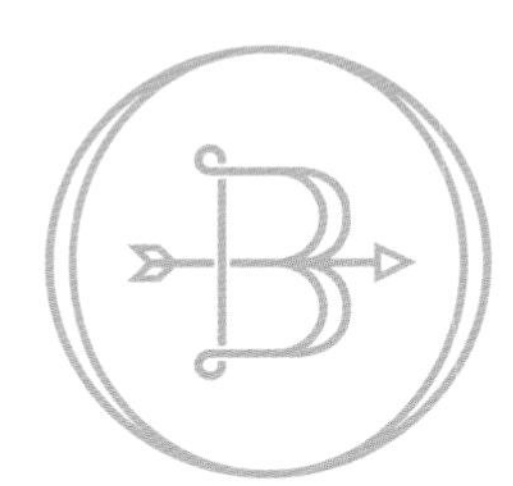		
3				
4				
5				

1A D Karl Design Vienna C Bienenstock **1B** D RetroMetro Designs C inbeen **1C** D J Fletcher Design C Briar Common **1D** D Grafixd C Budaors Antik
2A D Rami Hoballah C Book Binding Shop **2B** D Lukedesign C N/A **2C** D Karlis Dovnorovics C BEKSHTA **2D** D BrandFirst C In House
3A D Kairevicius C Bright North **3B** D Eleven19 C Brian Rhoten **3C** D Gustav Holtz Design C Wildfire Interactive **3D** D Stephen Lee Ogden Design Co. C Harned Bachert & Denton LLP
4A D Sophia Georgopoulou | Design C Theano Bella **4B** D HanleyCreative C BarnLight Eatery **4C** D 1 or Billion design C Baige Winery Group **4D** D Gizwiz Studio C Debra Corley
5A D M@OH! C The Blacksher Family **5B** D Green Ink Studio C Via Media **5C** D Effendy Design C CognitiveBits **5D** D Anthony Rees C Cleavage

A B C D

1

2

3

4

5

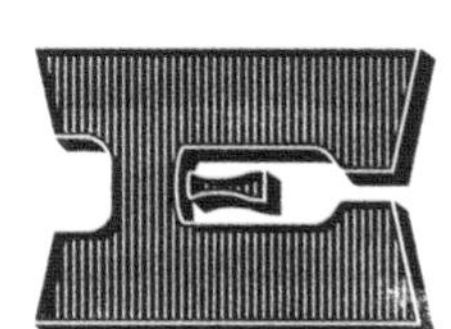

1A Ⓓ Gizwiz Studio Ⓒ John Wali **1B** Ⓓ DDB Sydney Ⓒ Knowledge Global **1C** Ⓓ Blocq Studio Ⓒ CROSTA PIZZA **1D** Ⓓ Tricia Hope Dugat Ⓒ Cathren Saunders, Horticulturalist & Floral Designer
2A Ⓓ Form Studio Ⓒ Projeto Conecta **2B** Ⓓ Dara Creative Ⓒ ConsumerChampion **2C** Ⓓ Jeffhalmos Ⓒ Clearoute **2D** Ⓓ PhD-mtl Ⓒ Christian Pigeon
3A Ⓓ Principals Pty Ltd Ⓒ Royal Botanic Gardens & Domain Trust **3B** Ⓓ Principals Pty Ltd Ⓒ Royal Botanic Gardens & Domain Trust
3C Ⓓ Principals Pty Ltd Ⓒ Royal Botanic Gardens & Domain Trust **3D** Ⓓ Principals Pty Ltd Ⓒ Royal Botanic Gardens & Domain Trust
4A Ⓓ Odney Ⓒ Dave Bruner Photography **4B** Ⓓ J Fletcher Design Ⓒ Dockhop **4C** Ⓓ Absolu communication marketing Ⓒ Delta **4D** Ⓓ Chadomoto / Dimiter Petrov Ⓒ Developica mobile software development
5A Ⓓ Parallele gestion de marques Ⓒ CEGEP a distance **5B** Ⓓ Effendy Design Ⓒ N/A **5C** Ⓓ Saywells Design Co. Ⓒ Ermanos Craft Beer & Wine Bar Mark **5D** Ⓓ Gizwiz Studio Ⓒ Ecava Sdn Bhd

	A	B	C	D
1				
2				
3				
4	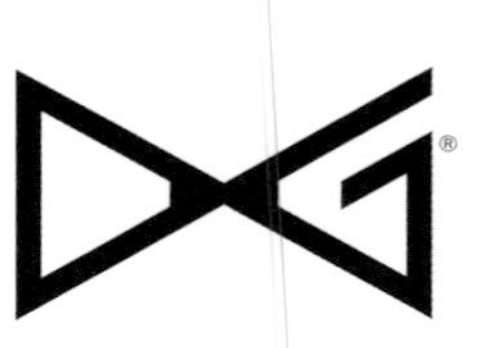	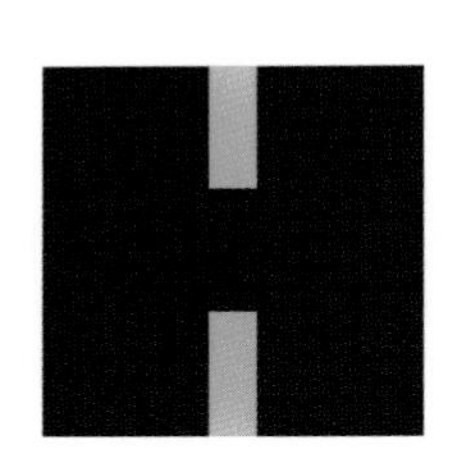	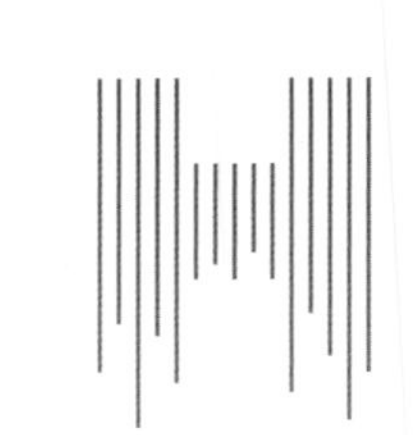	
5				

1A D SparrowDesign C WaryÅ„ski Grupa Holdingowa **1B** D RIJK Concept & Creation C fricflow consultancy **1C** D Kreativbuero Jonas Soeder C Personal **1D** D Grant Currie C Free Advertising
2A D ATOM Creative Agency C FITFIELDS **2B** D 01d C Fryville **2C** D Fuzzco C N/A **2D** D Flat 6 Concepts C Fieldstone Group
3A D MW Design Studio C Graham Translations **3B** D Allen Creative C Generation Empower **3C** D bartodell.com C Greenway Renovations & Custom Homes **3D** D Effendy Design C GARY SFEZ Video Productions
4A D Designer and Gentleman C Designer and Gentleman **4B** D Oxide Design Co. C Houck Transit Advertising **4C** D Anagraphic C Demographic Research Institute **4D** D Miriad C Holzfabrik
5A D Splash:Design C Evergreen Lands **5B** D KW43 BRANDDESIGN C Holy Haferl **5C** D Kairevicius C www.kairevicius.com **5D** D Hornall Anderson C Fred Hutch

	A	B	C	D
1				
2				
3				
4	LUXURY HOUSE			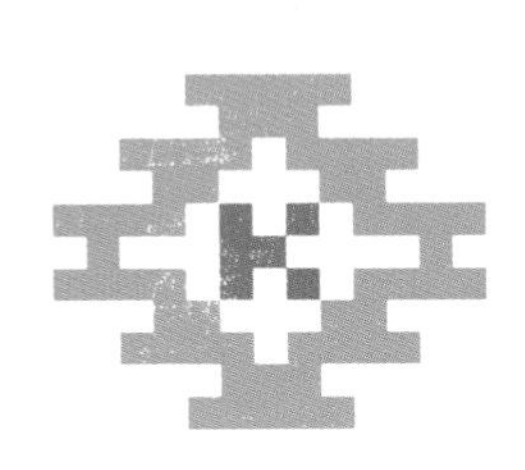
5				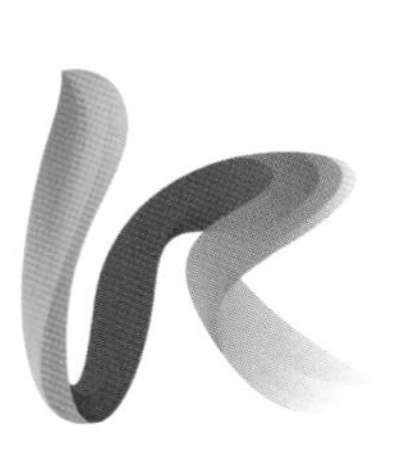

1A D 3 Advertising LLC C Humble Coffee Company **1B** D Alex Rinker C Stacey Hennessey **1C** D Yury Akulin | Logodiver C Right of Defence **1D** D Rebrander C Holocaust
2A D CF Napa Brand Design C Hahn Family Wines **2B** D Zync C Hangar 9 **2C** D Levogrin C Haut Monde **2D** D Kairevicius C Harisson Heights
3A D Type08 C HCC **3B** D Robert Finkel Design C HUNTER CONSTRUCTION **3C** D Creative Parc C Hill Country Tool Company **3D** D Blue Tongue Design Ltd C Heart Made Home
4A D Flat 6 Concepts C Luxury House **4B** D A.D. Creative Group C HQ **4C** D Jeffhalmos C ILO **4D** D J Fletcher Design C Kalakala Mercantile Co.
5A D Besapiens C Krasnokamsk Municipal Administration **5B** D Envision Creative Group C Keenagers **5C** D artslinger C Kohlman Kreative **5D** D Independent graphic designer C Known

A B C D

1

2

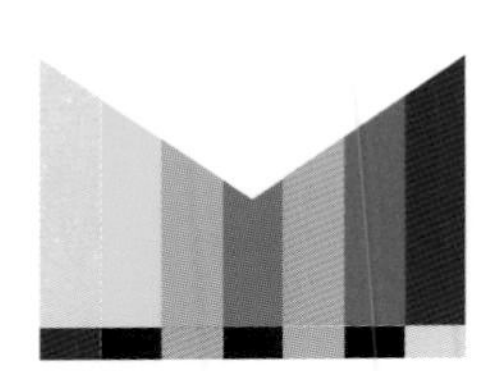

3

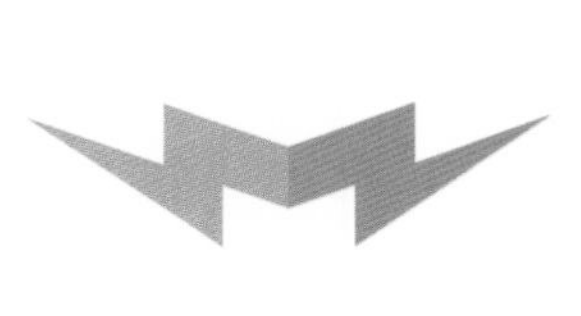

4

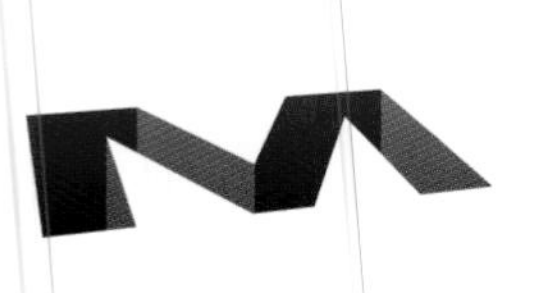

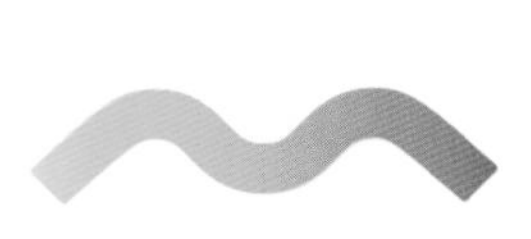

5

1A Ⓓ Rocksauce Studios Ⓒ Keyminder **1B** Ⓓ Brandburg Ⓒ Klenergy **1C** Ⓓ RedEffect Ⓒ LimeCreative / Karistianis **1D** Ⓓ Kreativbuero Jonas Soeder Ⓒ Kopf und Kragen Hamburg
2A Ⓓ Roy Smith Design Ⓒ LM **2B** Ⓓ Creation Ⓒ Warner Bros. **2C** Ⓓ Gardner Design Ⓒ Justin McClure Creative **2D** Ⓓ Rylander Design Ⓒ Meedan Labs
3A Ⓓ Oronoz Brandesign Ⓒ matchem **3B** Ⓓ Slagle Design Ⓒ Modern Medical **3C** Ⓓ RedSpark Creative Ltd Ⓒ Mastermind Business Solutions **3D** Ⓓ Pavel Saksin Ⓒ Multiplex energy
4A Ⓓ MVC Agency Ⓒ Medialogiq Systems **4B** Ⓓ MVC Agency Ⓒ Medialogiq Systems **4C** Ⓓ Oven Design Workshop Ⓒ Memorize it **4D** Ⓓ Farmboy Ⓒ Matrix Labs
5A Ⓓ Green Ink Studio Ⓒ MasterPeace Intimates **5B** Ⓓ Karl Design Vienna Ⓒ Mangiare **5C** Ⓓ Gardner Design Ⓒ Magic Talent **5D** Ⓓ Ulyanov Denis Ⓒ TMK

A B C D

1

2

3

4

5

1A D Fixer Creative Co. C The Machine Shop **1B** D Stan Designworks C MH Hotel Sdn. Bhd. **1C** D A.D. Creative Group C Moss Mansion **1D** D MODA Collaborative C MOJOHN CREATIVE DESIGN COMPANY
2A D Gardner Design C McCoy Petroleuem Corporation **2B** D Funnel C Mary DaRos **2C** D R&R Partners C museum month **2D** D BLVR C Mommy MD
3A D Galambos + Associates C Monark Guitars **3B** D 01d C AlmaMater **3C** D Kreativbuero Jonas Soeder C ARCA Records **3D** D A.D. Creative Group C The Myrtle Leaf
4A D Visual Lure, LLC C Flower Mountain Weddings & Receptions **4B** D re-robot C GGIT **4C** D Oluzen C Nelly **4D** D Visual Lure, LLC C NEWT
5A D Rickabaugh Graphics C Northwest Missouri State University **5B** D Gizwiz Studio C Charles Boudinot **5C** D Pix-I Graphx C Laurus Opes **5D** D O' Riordan Design C Orla Rice

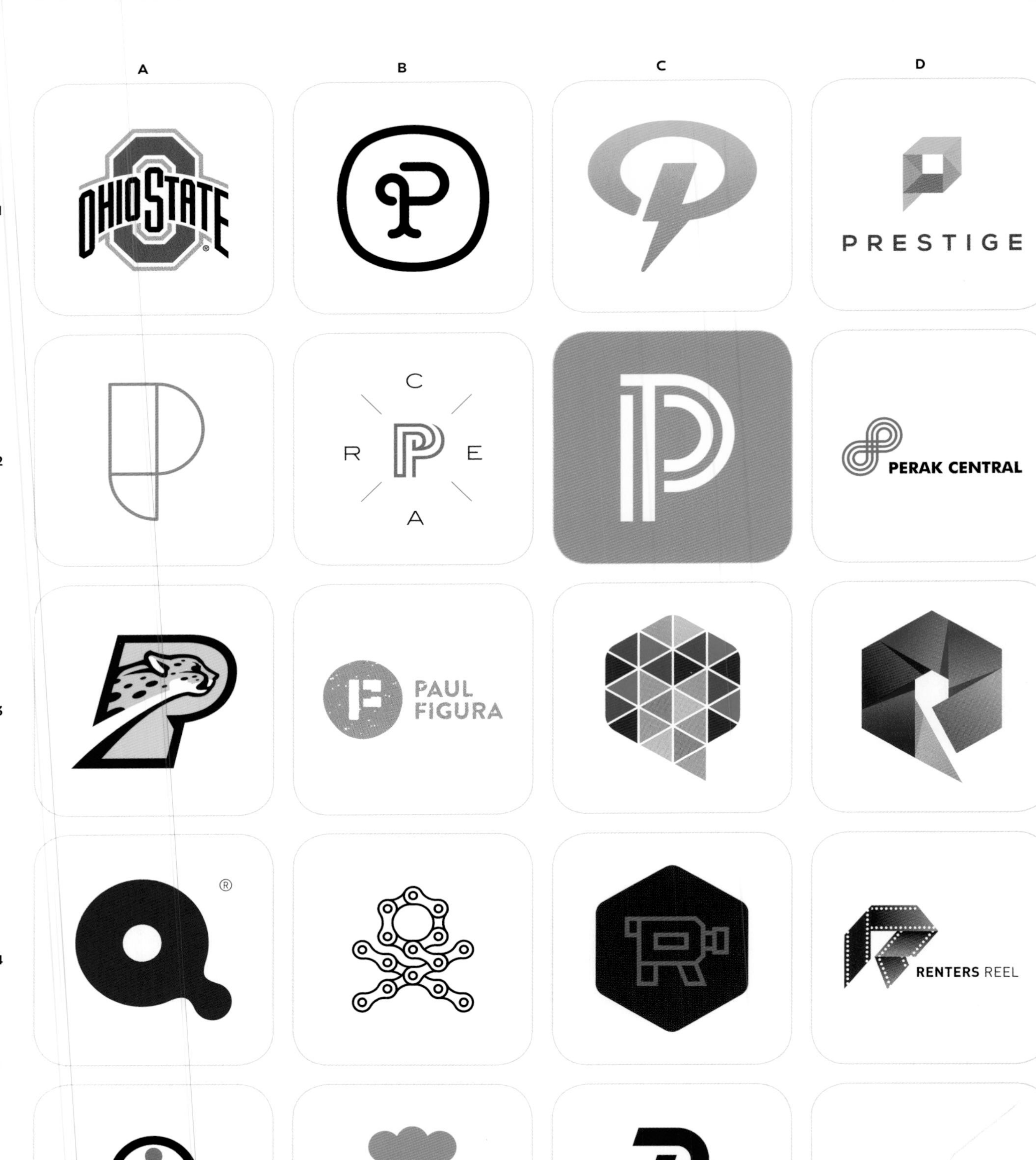

1A D Rickabaugh Graphics C The Ohio State University **1B** D Jeremiah Britton Design Co. C Pucker Makeup Studio **1C** D Oronoz Brandesign C N/A **1D** D Gizwiz Studio C Han Ming Ong
2A D Jody Worthington Graphic Design C EP Interiors **2B** D Studio Sudar d.o.o. C PERIS Ltd **2C** D idgroup C Pensacola Today **2D** D Stan Designworks C The Combined Bus Services Sdn. Bhd.
3A D HanleyCreative C Performance Indoor Training **3B** D Patrick Carter Design, Inc. C Paul Figura **3C** D Parallele gestion de marques C Federation quebecoise des municipalites **3D** D Graphics Factory CC C LogoGround
4A D Cezar Bianchi B+D C Quimicryl S/A **4B** D Quique Ollervides C Quimera **4C** D Luke Bott Design & Illustration C N/A **4D** D 36creative C ReReel
5A D KW43 BRANDDESIGN C everyone **5B** D Type08 C ER **5C** D Pavel Saksin C Rockstar **5D** D Zenetic C Revidere

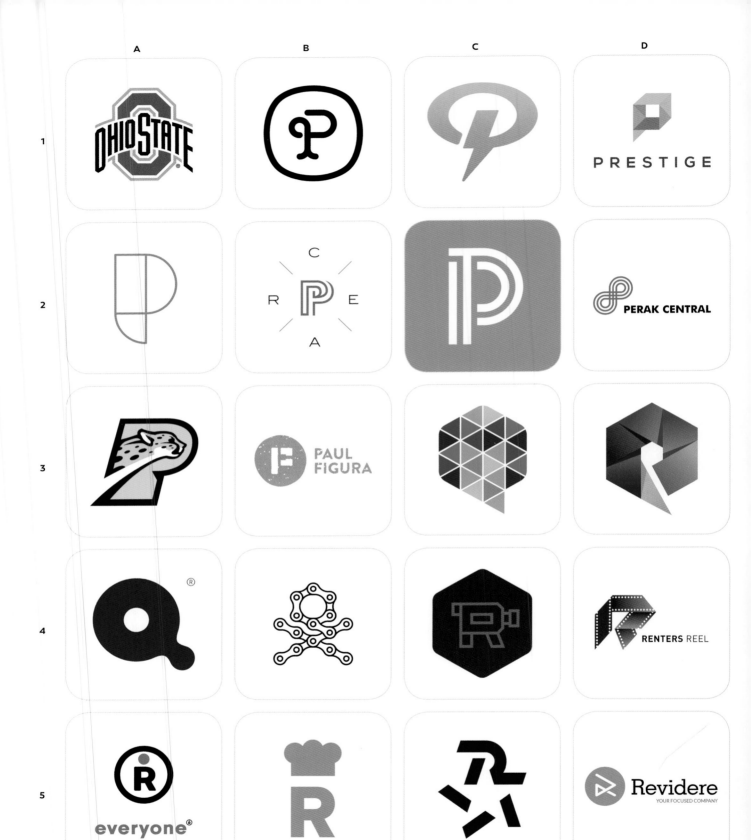

	A	B	C	D
1				
2				
3				
4			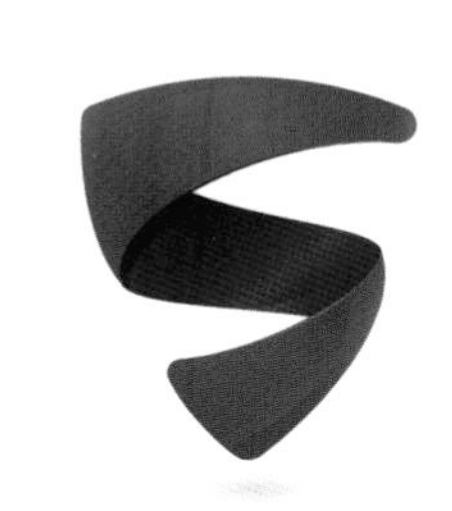	
5				

1A Ⓓ Brandforma Ⓒ N/A **1B** Ⓓ Rainmaker Creative Ⓒ Roots & Bloom Botanicals **1C** Ⓓ Miro Kozel Ⓒ Sportitan **1D** Ⓓ Gardner Design Ⓒ SiteBox Storage
2A Ⓓ David Gramblin Ⓒ SUPERIOR COMPANIES **2B** Ⓓ Alexander Wende Ⓒ skulpt **2C** Ⓓ WeLoveNoise Ⓒ Scorem **2D** Ⓓ Apex Creative Ⓒ Suntel Construction
3A Ⓓ Buzzbomb Creative Ⓒ Simpli.fi **3B** Ⓓ Daniel Schnitzer Design Ⓒ Schaefer Personal **3C** Ⓓ Paradigm New Media Group Ⓒ Fleur Di Lls Group **3D** Ⓓ Gardner Design Ⓒ Southwestern Community College
4A Ⓓ KW43 BRANDDESIGN Ⓒ Markus Schenkenberg **4B** Ⓓ Brandon Harrison Ⓒ Sam Hurd Photography **4C** Ⓓ Pavlodar School of Design Ⓒ Advline **4D** Ⓓ Gardner Design Ⓒ Southwestern Community College
5A Ⓓ J Fletcher Design Ⓒ Southeastern Construction **5B** Ⓓ Tactix Creative Ⓒ N/A **5C** Ⓓ The Blksmith Design Co. Ⓒ The Social Club **5D** Ⓓ Alex Rinker Ⓒ Small Giants

A B C D

1

45
MIDTOWN DINER

2

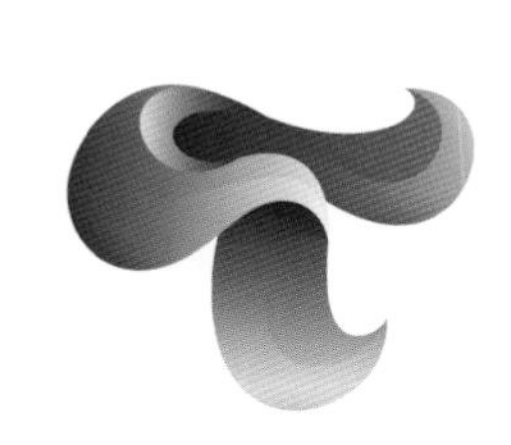

3

4

5

1A Ⓓ Thoburn Design & Illustration LLC Ⓒ TinSnips Metal Fabrication **1B** Ⓓ Banowetz + Company, Inc. Ⓒ Hyatt Times Square **1C** Ⓓ Tokshok Ⓒ Ufanet **1D** Ⓓ 1 or Billion design Ⓒ Tong Baoli
2A Ⓓ Pix-I Graphx Ⓒ Topic Creative **2B** Ⓓ Independent graphic designer Ⓒ Thrive **2C** Ⓓ Proof Positive Brand Design Ⓒ Terrarium Bar **2D** Ⓓ Fernandez Studio Ⓒ Tomnod
3A Ⓓ Braizen Ⓒ Tony Asgari **3B** Ⓓ Jerron Ames Ⓒ Three Defined **3C** Ⓓ Miro Kozel Ⓒ N/A **3D** Ⓓ The Brandit Ⓒ Tangled Roots Beverage Co.
4A Ⓓ John Mills Ltd Ⓒ TONE ZONE **4B** Ⓓ Unipen Ⓒ Unipen **4C** Ⓓ Logo Planet Laboratory Ⓒ Union Pipeline **4D** Ⓓ Karl Design Vienna Ⓒ United Electro
5A Ⓓ Greg Valdez Design Ⓒ Valdez Recycling Solutions, LLC **5B** Ⓓ Lippincott Ⓒ The Vitamin Shoppe **5C** Ⓓ Xplaye Ⓒ MNA de Mexico **5D** Ⓓ Sebastiany Branding & Design Ⓒ Vasa

A B C D

1

2

3

4

5

1A Ⓓ Keith Davis Young Ⓒ Vernetti **1B** Ⓓ Jody Worthington Graphic Design Ⓒ Kimberly Park Communications **1C** Ⓓ Braizen Ⓒ Viridian **1D** Ⓓ Grain Ⓒ Levvel
2A Ⓓ CRE8 DESIGN Ⓒ Vivas **2B** Ⓓ Jordahl Design Ⓒ VanGorp Landscaping **2C** Ⓓ CWP Design Studio Ⓒ Velano Vascular **2D** Ⓓ Alexander Wende Ⓒ vovovi
3A Ⓓ J Fletcher Design Ⓒ Wain Green Wood **3B** Ⓓ Pavel Saksin Ⓒ Welwer **3C** Ⓓ Visual Lure, LLC Ⓒ Whyman Studios **3D** Ⓓ Ulyanov Denis Ⓒ Natty Kristea
4A Ⓓ Noe Araujo Ⓒ Tttones **4B** Ⓓ DEI Creative Ⓒ The Schuster Group **4C** Ⓓ 3 Advertising LLC Ⓒ wanderable **4D** Ⓓ Graphic D-Signs, Inc. Ⓒ Wired Electrical Contractors
5A Ⓓ Galambos + Associates Ⓒ Wavetable **5B** Ⓓ Fancy Creative Ⓒ Wysong Glass of Charleston **5C** Ⓓ Chris Rooney Illustration/Design Ⓒ Wiener **5D** Ⓓ Chris Rooney Illustration/Design Ⓒ Wiener

A B C D

1

2

3

4

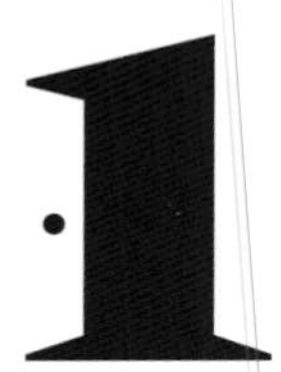

5

1A Ⓓ Daren Guillory Design Ⓒ White Nuckle Sports **1B** Ⓓ Type08 Ⓒ Wandering Table **1C** Ⓓ Sean Heisler Design Ⓒ The Acvitivity Exchange **1D** Ⓓ Denys Kotliarov Ⓒ x-change
2A Ⓓ Galambos + Associates Ⓒ MarkitX **2B** Ⓓ Emilio Correa Ⓒ ZenWay **2C** Ⓓ Jon Kay Design Ⓒ Kari Fry **2D** Ⓓ Steve Wolf Designs Ⓒ Zoetic Press
3A Ⓓ Never North Ⓒ ZipSeam **3B** Ⓓ Estudio Mezanino Ⓒ N/A **3C** Ⓓ 3x4 Design Studio Ⓒ www.a-one.company **3D** Ⓓ BLVR Ⓒ Synergy One Lending
4A Ⓓ Reghardt Ⓒ N/A **4B** Ⓓ Quique Ollervides Ⓒ Quique Ollervides **4C** Ⓓ Paradox Box Ⓒ Tright Trust **4D** Ⓓ YhankTou Creative Ⓒ N/A
5A Ⓓ ONY Ⓒ 9-18 Living Quarters **5B** Ⓓ DEI Creative Ⓒ UDR **5C** Ⓓ Unipen Ⓒ Eleven Two **5D** Ⓓ Square Feet Design Ⓒ Domain Companies

DESIGN /// DREW MELTON

CLIENT /// ANCHOR PAPER CO.

CATEGORY /// TYPOGRAPHY

Drew Melton wasn't one of those kids who was obsessed with lettering and pursued it as his life's calling. Quite the opposite, in fact. "This idea of becoming an illustrative letterer didn't occur to me until I dropped out of college and I was running my own design company. I was burnt out, and following amazing designers who were focused exclusively on lettering," Melton says. "I really sucked at it at first." So he took a few months to focus solely on lettering and started the Phraseology Project (http://phraseologyproject.com), where people would submit phrases and notations, and he would letter them and post them as practice. Talk about trial by fire and exposing yourself to possible critics! Well, it worked. He started getting hired for his lettering work, and he hasn't looked back.

In 2012, Melton and his wife, Kelsey Zahn, started Anchor Paper Co., a high-end online stationery store. "We were trying to find thank you cards after our wedding. Being a designer, I hated everything we looked at, so we decided to make our own. Unfortunately, we didn't get them made in time to use ourselves," he explains.

Although anchors are pretty prominent in logos (there is even another Anchor Paper, which is a wholesale paper distributor), Melton and Zahn have an aversion to the symbol. "My wife and I have anchor tattoos on our wrists—we got them done on a whim in Colorado before we got married. It's been an icon in our relationship, and since this is our side project together, we decided to call it *Anchor*, even though anchors are everywhere," Melton says, laughing.

> "The cards are very minimal. I wanted to create a product that allows users to add value to it with their handwriting."
> —Drew Melton

After crafting the anchor logo, Melton hand-lettered the company name. He says, "The lettering is absolutely meant to look 'anchored.' My goal with the branding and design of the cards is meant to be timeless and reliable for years to come. I am trying to stay away from current trends with 'anchor,' because keeping up with trends is impossible."

Each greeting card takes on its own distinct typographic style as well. For instance, "Good Morning" feels sunny and bright, and "Remarkable" feels bold and proud. "The biggest thing I had to do was keep from overdesigning," Melton says. "We letterpressed the designs onto 180 pound paper, it's beautiful, but at the end of the day what makes the card valuable to someone is that there is all this white space for them to write a personal note. The design just elevates the importance of the interactions."

The serifs on the letters provide a certain stability, and the flourish from the *h* seems to hook inside the *c* in *anchor*. The curve of the elegant lettering creates a nice juxtaposition with the anchor symbol and the words beneath it.

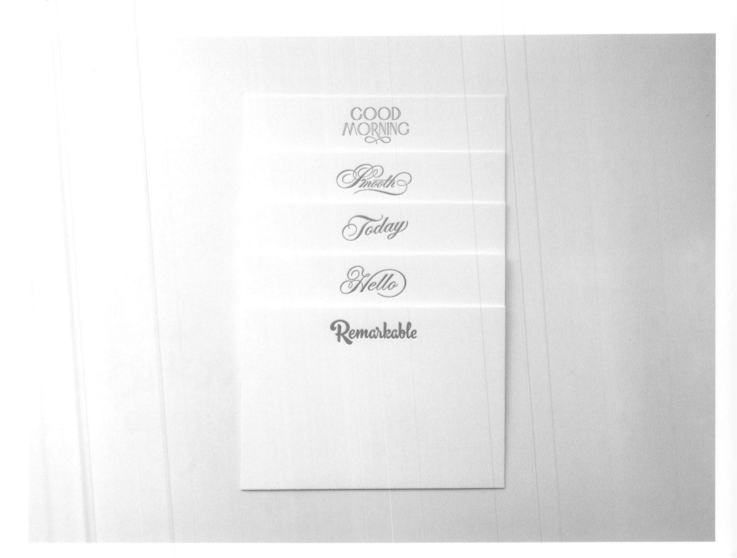

Various greetings hand-lettered by Melton.

WORDS FROM DREW MELTON

THE CURATED LIFE

LA / CA

DASHING DISH

"I've worked with Sean Farrell on this project for the past four years. I put together the original logo when I was living in Michigan. He is a talented icon designer, but he doesn't do lettering. We often worked on branding projects collaboratively. His wife runs a large online food blog called *Dashing Dish* where she posts beautifully photographed healthy recipes regularly.

"Since designing the first logo, Sean has commissioned me to do redesigns twice, and we may even be working together again soon on another redesign. As *Dashing Dish* grows and matures, we are discovering the needs and personality needs to change. This is not efficient, but it keeps *Dashing Dish* from getting stuck in the past. The project has grown up with us. Every time we work together we create something great. It's a fun project to be connected to.

THE CURATED LIFE

"This project was started by my wife Kelsey Zahn (http://kelseyzahn.com) two and a half years ago when we moved to Los Angeles. We had just gotten married and she was going through a major career shift from a steady, well-paying job to freelance styling. In the meantime, to keep busy, she started this project in order to maintain her curiosity about food, life and style. This project has never been a commercial success, but I love the purity of this personal product. It has an ease about it both in the design and the content. She still posts five days a week even after her freelance has picked up considerably."

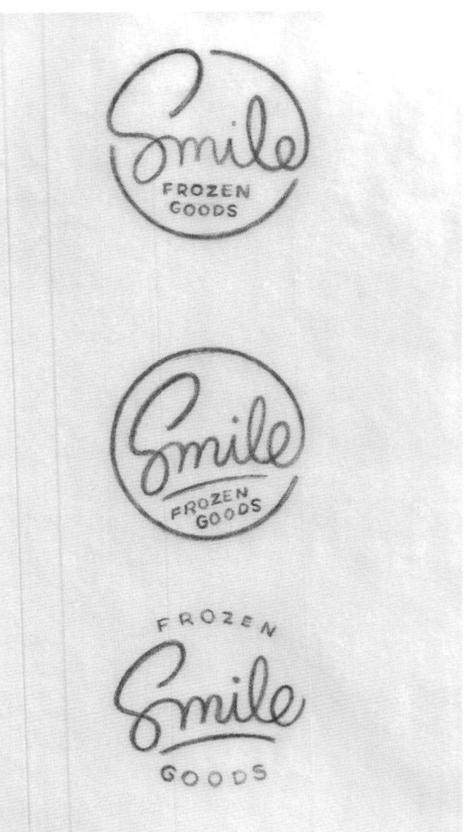

SMILE FROZEN GOODS

Jon Setzen and Kevin Hockin devised the designer/foodie dream project. They came up with the idea of doing a boutique ice cream truck business around Los Angeles based around quality ingredients. The Smile logo is simple and straightforward and looks amazing on the 1950s-era ice cream truck.

CATEGORY ///

TYPOGRAPHY

	A	B	C	D
1			j:)y	SVC
2	siba STEVENS – THE INSTITUTE OF BUSINESS & ARTS	snotes	dean CREATIVE	Elianne Ramos
3		PROOF COOKERY AND DRINKERY	MARK	FARM
4	S°MAIN KITCHEN	PAPERCVLT	DESTINATI°NS	THE SPECTATOR HOTEL
5	J. RICHARD HILL &CO.		ANCHOR PAPER Co.	NORTH INLET

1C Ⓓ Joy Rubin Creative Ⓒ Joy Rubin Creative **1D** Ⓓ 903 Creative, LLC Ⓒ SVC Construction
2A Ⓓ Grain Ⓒ Stevens – The Institute of Business & Arts **2B** Ⓓ Paradigm New Media Group Ⓒ Fleur Di Lis Group **2C** Ⓓ Brandjamin Ⓒ Dean Creative **2D** Ⓓ Pix-I Graphx Ⓒ Elianne Ramos
3A Ⓓ Crooked Tree Creative Ⓒ Franklin, NC **3B** Ⓓ Scott Oeschger Design Ⓒ Star Group **3C** Ⓓ Alex Tass Ⓒ ArtMark **3D** Ⓓ Farm Design Ⓒ Farm Design
4A Ⓓ Colleen Coolidge Lindner Ⓒ Louis Soon **4B** Ⓓ Jordahl Design Ⓒ papercult **4C** Ⓓ Doc4 Ⓒ Destinations **4D** Ⓓ Stitch Design Co. Ⓒ The Spectator Hotel
5A Ⓓ GOOD CANOE, INC Ⓒ J. Richard Hill & Co. **5B** Ⓓ Clark & Co. Ⓒ The Frontier Fund **5C** Ⓓ Your Just Lucky Ⓒ Anchor Paper Co. **5D** Ⓓ J Fletcher Design Ⓒ North Inlet

1A D Maurizio Pagnozzi C logo **1B** D Daniel Eris C ripple **1C** D PytchBlack C exeso **1D** D Rebrander C flood
2A D Jibe C Marketer's Interface **2B** D Burocratik C Quiver **2C** D Lippincott C Cox **2D** D Eder Saos C Kengo
3A D Luka Balic C Kratki i Slatki **3B** D Scott Oeschger Design C Star Group **3C** D Erwin Bindeman C Blue Bridge Search **3D** D Effendy Design C Seriously Open
4A D Hornall Anderson C Seattle Art Museum **4B** D Maurizio Pagnozzi C one **4C** D Reghardt C Only Real Estate **4D** D Blackletter C MKSK
5A D Think to Make C 1 Kick Canned Mule **5B** D Sam Dallyn C UP DROID **5C** D A.D. Creative Group C INDUSTRY **5D** D Second Street Creative C Proof

A B C D

1

ZER011

2

OCEAN

STANLEY.

3

LINEA

CLICK

LIQUID

ENTER

4

LESS

RETRO

LAUNCH

QUINN

5

MELIUS

ARGEPLAN

WESTREEF

AFTERHOURS

1A D Jibe C Jibe Media **1B** D Oxide Design Co. C Rez Roasters **1C** D Steven Schroeder C EDGE **1D** D zero11 C zero11
2A D Kovach Studio C Galery Singidunum **2B** D Deksia C Code 3 **2C** D Fernandez Studio C Anheuser-Busch **2D** D Lippincott C Stanley
3A D Parallele gestion de marques C Societe de transport de Levis **3B** D Budanov. Branding & Identity C Oleg Emelyanov Group **3C** D Kovach Studio C On Architecture **3D** D RolandRekeczki C Enter offices
4A D Rebrander C LESS **4B** D Braley Design C No Angel T's **4C** D Launch C Launch **4D** D Blackletter C Quinn & Co.
5A D Alama Design C Ciarla Group **5B** D Sebastiany Branding & Design C Argeplan **5C** D p11creative C Pinnacle Residential **5D** D SUMO C Natural History Museum

	A	B	C	D
1	WHYFLY	GOVER	AQUILINE	HAYDEN
2	BODYART	SHORTY·140	EMPHASIS™	GREEN ROOF INTELLIGENCE INHABITECT
3	BUDERKA	PLAYTURN		
4	LUCKY BRAND EST. 1990	CRE8TOR INDUSTRIES	LOOK! MOSCOW	THE BERNDALES FOOD-CO.
5	THE BRANDI PROJECT	FRED + ERIC	COOKE EST. 1999 HELMS	MA RA KA DESIGN

1A D Besapiens C Why Fly Telecom **1B** D Pavel Saksin C Gover **1C** D Anthony Rees C Aquiline **1D** D Type08 C VdH Yachts
2A D petervasvari.com C Kallos Cosmetics **2B** D Hubbell Design Works C Shorty-140 Entertainment **2C** D Rule29 C Emphasis **2D** D Proof Positive Brand Design C Inhabitect
3A D Voov Ltd. C Buderka Jewellery **3B** D Jon Kay Design C Ryan Novak **3C** D Just Creative Design C Phone Division **3D** D Sabingrafik, Inc. C Puerto Cancun
4A D J Fletcher Design C Lucky Brand **4B** D Clark & Co. C CRE8TOR INDUSTRIES **4C** D Roman Zolotorevich C Look! Moscow **4D** D NO-BAD C THE BERNDALES FOOD-CO.
5A D Stebbings Partners C The Brandi Project **5B** D FRED+ERIC C FRED+ERIC **5C** D Atypic C Seafoods.com **5D** D Marakasdesign C MARAKAS_DESIGN studio

	A	B	C	D
1	CATEGORY /// **ENCLOSURES**			
2				
3				
4				
5				

1C D Parallele gestion de marques C Je coop **1D** D Sakkal Design C Mindy Peters Arabians
2A D Kreativbuero Jonas Soeder C Rhythm Kicker **2B** D Stebbings Partners C Boston Nightlife Ventures **2C** D Tamer Koseli C cangorkem.com **2D** D Doublenaut C Town Moto
3A D Just Creative Design C The Tasty Baker **3B** D Swin Huang Design C 3 HOUSES **3C** D RedEffect C ExploreGreece.ru **3D** D Peppermill Projects C Old Ox BREWERY
4A D Colleen Coolidge Lindner C Stephen Voss **4B** D Colleen Coolidge Lindner C Louis Soon **4C** D Unipen C Before Deco **4D** D GL Creative Design C GL Creative Design
5A D Xplaye C Suites Alce **5B** D Niedermeier Design C Expedia **5C** D Gizwiz Studio C Victoria Thomas **5D** D FS Grafik Design C N/A

	A	B	C	D
1				
2				
3				
4				
5				

1A Ⓓ Denys Kotliarov Ⓒ Brick technology **1B** Ⓓ Julian Peck Creative Ⓒ Artisan Bistro **1C** Ⓓ Xplaye Ⓒ Fujiro **1D** Ⓓ Steve DeCusatis Design Ⓒ Skillet Creative
2A Ⓓ The Blksmith Design Co. Ⓒ Otis & Sons **2B** Ⓓ Slagle Design Ⓒ Slagle Design **2C** Ⓓ DEI Creative Ⓒ Red Propeller **2D** Ⓓ Ye Olde Studio Ⓒ Artillery Drums
3A Ⓓ Varick Rosete Studio Ⓒ One Spark **3B** Ⓓ Mindgruve Ⓒ SDX **3C** Ⓓ Noriu Menulio Ⓒ ART AGENCY ARTSCAPE **3D** Ⓓ Shadia Design Ⓒ Darian Milburn
4A Ⓓ Haffelder Studios Ⓒ www.haffelderstudios.com **4B** Ⓓ MKJ Creative Ⓒ Performing Arts **4C** Ⓓ Jarheadesign Ⓒ Yes Drinks **4D** Ⓓ Chris Rooney Illustration / Design C: BMC Ⓒ spun ICE CREAM
5A Ⓓ Patrick Carter Design, Inc. Ⓒ Wicked Barley **5B** Ⓓ Principals Pty Ltd Ⓒ Opal Specialised Aged Care **5C** Ⓓ Sophia Georgopoulou | Design Ⓒ Zeea Canada **5D** Ⓓ Muhina Design Ⓒ LLC Wine club

A B C D

1

2

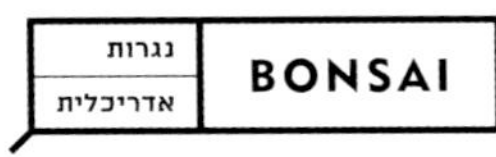

3

4

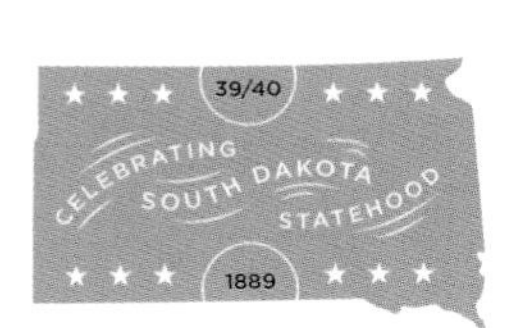

5

1A D reedesign studio C fitness-gaming.com **1B** D Stitch Design Co. C Garden & Gun Magazine **1C** D Denys Kotliarov C Brick technology **1D** D Just Creative Design C Spice Sage
2A D Kreativbuero Jonas Soeder C Personal **2B** D Liquid Agency C Roseburg Forest Products **2C** D OPEN C BONSAI **2D** D AkarStudios C Picnik
3A D Marakasdesign C Miles Company **3B** D Scott Oeschger Design C DB, Inc. **3C** D Sudduth Design Co. C Brightwing Custom Exteriors **3D** D Buzzbomb Creative C HFTY
4A D Clark & Co. C French Press Roasters **4B** D Clark & Co. C The Frontier Fund **4C** D Cinq Partners C TOLSTOI **4D** D Lippincott C BLACK + DECKER
5A D Latinbrand C Faina **5B** D Gardner Design C Design Business Interiors **5C** D Second Street Creative C Alee J **5D** D Visual Dialogue C Donghue Barrett and Singal

A B C D

1

2

3

4

5

1A D Tribambuka C The Ben Faulkner Band **1B** D Todytod C Booking.com **1C** D SALT Branding C Salt Branding **1D** D Oxide Design Co. C Center for Civic Design
2A D Almanac C Jay Fram **2B** D Tokshok C Ufanet **2C** D Apus Agency C Art Quadrum **2D** D Karl Design Vienna C biiid Germany
3A D T&E Polydorou Design Ltd C Faros Hotel **3B** D J Fletcher Design C Richard Hurford **3C** D Wheelhouse Collective C Creighton University **3D** D Tokshok C Ufanet
4A D Outdoor Cap C Watershop **4B** D Liquid Agency C Roseburg Forest Products **4C** D Jakshop C WILEY ROOTS BREWING CO. **4D** D Josh Carnley C JAY LANDINGS MARINA & RV PARK
5A D Banowetz + Company, Inc. C Hyatt Times Square **5B** D Anthony Rees C HQ Network **5C** D Alex Rinker C Race Corps **5D** D Chadomoto / Dimiter Petrov C Funbox street wear shop

	A	B	C	D
1				
2				
3				
4				
5				

1A Ⓓ WestmorelandFlint Ⓒ Urban Moose Brewing Co. **1B** Ⓓ Salih Kucukaga Design Studio Ⓒ MODMODS **1C** Ⓓ Amy McAdams Design Ⓒ Jordan Updike/Forage **1D** Ⓓ smARTer Ⓒ Macleod & Co
2A Ⓓ Type08 Ⓒ Alumni Golf Classics **2B** Ⓓ Sunday Lounge Ⓒ Paul Inge Building LLC **2C** Ⓓ Mark Huffman Creative Ⓒ Infinity Fitness **2D** Ⓓ Braue: Brand Design Experts Ⓒ J.W. Döscher Ww.
3A Ⓓ Maurizio Pagnozzi Ⓒ MACRIDE **3B** Ⓓ Kay Loves Candy Ⓒ Savannah Community Radio **3C** Ⓓ Banowetz + Company, Inc. Ⓒ Stash Design **3D** Ⓓ Fuzzco Ⓒ DOTTIE'S Toffee
4A Ⓓ Scott McFadden Creative Ⓒ Scott McFadden Creative **4B** Ⓓ Naughtyfish Garbett Ⓒ Sydney Opera House **4C** Ⓓ Braizen Ⓒ Sarah Catherine **4D** Ⓓ Bethany Heck Ⓒ N/A
5A Ⓓ Niedermeier Design Ⓒ Don't Call Me Ma'am **5B** Ⓓ Riddle Design Co. Ⓒ Lazy Hiker Brewing Company **5C** Ⓓ zero11 Ⓒ Samboka Restaurant **5D** Ⓓ Juicebox Interactive Ⓒ Touche Collections

A B C D

1

2

3

4

5

1A Ⓓ Chris Rooney Illustration/Design Ⓒ California State Fair **1B** Ⓓ Parallele gestion de marques Ⓒ Fromagerie La Chaudiere **1C** Ⓓ Estudio Brado Ⓒ Plozy **1D** Ⓓ TerriLowry.com Ⓒ N/A
2A Ⓓ KW43 BRANDDESIGN Ⓒ GREY Düsseldorf **2B** Ⓓ Dotzero Design Ⓒ Dotzero **2C** Ⓓ Keystone Resources Ⓒ Accent Guru **2D** Ⓓ Z&G Ⓒ N/A
3A Ⓓ TYPE AND SIGNS Ⓒ Julia Testa **3B** Ⓓ Cezar Bianchi B+D Ⓒ Suits and Tables **3C** Ⓓ DEI Creative Ⓒ Skotdal Real Estate **3D** Ⓓ J Fletcher Design Ⓒ Rutledge Cab Company
4A Ⓓ EMC illustration & design Ⓒ Jeanie Randazzo **4B** Ⓓ Karl Design Vienna Ⓒ Momentum **4C** Ⓓ Jesse Arneson Ⓒ Daniel F. Ward **4D** Ⓓ MODA Collaborative Ⓒ N/A
5A Ⓓ James Dean & Company Ⓒ The Hungry Heart **5B** Ⓓ Flight Deck Creative Ⓒ The Midwest Clinic **5C** Ⓓ Keyword Design Ⓒ Towle Theater **5D** Ⓓ Oronoz Brandesign Ⓒ N/A

DESIGN /// OCD

CLIENT /// MARCUS SAMUELSSON GROUP AND KARLITZ & COMPANY

CATEGORY /// DISPLAY TYPE

Harlem EatUp! is a four-day festival in Harlem, New York, celebrating the culinary, fine and performing arts in the community. The festival is the brainchild of Marcus Samuelsson, a well-known chef who owns several restaurants, among them Red Rooster Harlem. Samuelsson partnered with Karlitz & Company to develop the festival, and they hired OCD to create the identity. Bobby C. Martin Jr., founding partner at OCD says, "It was important for the Harlem EatUp! identity to reflect the vibrancy of the community in a bold, beautiful and contemporary way, but to stay away from the typical, cliché elements of Harlem."

Samuelsson and Herb Karlitz had specific ideas about what should and should not be included as part of the design. "When they describe Harlem, they talk about the nature of the mosaic of so many diverse cultures coming together, so the identity should have this color and pop and vibrancy to it," Martin says. "We wanted to make sure the identity embodies a soulful mix of cultures, but it's also a sensitive topic. It has to push past stereotypes and, instead, focus on the vibrancy, energy and spirit of the community. The festival needs to be inclusive so those born and raised in Harlem are proud to be a part of it."

The designers walked the streets of Harlem snapping pictures of signage and tile work, storefronts and church facades, to document the evolving cultural landscape. In particular, the designers were inspired by colorful mosaic illustrations found at the 125th Street subway station and the typography used in many storefront signs throughout the neighborhood. "The result was a collage of incredible lettering, which served as the starting point for our design exploration," Martin recalls.

The chunky, hand-drawn, sans serif letterforms were inspired by the reference material they collected. The designers arranged the type with extra-tight letter spacing to form a mosaic pattern. Harlem's architecture informed the stacked logo which also pays an homage to the iconic subway system tiles. A certain visual excitement was achieved with the combination of the stacked letters and vibrant colors. But when OCD presented the typographic set to Samuelsson and Karlitz, they wanted more overt visual references to food and music.

Back at the drawing board, the OCD designers drew musical notes and a fork, knife and spoon to counter the type without being too obvious. The weight and scale of the icons played well with the letterforms, creating fluidity and excitement, while the tag, "A celebration of food, culture and spirit," anchors it together.

Choosing the right colors was just as important as the typography. "Marcus specifically said he wanted this to feel high-end, like the Oscars of food and art festivals," Martin says. "We showed him the logo in gold and he loved it, but we felt one color wasn't enough. We wanted to use colors that are less expected for a food festival, so we chose purple and teal as secondary colors to complement the gold."

The vertical format was designed with modularity in mind. The stacked logo expands and contracts according to the type of content needing to be displayed. OCD also designed a horizontal format in order for the logo to have multiple uses. "Knowing we'd need to hand it off to other agencies, we wanted to be sure we gave them different ways to use the logo," Martin notes.

> "The final arrangement of forms came out of a broad exploration. We started with the obvious then pushed ourselves to make it uniquely Harlem by adding height and pushing legibility."
>
> —Bobby C. Martin Jr.

The eclectic signs, architecture and illustrations around Harlem are a cacophony of color, type and imagery. OCD designers used this visual reference as inspiration for the Harlem EatUp! logo.

The initial type-only logo.

The final vertical logo incorporating the musical and food icons representative of the festival in all three colors.

OCD created this horizontal logo format to give other agencies who'll use the logo more than one option.

WNBA LOGO

The WNBA is the top professional women's sports league in the world. In 2012, U.S. Women's Basketball won their fifth straight gold and forty-first straight Olympic game. The players are breaking every record in the books and have compelling individual stories to boot. That was the brief. OCD worked with the WNBA to create an identity system that puts an amplifier to the league's players and their remarkable game.

"Logo woman" is an evolution of the original WNBA shield. The silhouette was redrawn to better symbolize the athleticism and diversity of today's players. The orange and oatmeal were brought in from the league's most recognizable feature: the WNBA game ball. Referee uniforms and in-house communications had been leveraging the unique palette for some time, but it was never brought to the fans. And, of course, great pride, power and opportunity come from being part of the larger NBA family. To reinforce that relationship, the pointed shield was replaced with the rounded rectangular lozenge that has become synonymous with professional basketball worldwide.

Fans, partners, players and coaches all talk about a new swagger in the league. Going on twenty years, it's maturing into something that's increasingly tough and confident. That swagger needed a typographic voice. We recommended Cyclone because it incorporates a seam inspired by the seams of the basketball itself. It has great height and it was flexible enough to work on an angle, so it could come alive like the players.

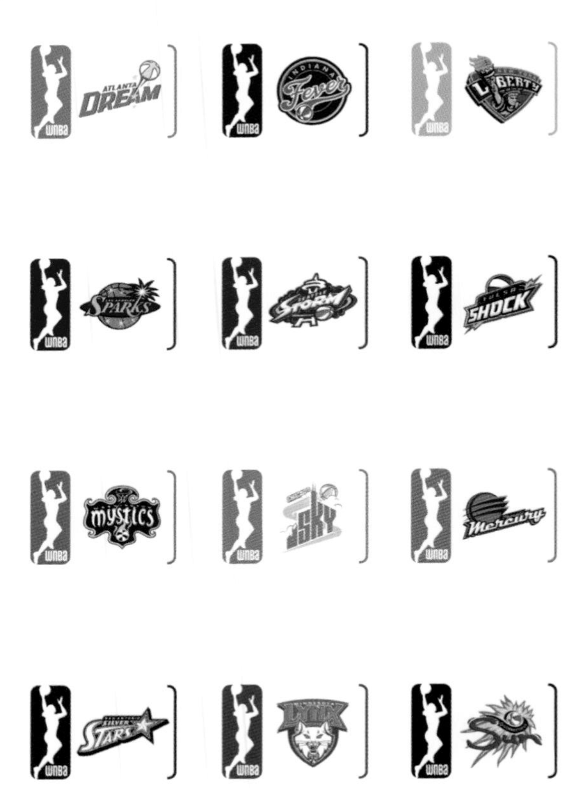

The vitality of the WNBA logo is represented in various forms, from the silhouette of a player to the logotype to representation in different colors when displayed with team logos.

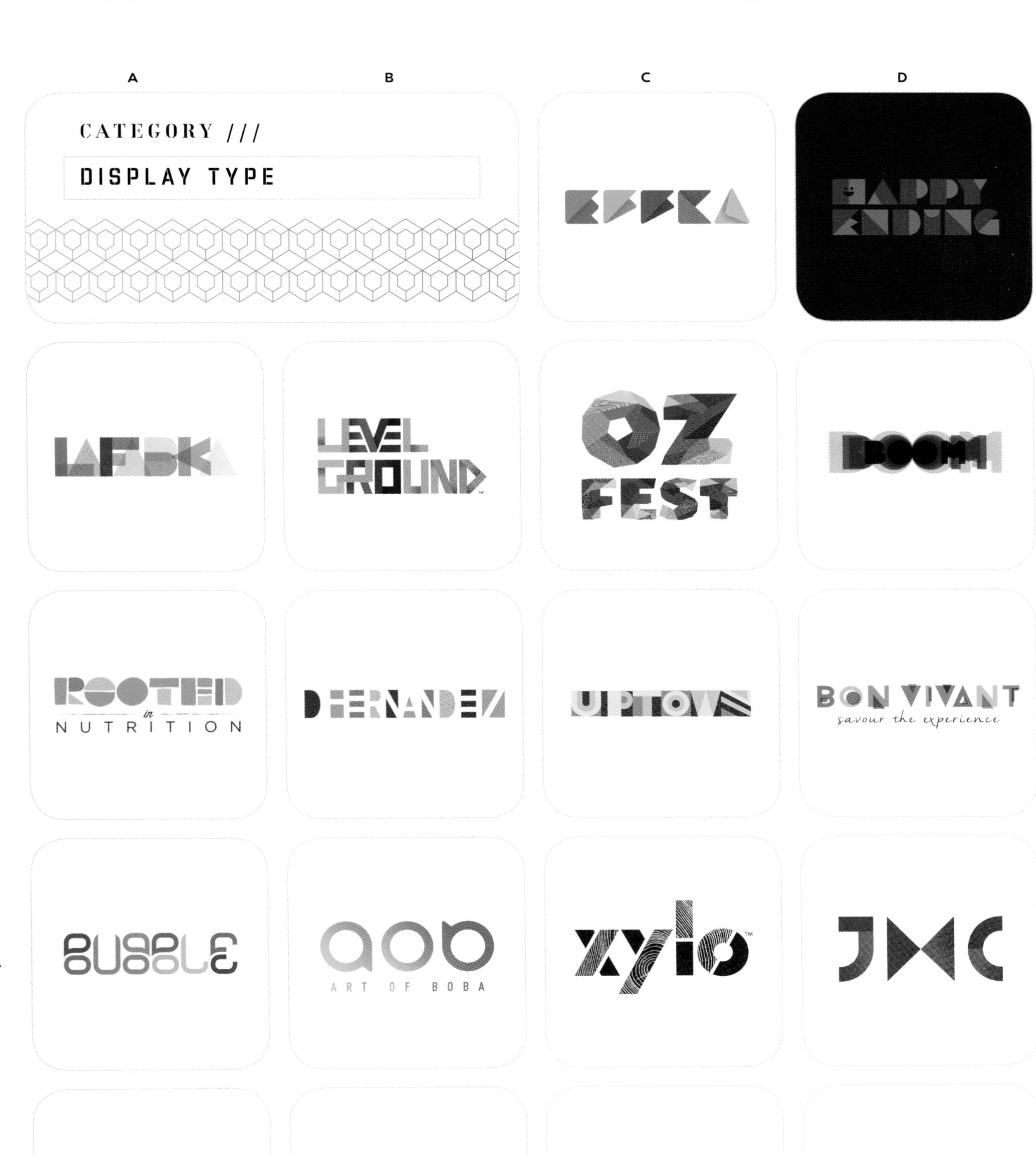

1C D Musab C EffKa **1D** D Quique Ollervides C Happy Ending
2A D Think to Make C La FabKa **2B** D Rule29 C Level Ground **2C** D Ishan Khosla Design C Australian High Commission **2D** D CINDERBLOC INC. C The School of Design (George Brown College)
3A D Think to Make C Rooted in Nutrition **3B** D Daniel Fernandez C Self **3C** D Keyword Design C Uptown United **3D** D Jeff Phillips Design C Bon Vivant
4A D Alex Tass C Bubble **4B** D AkarStudios C Art Of Boba **4C** D 70kft C Cyclewood Solutions **4D** D Gardner Design C Justin McClure Creative
5A D Voov Ltd. C Mobon **5B** D Fabio Okamoto Design C Okha **5C** D Tokshok C tokshok **5D** D smARTer C Kingstone Comics

A B C D

1

2

3

4

5

1A D South C art **1B** D Essex Two C Gretel, LLC **1C** D Alex Tass C Experimental work **1D** D Live Nation Labs C Live Nation
2A D Tangens C Refazenda **2B** D Levogrin C Solente **2C** D Jody Worthington Graphic Design C Kimberly Park Communications **2D** D Charm Creative C Red Calaca
3A D Creativille C Mama Said No Rock Band **3B** D Amy McAdams Design C Sherri Dugger **3C** D Quique Ollervides C Güeros / Alonso Ruizpalacios **3D** D M@OH! C Locally Laid Egg Company
4A D Glitschka Studios C Lord Maude **4B** D 903 Creative, LLC C 903 Creative **4C** D Tribambuka C Hot Teeth **4D** D Grafixd C DVD King
5A D Justin Gammon | Design + Illustration C Weirdo Toys **5B** D Longo Designs C Personal Project **5C** D Gyula Nemeth C Panini America **5D** D J Fletcher Design C Southern Craft Creamery

	A	B	C	D
1				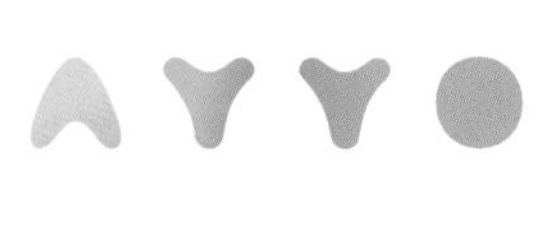
2				
3				
4				
5				

1A Ⓓ Larry Levine Ⓒ The Urban Tap **1B** Ⓓ Quique Ollervides Ⓒ Fan Art **1C** Ⓓ Ishan Khosla Design Ⓒ Australian High Commission **1D** Ⓓ ONY Ⓒ AYYO
2A Ⓓ Alex Tass Ⓒ DawnTown **2B** Ⓓ Jerron Ames Ⓒ Arties **2C** Ⓓ Creation Ⓒ Noise Communication Solutions **2D** Ⓓ Jeff Phillips Design Ⓒ myOZexp
3A Ⓓ Arcane / HONEY Ⓒ Maple and Moose **3B** Ⓓ Misign - Visual Communication Ⓒ BURZ **3C** Ⓓ Amy McAdams Design Ⓒ Sherri Dugger **3D** Ⓓ Creative Parc Ⓒ Colors of Hope
4A Ⓓ Tokshok Ⓒ Ufanet **4B** Ⓓ Andrius Vilbrantas Ⓒ Pandowear.com **4C** Ⓓ Pavel Saksin Ⓒ Tahuna **4D** Ⓓ Alama Design Ⓒ Sweet Ideas Cafe
5A Ⓓ THINKMULE Ⓒ Sailor's Rest Farm **5B** Ⓓ Kreativbuero Jonas Soeder Ⓒ Hook Music **5C** Ⓓ Quique Ollervides Ⓒ Siete Lobos Rojos **5D** Ⓓ Brandon Harrison Ⓒ Living Word Christian Center

DESIGNER /// DANA TANAMACHI

CLIENT /// NIKE

CATEGORY /// CALLIGRAPHY

Nike wanted to commemorate the 2013 Nike Women's Marathon in San Francisco with a special identity program to celebrate the marathon's tenth anniversary. To give the marks a distinguished, handmade look, Nike design director Emily Duell hired Dana Tanamachi as the artist-in-residence for the campaign. Tanamachi's hand-drawn style has a definitively bold yet elegant aesthetic, perfect for the event.

The design brief had several objectives, including: to encourage and inspire, to celebrate accomplishments, to be authentic, to be youthful, and to be local to San Francisco. With these goals in mind, Tanamachi first started drawing the "We Run" logo in pencil. "I did a few rough sketches, a bit blockier with the words stacked like wood type," she says. "I then drew the logotype on a swash baseline so it moves from low to high, showing forward movement, positive thinking and fluidity. There are a ton of hills in San Francisco so the upward movement is a nod to that."

The lettering was accompanied by cityscape illustrations that captured the essence of the city with the iconic Golden Gate Bridge, rocks, cliffs and waves. "Nike wanted the illustration to tell a story within this enclosure. I have a collection of books on circular Japanese ornamental designs that I referred to when developing these vignettes. You can see the Japanese influence in the waves and sky, but I also tried to incorporate modern elements such as the geometric rocks and a bridge made from almost tribal shapes," Tanamachi says.

Nike also asked Tanamachi to design a separate Nike Women's logo that would be used on signage and promotions for the event. In contrast to the bold, blockier We Run logo, Nike wanted a more elegant script style for this logo.

Duell says, "Dana did an excellent job creating a variety of different branding elements that provided us with a robust toolkit. She helped create an aesthetic that felt feminine and relevant and brought a fresh look to the race series."

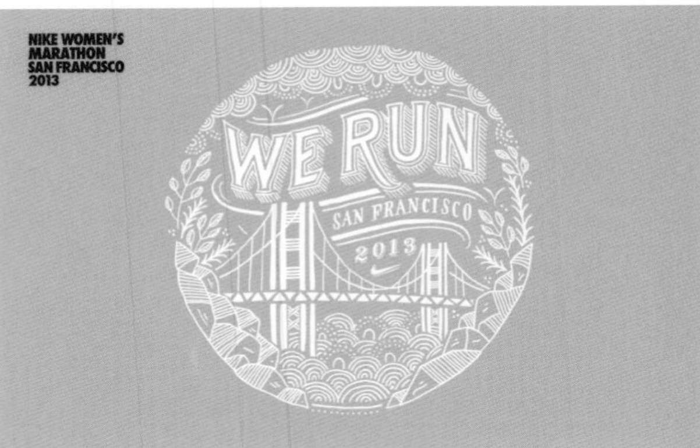

The We Run enclosure had to encompass several elements related to San Francisco, the 2013 Nike Women's Marathon host city. Tanamachi elegantly captured these elements within the circular enclosure.

The We Run logotype is used by itself for merchandise, printed over a female runner silhouette, illustrated by Hiroshi Tanabe. The fluidity and movement of the runner work seamlessly with the logotype, capturing the essence of the event. Even the Nike swoosh perfectly flows with the design.

In keeping with the forward movement of the other logotypes, Tanamachi incorporated the upward swoosh below the script for the secondary type. She used her own handwriting as the basis for the script, though she embellished the capitals.

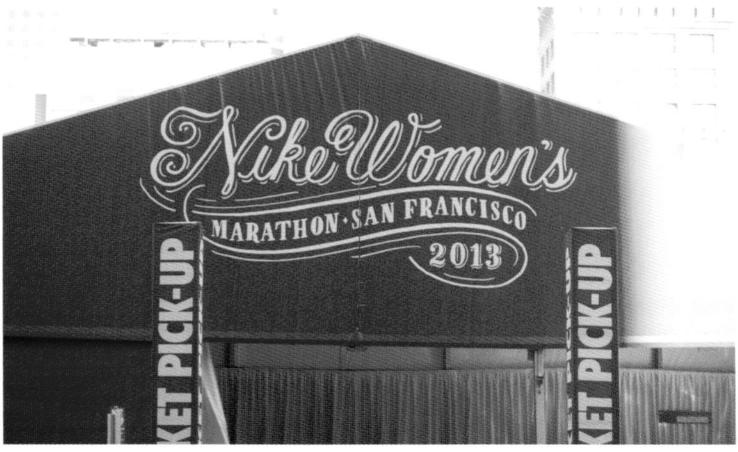

DESIGN /// LUKE LUCAS

CLIENT /// ALL GOOD ORGANICS

CATEGORY /// CALLIGRAPHY

All Good Organics, based in New Zealand, works with organic fair trade farmers to provide healthy, organic fruits and vegetables to consumers. Its offerings include organic sparkling fruit juices. AGO wanted to avoid the usual clichés associated with organics when rolling out this new product to consumers, such as folksy illustrations and raw materials like kraft paper. Simon Coley, AGO creative director sums it up: "The brief, in one line, was to make organics glamorous, and do something new."

To do this, he hired lettering artist Luke Lucas to come up with typographic styles for each flavor that could comfortably hug the shape of the bottle and be highly legible. Lucas, who's based in Sydney, Australia, is primarily known for his editorial and advertising work, so he was particularly excited to work on a logo for an actual product. It also helped that Coley is a fan of the late, great designer Herb Lubalin. "Luke is just as big of a fan, so when we met and talked about the project we hit it off. This made the creative process straightforward and really enjoyable," Coley says.

Each flavor of All Good Organics has its own logotype with the bird icon cleverly integrated in each design. The focus was on creating a beautiful shape, colors to complement the juice, and typographic treatment that would delight the eyes—just like the juice delights the tongue.

"It's rare for a client to have a passion for design and typography, let alone be familiar with the design legacy of the late Herb Lubalin, so it was a very pleasant surprise," Lucas says. "They wanted the type to be truly custom, juicy, and to take inspiration from Lubalin's use of ligatures and swashy typographic forms."

Lucas took that inspiration and developed his own type styles for the fruit juices, but the biggest challenge wasn't rendering the letters, it was the space it had to live on. "The shape of the bottle is like a teardrop, and the application space for printing the lettering is an awkward tapered rectangle, so this defined the overall shape and presence of the lettering on the bottles," he says. "Each of the flavors consisted of words of different lengths and line breaks, but as a range they needed to have a consistent proportional weight on the bottle."

To get the right balance, Lucas ended up going through several rounds of refinements. "After Luke had done a couple of preliminary sketches and we got the balance between letterforms and the swashes and curlicues that make the type look fruit-like and plant-like, it was a case of going back and forth with a number of refinements to fit the shape of the bottle and balance all five of the flavor names so the full set of bottles and flavors looked and felt like a family," Coley notes.

In addition to hitting the right balance for each flavor name, Lucas had to accommodate the AGO bird logo into each design. "The aim was to integrate the brand into the flavor lettering in the subtlest of ways to allow a single design piece to sit front and center on the bottle, with no further distractions or unnecessary visual clutter," Lucas explains. All the visual elements, including the juice itself, create a clear, sophisticated, mouth-watering identity for each organic flavor.

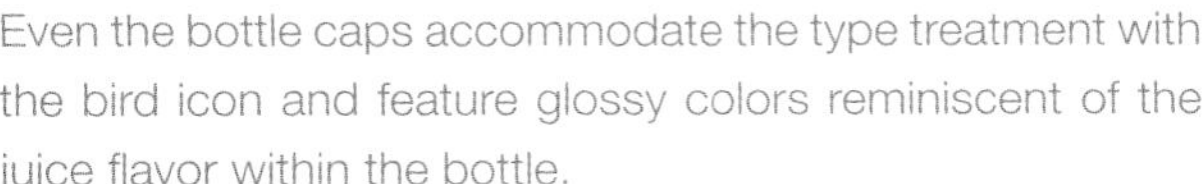

Even the bottle caps accommodate the type treatment with the bird icon and feature glossy colors reminiscent of the juice flavor within the bottle.

Lucas had an especially difficult challenge incorporating this long flavor name into the same space as the other fruit juice logos.

The sophisticated logotype and sparse flavor descriptions let the product speak for itself.

The logo was also featured on the juice cases.

A B C D

CATEGORY ///

CALLIGRAPHY

1

2

3

4

5

1C D FiftyIFifty C FiftyIFifty **1D** D Karl Design Vienna C biiid Germany
2A D Luka Balic C Leo Burnett, Open Brand **2B** D Luka Balic C Leo Burnett, Open Brand **2C** D Luka Balic C Jam Ritual **2D** D Rami Hoballah C Alaa Sheet
3A D Oven Design Workshop C Fiori **3B** D Samarskaya & Partners C Sweethaus **3C** D Quiskal C Boutique L'Arrivage **3D** D zero11 C Lebaneesh restaurant
4A D Xplaye C Brava AB **4B** D Fixer Creative Co. C Hannah Parsons **4C** D Pavel Saksin C Smine **4D** D Pavel Saksin C Moka
5A D Brandberry C Varmara **5B** D J Fletcher Design C Fatty's Brewing Co. **5C** D Odney C MBTs **5D** D Sunday Lounge C Becky Hersch

	A	B	C	D
1				
2	Haymaker			
3	Astra INTERACTIVE		Grattitude	Purple Heist
4				
5			Lozeau	Telly

1A Ⓓ Linda Bourdeaux Ⓒ Amber Beckham Photography **1B** Ⓓ Chad Michael Studio Ⓒ The Avala Wine Company **1C** Ⓓ Sunday Lounge Ⓒ Wanderlust Road **1D** Ⓓ Thomas Cook Designs Ⓒ Real McCoy's
2A Ⓓ Robot Agency Studios Ⓒ Haymaker Clothing **2B** Ⓓ Paul von Excite Ⓒ Baylife **2C** Ⓓ Paul von Excite Ⓒ TeeJay Delacruz **2D** Ⓓ Tortugastudio Ⓒ Savoy
3A Ⓓ Unipen Ⓒ Astra Interactive **3B** Ⓓ Paul von Excite Ⓒ Graph Paper Press **3C** Ⓓ NO-BAD Ⓒ Grattitude **3D** Ⓓ Just Creative Design Ⓒ Purple Heist
4A Ⓓ Type08 Ⓒ Noom **4B** Ⓓ Mindgruve Ⓒ SDX **4C** Ⓓ Marakasdesign Ⓒ LOLO Cakes Boutique **4D** Ⓓ Pixonal Ⓒ N/A
5A Ⓓ Maximo Gavete Ⓒ Pilar Astola **5B** Ⓓ Slagle Design Ⓒ Slagle Design **5C** Ⓓ Parallele gestion de marques Ⓒ Lozeau **5D** Ⓓ Pavel Saksin Ⓒ Telly

	A	B	C	D
1				
2				
3				
4				
5				

1A Ⓓ The Blksmith Design Co. Ⓒ Otis & Sons **1B** Ⓓ Stephen Lee Ogden Design Co. Ⓒ Debo's Diners (Steak & Shake Franchise Owner) **1C** Ⓓ Unipen Ⓒ Decor **1D** Ⓓ Helms Workshop Ⓒ Howler Bros
2A Ⓓ Haffelder Studios Ⓒ Electric Tattoo Parlor **2B** Ⓓ Roost Designs Ⓒ Panera Bread **2C** Ⓓ Letter Shoppe Ⓒ Caryn Wooldridge **2D** Ⓓ Austin Logo Designs Ⓒ Flat Bill Bat Co.
3A Ⓓ CWP Design Studio Ⓒ Cakewalk **3B** Ⓓ Tortoiseshell Black Ⓒ P&MM **3C** Ⓓ Refinery 43 Ⓒ Cindy Giovagnoli **3D** Ⓓ Akhmatov Studio Ⓒ Comfort
4A Ⓓ Jody Worthington Graphic Design Ⓒ Drift Boat Co. **4B** Ⓓ Paul von Excite Ⓒ Haven & Florin **4C** Ⓓ Paul von Excite Ⓒ Theme Designer **4D** Ⓓ Oronoz Brandesign Ⓒ Better Fellow
5A Ⓓ Jody Worthington Graphic Design Ⓒ Hello, Sailor! **5B** Ⓓ Farmboy Ⓒ Healthwise Essential Oils **5C** Ⓓ Studio Botes Ⓒ 360eight **5D** Ⓓ 903 Creative, LLC Ⓒ NatureServe

DESIGN /// CHAD MICHAEL

CLIENT /// DISTRÖYA SPICED SPIRIT

CATEGORY /// CRESTS

Chad Michael has always loved art and design, so he pursued drawing and painting when he went to university. Unfortunately, a devastating accident badly injured his right hand and damaged 70 percent of the ligaments and tendons, leaving him unable to draw for any length of time. Still wanting a career in the arts, Michael pursued graphic design. He works completely digitally, but you wouldn't know it from looking at his work, which has a decidedly handcrafted feel. "I tend to operate in a similar manner as if by hand. I rough together initial concepts with hundreds of different pieces I've developed over the years to grasp the main idea. Then I craft and evolve the piece until I have a gut feeling that the design is where it should be," he notes.

This meticulous approach to design is why his crest logos are so good. When Diströya Spiced Spirit wanted to expand its brand and have a separate and distinct logo mark for T-shirts, coasters and the like, they asked Michael to do it. He was no stranger to the company: He designed the packaging the year before, working with illustrator Steven Noble. The packaging features a woodcut illustration of a Viking, below the product name set in a blackletter typeface. "I took the feeling of the Diströya brand that I had developed prior, which is medieval, authentic and masculine, and pushed it further to show the brand's wide visual range. I gained inspiration from old bookplates and manuscript drop caps," Michael says.

"I always start with a foundation, which in this case was the *D* drop cap, and work out from there until there is a fluidity between space and design elements," he says. "Even though much of my work lends itself to be condensed with ornamentation and typography, there is always a level of breathing room where the viewers eyes may rest." Crisp lines separate the elements, so even the tiniest details aren't lost when printed.

The evolution of the logo starts with the *D* at the center. Michael gradually builds each layer from the inside out and reverses the background midway through the exploratory phase.

The final logo design was printed by letterpress on coasters by Studio on Fire.

The Diströya packaging designed by Michael and illustrated by Steven Noble.

Migrant

German-based Trautwein Distillery Company wanted its brand to focus on the owner's late grandfather and his 1930s migration to the United States. The crest logo takes visual cues from the sea by way of the anchor symbol, rope-like looping of the *M*, and outer circles that evoke an abstract water ripple.

AUSTIN COCKTAILS

Michael developed this primary crest for Texas-based natural cocktail company. The aim was develop a mark that felt organic and modern with a touch of luxury.

DAGGER & CO.

This tattoo company, based on the island of Malta, is operated by two eccentric owners who wanted to stray from the typical tattoo shop identity. They wanted a single memorable mark that reflected the shop's personality and commitment to high quality.

DESIGN /// JOE WHITE

CLIENT /// ARTILLERY DRUMS

CATEGORY /// CRESTS

Artillery Drums is a drum manufacturer in the United Kingdom, processing military grade metals into top range drums. They hired Joe White of Ye Olde Studio in London to create a logo design and emblem for their product. "The main idea for this brand was to create something in line with the industry, but also show a military theme," White says.

"When I'm asked to produce a brand, often a crest will be a part of this, along with many other elements. I often refer to my designs as badges or emblems."

Artillery Drums wanted the full monty with this brand—custom lettering and an emblem similar to a military insignia. "They wanted a custom typeface to distinguish their company from the others and work well as a logotype without any exterior decorations or symbols," he notes. He produced several custom typefaces, each referencing a heavy metal music style, for the client to choose from, along with four different design directions.

"In the final stages, I also produced a detailed badge along with several other branding elements. Some of the elements are a little worn, where as others are much cleaner," White notes. "This allows the company to dress up or dress down to suit any event or product without losing sight of the original brand."

ARTILLERY DRUMS
ARTILLERY DRUMS
ARTILLERY DRUMS
ARTILLERY DRUMS
ARTILLERY DRUMS
ARTILLERY DRUMS
ARTILLERY DRUMS
Artillery Drums

White did several hand-lettering samples for the client to choose from.

> "What's great in this day and age is that we are free to explore all of these old styles into new, modern approaches for branding."
> —Joe White

Taking his initial lettering samples, White did some preliminary logo designs, mixing and matching type styles to see what would work with each design.

Here he focused on trademarks for Artillery Drums.

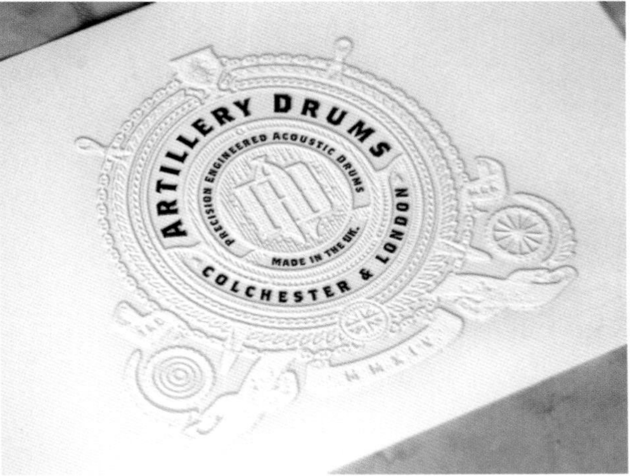

There are two versions of the final crest logos, which can be used in either white or black. On the detailed, letterpress-printed logo, the drum sticks emerge from the top and bottom of the crest.

A B C D

1

CATEGORY ///

CRESTS

2

3

4

5

1C Ⓓ Tim Frame Design Ⓒ TIM-O-TEE **1D** Ⓓ Roger Strunk Ⓒ Doo-Dah Merch
2A Ⓓ Ye Olde Studio Ⓒ Ye Olde Studio **2B** Ⓓ Keith Davis Young Ⓒ Vernetti **2C** Ⓓ Oxide Design Co. Ⓒ Nebraskans for Civic Reform **2D** Ⓓ 903 Creative, LLC Ⓒ StyleCraft Homes
3A Ⓓ Proof Positive Brand Design Ⓒ The Tribune **3B** Ⓓ McGuire Design Ⓒ Christina Cruz **3C** Ⓓ Type08 Ⓒ Pollaro **3D** Ⓓ Cinq Partners Ⓒ SCHLADMING VIENNA AUSTRIA
4A Ⓓ Tamer Koseli Ⓒ symbolicities.com **4B** Ⓓ Steven Schroeder Ⓒ PAIR OF HEIRS FAITH & STYLE **4C** Ⓓ Stebbings Partners Ⓒ Boston Nightlife Ventures **4D** Ⓓ Clark & Co. Ⓒ The Sweat Life Shop
5A Ⓓ Bryan Couchman Design Ⓒ The Fox's Hollow **5B** Ⓓ Steve Wolf Designs Ⓒ Hayes & Taylor Clothing **5C** Ⓓ MODA Collaborative Ⓒ Collaborative American Made Creative Design **5D** Ⓓ Paul Tynes Design Ⓒ Swindoll Drums

A B C D

1

2

3

4

5

1A Ⓓ danielguillermo.com Ⓒ SVA **1B** Ⓓ Jerron Ames Ⓒ Fivestar Branding Agency **1C** Ⓓ Jonathan Schubert Ⓒ HONEY BEE LOCAL RAW UNFILTERED HONEY **1D** Ⓓ Sunday Lounge Ⓒ River's Edge Brewing Co
2A Ⓓ Sudduth Design Co. Ⓒ Mighty Fit **2B** Ⓓ Stevaker Design Ⓒ SupplyHog **2C** Ⓓ created by South Ⓒ DAILY KITCHEN & PRESSED JUICERY **2D** Ⓓ Unboxedesign Ⓒ Doug Mundt
3A Ⓓ Braizen Ⓒ Steve Barrett **3B** Ⓓ Stitch Design Co. Ⓒ Monamie Ice Cream **3C** Ⓓ Funnel Ⓒ Leza Tellam **3D** Ⓓ Second Street Creative Ⓒ Center for Inquiry
4A Ⓓ Odney Ⓒ Millers Homestead **4B** Ⓓ Glitschka Studios Ⓒ Lorain County Tourism Board **4C** Ⓓ Husbandmen Ⓒ Pretty City Gardens & Landscaping **4D** Ⓓ Braizen Ⓒ Samantha Pattillo
5A Ⓓ Sunday Lounge Ⓒ Caveman Brewing Co **5B** Ⓓ Keith Davis Young Ⓒ Transpecos **5C** Ⓓ Dessein Ⓒ Beerland Brewing Co **5D** Ⓓ AcrobatAnt Ⓒ BOK Center

A B C D

1

2

3

4

5

1A Ⓓ Salih Kucukaga Design Studio Ⓒ S.C. **1B** Ⓓ MODA Collaborative Ⓒ The Kaiser **1C** Ⓓ James Dean & Company Ⓒ Sunflower Espresso **1D** Ⓓ Projektor Brand Image Ⓒ Switchback Cyclery
2A Ⓓ Jon Eslinger / Design Ⓒ Calliope Piano Service **2B** Ⓓ Jerron Ames Ⓒ Wine Broker **2C** Ⓓ Chad Michael Studio Ⓒ Self Branding **2D** Ⓓ Chad Michael Studio Ⓒ Mirko Merchiori Photography
3A Ⓓ Jerron Ames Ⓒ Rocky Mountain Timber Frame **3B** Ⓓ Greg Valdez Design Ⓒ Birdie's Best **3C** Ⓓ THINKMULE Ⓒ Summer House Films **3D** Ⓓ GreyBox Creative Ⓒ Luxury Big Island
4A Ⓓ Studio Ink Ⓒ Bike Bendigo Inc. **4B** Ⓓ Nosh Creative Ⓒ Scott Jones **4C** Ⓓ Sunday Lounge Ⓒ COLORADO SKY Brewing Company **4D** Ⓓ Type08 Ⓒ Almost Famous
5A Ⓓ Raineri Design Srl Ⓒ Vignenote **5B** Ⓓ Mikey Burton Ⓒ Esquire **5C** Ⓓ Flight Deck Creative Ⓒ Jesper Jensen **5D** Ⓓ Banowetz + Company, Inc. Ⓒ White Rock Lake Conservancy

	A	B	C	D
1				
2				
3				
4				
5				

1A Ⓓ Sudduth Design Co. Ⓒ Mighty Fit **1B** Ⓓ Sloane Design Ⓒ North Carolina State Parks **1C** Ⓓ Jack in the Box Ⓒ Margaret River Ale Company **1D** Ⓓ Tribe Ⓒ Old Bust Head Brewing Company
2A Ⓓ Chad Michael Studio Ⓒ Dagger & Co. Tattoo Shop **2B** Ⓓ bartodell.com Ⓒ SlateStudio.com **2C** Ⓓ Funnel Ⓒ Gail Payne **2D** Ⓓ Jon Kay Design Ⓒ Fangamer
3A Ⓓ Alexander Wende Ⓒ Corte Corvo **3B** Ⓓ Sean Heisler Design Ⓒ Raleigh Beer Garden **3C** Ⓓ Sunday Lounge Ⓒ Sunday Lounge **3D** Ⓓ The Blksmith Design Co. Ⓒ Prince Ink Co.
4A Ⓓ Sunday Lounge Ⓒ Salida Hydroponic Supply **4B** Ⓓ Courtney Windham Design Ⓒ Department of Industrial + Graphic Design, Auburn University **4C** Ⓓ Alphabet Arm Design Ⓒ G2 Technology Group, Inc. **4D** Ⓓ Stevan Rodic Ⓒ Campers 4a Cause **5A** Ⓓ Airtype Studio Ⓒ Krankies Coffee **5B** Ⓓ Resource Branding & Design Ⓒ Carter USA **5C** Ⓓ The Brandit Ⓒ Markstein Beverage Co. **5D** Ⓓ Resource Branding & Design Ⓒ CF Lane

	A	B	C	D
1				
2				
3				
4				
5				

1A Ⓓ Courtney Windham Design Ⓒ Rockhurst Farm **1B** Ⓓ Austin Logo Designs Ⓒ BLACKBERRY Blossom Foods **1C** Ⓓ Stan Designworks Ⓒ Gaharu Technologies Sdn. Bhd. **1D** Ⓓ Grason Studio Ⓒ Tacos Banditas
2A Ⓓ Ⓒ Big Sky Burger **2B** Ⓓ Norfolk Southern Corp. Ⓒ Norfolk Southern **2C** Ⓓ Graphic D-Signs, Inc. Ⓒ The Renovation Company **2D** Ⓓ James Dean & Company Ⓒ Superior Rubber Stamp & Seal
3A Ⓓ Chad Michael Studio Ⓒ Old Town Distilling Co. **3B** Ⓓ Tin Bacic Ⓒ Twilight Pizza Bistro **3C** Ⓓ Sabingrafik, Inc. Ⓒ Malahat Spirits Co. **3D** Ⓓ Nox Creative Ⓒ Dock and Roll Diner
4A Ⓓ Ye Olde Studio Ⓒ Manor Barn **4B** Ⓓ Ye Olde Studio Ⓒ Coffee Works **4C** Ⓓ Ye Olde Studio Ⓒ Amica **4D** Ⓓ Jon Kay Design Ⓒ Jeff Benson
5A Ⓓ Glitschka Studios Ⓒ Fidelis Farm & Vineyard **5B** Ⓓ Amy McAdams Design Ⓒ Redemption Cider **5C** Ⓓ bartodell.com Ⓒ Bomb City Supply Co. **5D** Ⓓ Ⓒ Great Rhytm Brewing Company

A B C D

1

2

3

4

5

1A Ⓓ Glitschka Studios Ⓒ Fidelis Farm & Vineyard **1B** Ⓓ Ye Olde Studio Ⓒ Artillery Drums **1C** Ⓓ Patrick Carter Design, Inc. Ⓒ Make My Freshener **1D** Ⓓ johnshoward Ⓒ Sisters Cove
2A Ⓓ James Dean & Company Ⓒ The Humidor Cigars & Lounge **2B** Ⓓ Sunday Lounge Ⓒ Seasons Cafe **2C** Ⓓ Unboxedesign Ⓒ Jennifer Williams **2D** Ⓓ Graphic D-Signs, Inc. Ⓒ Pint
3A Ⓓ Fuzzco Ⓒ COAST BREWING **3B** Ⓓ Sunday Lounge Ⓒ Colorado Sky Brewing Co **3C** Ⓓ Sunday Lounge Ⓒ Guidestone Colorado **3D** Ⓓ Timber Design Company Ⓒ Black Acre Brewing Co.
4A Ⓓ Graphic D-Signs, Inc. Ⓒ The Great Divide Campground **4B** Ⓓ Jerron Ames Ⓒ Presidio Sports Management **4C** Ⓓ David Cran Design Ⓒ Kerrisdale Farmers Market **4D** Ⓓ LETR & Co. Ⓒ SAVANNAH COFFEE ROASTERS
5A Ⓓ Ye Olde Studio Ⓒ Club Scale **5B** Ⓓ Sudduth Design Co. Ⓒ Moonshine Tea Co. **5C** Ⓓ Proof Positive Brand Design Ⓒ The Tribune **5D** Ⓓ David Cran Design Ⓒ Tazito Burrito

A B C D

1

2

3

4

5

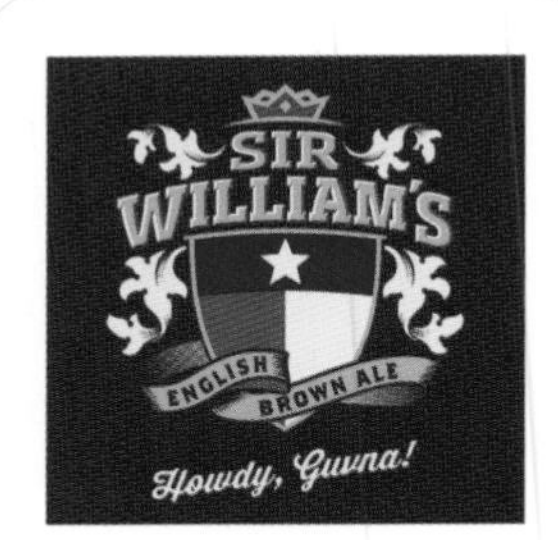

1A Ⓓ Sudduth Design Co. Ⓒ Moonshine Tea Co. **1B** Ⓓ Roger Strunk Ⓒ Robostangs VEX Robotics Team 6133 **1C** Ⓓ Josh Carnley Ⓒ ROOTER PENNANT SUPPLY **1D** Ⓓ Patrick Carter Design, Inc. Ⓒ Kick Butts Vapor
2A Ⓓ Roger Strunk Ⓒ Hutton Block Party **2B** Ⓓ Tim Frame Design Ⓒ TIM-O-TEE **2C** Ⓓ McGuire Design Ⓒ Alamo Heights Booster Club **2D** Ⓓ Dalton Agency Ⓒ Sunshine Soccer Group
3A Ⓓ 144design Inc Ⓒ North American Hockey League **3B** Ⓓ Glitschka Studios Ⓒ Caldejon Justice Foundation **3C** Ⓓ Amy McAdams Design Ⓒ Indianapolis Public Schools (IPS) **3D** Ⓓ Alex Rinker Ⓒ NSMW
4A Ⓓ Fraser Davidson Ⓒ Chicago Knights **4B** Ⓓ Sunday Lounge Ⓒ Colorado Sky Brewing Co **4C** Ⓓ Deuxtone Ⓒ Baylor Student Foundation **4D** Ⓓ Jerron Ames Ⓒ Vacation Races
5A Ⓓ Steve Wolf Designs Ⓒ LEHOME Vintage Furniture **5B** Ⓓ Dotzero Design Ⓒ Pendlton Woolen Mills **5C** Ⓓ Buzzbomb Creative Ⓒ Grapevine Craft Brewery **5D** Ⓓ Timber Design Company Ⓒ Hubbard & Cravens Coffee and Tea

	A	B	C	D
1				
2				
3				
4				
5				

1A D Headron Collider C Wayde Carroll Photography LLC **1B** D Jerron Ames C Fivestar Branding Agency **1C** D Studio Absolute C The Provision **1D** D Jody Worthington Graphic Design C Kimberly Park Communications
2A D Right Angle C Lafayette Science Museum **2B** D Severance Digital Studio C Fulton Cycle Works **2C** D Clark & Co. C Sail Away **2D** D Letter Shoppe C Daniel Nguyen
3A D Glitschka Studios C White Hat **3B** D A.D. Creative Group C DNC **3C** D Jon Kay Design C Fangamer **3D** D Stiles Design C Roaring Fork Beer Company
4A D eggnerd C Dragons Soccer **4B** D Outdoor Cap C Marley's Pizzeria **4C** D Eder Saos C Marley's Pizzeria **4D** D Ninet6 Ltd C Richmond Republic
5A D Chris Millspaugh Design C Beautiful Music Violin Shop **5B** D Tortugastudio C N/A **5C** D David Cran Design C Crisp and Co. Pickles **5D** D Sunday Lounge C Salida Hydroponic Supply

	A	B	C	D
1				
2				
3				
4	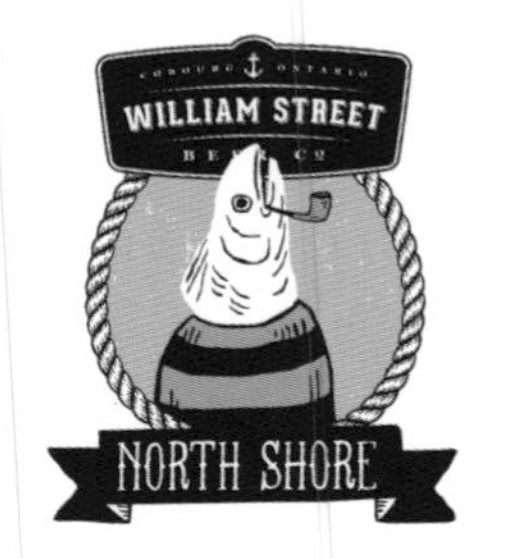			
5				

1A Ⓓ Tortoiseshell Black Ⓒ Geeky Jerseys **1B** Ⓓ Jon Kay Design Ⓒ fangamer **1C** Ⓓ Oronoz Brandesign Ⓒ Funny or Die **1D** Ⓓ R&R Partners Ⓒ Mark Naparstek
2A Ⓓ TYPE AND SIGNS Ⓒ El Trapiche **2B** Ⓓ Hubbell Design Works Ⓒ MOUNTAINEERS **2C** Ⓓ Wray Ward Ⓒ Self Promotion **2D** Ⓓ Dessein Ⓒ Beerland Brewing Co
3A Ⓓ Jackson Spalding Ⓒ Sinister Sound **3B** Ⓓ sodesign Ⓒ N/A **3C** Ⓓ Glitschka Studios Ⓒ The Wicked Wheel **3D** Ⓓ Gardner Design Ⓒ Willow Creek Ranch
4A Ⓓ Luke Despatie & The Design Firm Ⓒ William Street Beer Co. **4B** Ⓓ Dave Smith Artist Ⓒ John Mayer **4C** Ⓓ Bethany Heck Ⓒ N/A **4D** Ⓓ Resource Branding & Design Ⓒ CF Lane
5A Ⓓ 144design Inc Ⓒ Old School Outfitters **5B** Ⓓ 903 Creative, LLC Ⓒ yogg **5C** Ⓓ Sudduth Design Co. Ⓒ Tommy's Superfoods **5D** Ⓓ Ninet6 Ltd Ⓒ Bronx Brew & Brew

A B C D

1

2

3

4

5

1A D Glitschka Studios C Printers Distillery **1B** D Wray Ward C Brandon Scharr / Patrick McLean **1C** D Amy McAdams Design C Indy Reads & The Simon Family Foundation **1D** D Second Street Creative C Grace Community Church
2A D Clark & Co. C CRE8TOR INDUSTRIES **2B** D Second Street Creative C South Circle Farm **2C** D Funnel C Bryon Larrance **2D** D Stitch Design Co. C Remington Roasters
3A D Josh Carnley C Granite City Running **3B** D Sudduth Design Co. C Moonshine Tea Co. **3C** D Timber Design Company C Big Red Liquors **3D** D Timber Design Company C The North End
4A D Handsome C Lucas Bols **4B** D Wray Ward C Aviator Brewing **4C** D Jerron Ames C The Roughout Rose **4D** D Keith Davis Young C Paul Octavious
5A D Jon Kay Design C Desert Bus For Hope Chairty **5B** D CF Napa Brand Design C Canopy Management **5C** D Steve Wolf Designs C Hook & Irons Clothing **5D** D Chad Michael Studio C The Beauty Kitchen

DESIGN /// BRANDIOSE

CLIENT /// EL PASO CHIHUAHUAS

CATEGORY /// SPORTS

Jason Klein and Casey White are lifelong friends who started their design career together while still in high school in San Diego, California, by designing mascots and uniforms for local football teams. During summer break in college, they put together their portfolios and sent them to all 160 minor league baseball teams in hopes of getting a gig. One team responded, and that was the beginning of their careers designing logos for minor league baseball, which is still the foundation of their business at Brandiose fifteen years later. White does most of the design and illustration work, and Klein focuses on client relations and early concept development.

"Brands for minor league baseball teams are really integrated with stories about the towns," says White, so for every logo project, they travel to the town and find out what's unique and important in each community. "The club owner has no say about the product on the field [i.e. the players and the game], so they control everything off the field, and that's what we do. It's about implementing that brand at the park through signage, wayfinding, mascots and special promotions. The theme and story of the entire ball park experience is the most important to us."

Such was the case with the El Paso minor league baseball team. "El Paso is a really unique border town, but it has a chip on its shoulder because of its reputation of being next to Juarez and the violence there. It's a dusty western town with a Mexican and cowboy vibe," he says. "The process of being there helped us understand that they needed to be famous. Every attempt in the past was sort of a parody of the big kids. It needed its own identity, something very authentic."

In addition to creating a logo for the team, Brandiose suggested Chihuahuas for the team name and mascot. Another early contender was the Buckaroos, which came from the owners. "The town is in the Chihuahuan Desert. It's a scrappy underdog town. That's also the story of minor league baseball, trying to make it to the big leagues, so Chihuahuas were a great fit," explains White. "You have to consider how the name and mascot will contribute to the overall experience at the ballpark and the ideas of family and fun."

After visiting El Paso, Brandiose put together a brief listing the town's values, vision, aspirations and unique qualities, combined with photos they gathered of the locals, public buildings, art and industry. Armed with this information, White did a first round of tight sketches to present to the team owners, including elements that could be used for both Buckaroos and Chihuahuas. "We call this our shotgun approach. I sketch really tiny so I can get a lot done quickly," he says. "The tight sketches keep the conversation on track to focus on the story. I know that once we take it into Illustrator it will evolve a lot, so I'm not worried about getting it totally accurate at this stage."

By the third round of sketches, the Buckaroos direction was eliminated to focus on the dog's attributes instead. "In round three we made him a little more psycho than he should be. His proportions changed a bit. We gave him dark bags under his eyes, like he was up all night digging in the junkyard. There's also an eye patch. In the final version there's a scar under his eye," White says. As he refined the Chihuahua, he also worked on the lettering: "The font is inspired by the architecture and the town."

When working with any major sports team, it's imperative that the design can be translated to embroidery. "That's really where baseball brands exist for most people, and designing for embroidery is very specific," White notes. Twelve years ago he and Klein visited the headquarters of New Era in Buffalo, New York, which embroiders the official caps of Minor and Major League Baseball. "We spent the whole day standing over the shoulders of the digitizers as they retraced our designs, learning their techniques and what's possible. All of our designs are built with that capability in mind. They need to be illustrative while also keeping it simple enough to be embroidered."

White and Klein are pleased with how well the mascot has played out in the overarching brand experience at the ballpark. Nachos are served in dog bowls, and restroom signage includes hydrants—themes that were devised by Brandiose and carried out in "Disneyesque style throughout the park," notes White, who admits that he and Klein are Disney fanatics, and they like to think of themselves as the Disney imagineers of baseball.

"The town was really excited and had a beautiful ballpark, but they hated the name," he says with a laugh. "But that's really common."

"We come to these projects with the best intentions. When it comes to naming we've got a really good track record. Now the Chihuahua is a beloved icon in El Paso, and it's breaking all kinds of merchandising records. Attendance is excellent. It's very cool to see that transformation," White says.

EL PASO

EL PASO PERSONALITY

"WE CAN MAKE FUN OF US, BUT YOU CAN'T"
"WHY NOT ME?"
AWKWARD
BICULTURAL
BRASH
CHIP ON SHOULDER
DOESN'T NECESSARILY ASSIMILATE
DON'T TELL US WHAT TO DO
FRIENDLY
INDEPENDENT
IRREVERENT
LEFT OUT
LONER
LOW SELF ESTEEM
(WE ARE WHAT WE THINK WE ARE)
MIDDLE CHILD
MISUNDERSTOOD
PARTY ANIMAL
POOR
QUIET
SHY
SMART KID
TOOK THE WRONG PATH
UNDERDOG
UNDERESTIMATED
UNSURE
VERY TOUCH
YOUNG

EL PASO VALUES

"REAL" MEXICAN FOOD
CULTURALLY TOLERANT
FEISTY
FIERCELY PROTECTIVE
FOOD-ORIENTED
HOSPITALITY
ISLAND VIBE
NOT PART OF TEXAS
NOT PRETENTIOUS
POLITE
REBELLIOUS
SUPER LAID BACK
TAILGATING
TRANSITIONAL FAMILY VALUES
WARM TO OUTSIDERS
WELCOMING

EL PASO ASPIRATIONS

"LA FRONTERA"
CAMARADERIE
COMMITMENT
FUN ESCAPE
GOING PLACES
GREAT SMALL TOWN
HEROS & RITUALS
HIP / COOL
OPTIMISM
PALATABLE DOWNTOWN ENERGY
PLACE TO BE SEEN
POSSIBILITIES
PRIDE
PROGRESS
RESPECT

BRAND VISION

IRREVERENT
UNIQUE
EDGY
COOL
PROGRESSIVE
HUMOROUS

DALLAS

BRAND AWARENESS
COMPETITIVE
EXCLUSIVE
MINI LOS ANGELES
PREPPY
PUSHY
RICH
SHOWY
SNOB
PRETENTIOUS
UNNECESSARY

EL PASO STEREOTYPES

DRY
DUSTY BORDER TOWN
HOT

BRAND IDEAS

- FLAME OR STAR CHANGE COLOR FOR WIN / GAME TONIGHT
- CHUCOLEAKS (BATHROOM)
- BAR CALLED "CITY HALL"

EL PASO ICONS

"CHUO-TOWN"
BOOTS
BUDWEISER BEER
CHIPS
ENCHILADAS
LONGEST RUNNING RODEO
MARGARITA
MOUNTAIN
OLD WEST / OLDEST MISSION
SMOKE STACK
SOMBRERO
STAR
SUN
TACO
TEQUILA
THUNDERBIRD

Brandiose

When embarking on any logo project, White and Klein compile a brief that details not only prospective brand attributes, but community values and local icons. They compile photos from around town of the people, architecture, and popular hot spots.

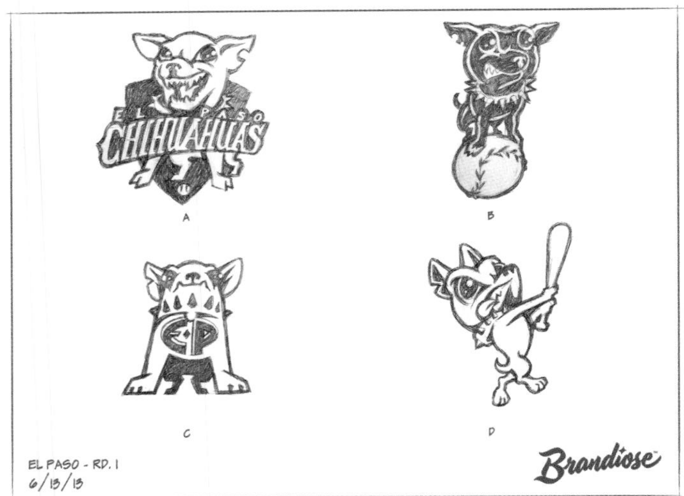

Brandiose's first round of sketches includes several fierce-looking Chihuahuas, lettering trials, and a couple of Buckaroos sketches, since that name was still in the running. "These are illustrative, complex logos and very narrative, so details can run away with themselves at this stage," White notes.

In the second round of sketches, Brandiose experimented with different eyes for the dog and continued tweaking the letters. The swinging character references the big league club, the San Diego Padres.

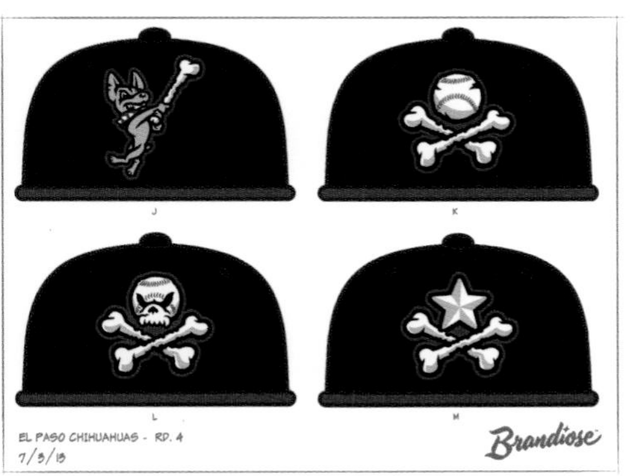

By the fourth round of sketches, the Chihuahua was the chosen direction. Brandiose experimented with different facial expressions, as well as playing with eye patches or dark bags under the eyes. "We have a sweet spot that we try to work toward—tenacious." The dog looks fierce but not maniacal; cute but not cartoony. They also created other elements for hats, such as a skull with dog bones and the city initials.

The final logo design has been implemented throughout the ballpark, and fans are buying the merchandise in droves.

	A	B	C	D
1				
2				
3				
4				
5				

1C Ⓓ brandon Ⓒ Amchit Club **1D** Ⓓ petervasvari.com Ⓒ Hungarian Leisure Sport Association
2A Ⓓ Rickabaugh Graphics Ⓒ American Athletic Conference **2B** Ⓓ Fraser Davidson Ⓒ Champion **2C** Ⓓ Riggalicious Design, LLC Ⓒ Personal Project **2D** Ⓓ Riggalicious Design, LLC Ⓒ Personal Project
3A Ⓓ Swanson Russell Ⓒ Food Bank for the Heartland **3B** Ⓓ Luke Bott Design & Illustration Ⓒ N/A **3C** Ⓓ bartodell.com Ⓒ Amarillo Fire FC **3D** Ⓓ bartodell.com Ⓒ High Plains Drifters
4A Ⓓ Design Studio Minin and Pozharsky Ⓒ FC Zenit, Saint-Petersburg, Russia **4B** Ⓓ petervasvari.com Ⓒ Somos Broadcast Media Zrt. **4C** Ⓓ eggnerd Ⓒ Dragons Soccer **4D** Ⓓ Gardner Design Ⓒ Flying Squirrel
5A Ⓓ Gyula Nemeth Ⓒ Team Hungary **5B** Ⓓ Bethany Heck Ⓒ N/A **5C** Ⓓ Type08 Ⓒ Tim Carter Foundation **5D** Ⓓ R&R Partners Ⓒ Las Vegas Convention & Visitors Authority

A B C D

1

2

3

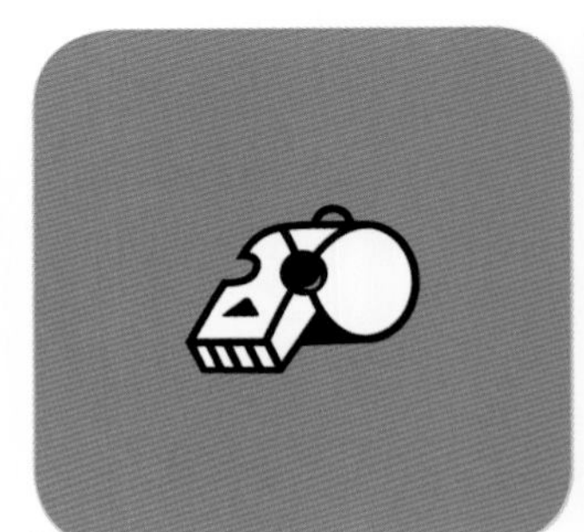

4

5

1A D Fraser Davidson C London Warriors **1B** D Fraser Davidson C West Sydney Pirates **1C** D Hubbell Design Works C 98 Skulls **1D** D Rickabaugh Graphics C American Athletic Conference
2A D AcrobatAnt C BOK Center **2B** D Link Creative C JRM Hornets **2C** D Jerron Ames C Arteis **2D** D Karl Design Vienna C Fairliners
3A D Torch Creative C National Hockey League **3B** D WestmorelandFlint C N/A **3C** D iTortoiseshell Black C Milton Keynes Shadows **3D** D Stevan Rodic C N/A
4A D Jerron Ames C N/A **4B** D Denys Kotliarov C Brick technology **4C** D notamedia C Russian swimming federation **4D** D Double A Creative C N/A
5A D Roger Strunk C Unused **5B** D Independent graphic designer C Runifly **5C** D Associated Integrated Marketing C Associated Integrated Marketing **5D** D Helikopter Brand Design C Pite Havsbad group

DESIGN /// GYULA NEMETH

CLIENT /// BUDAPEST COWBELLS

CATEGORY /// HEADS

In the last ten years, football has increasingly gained popularity in Budapest, Hungary. It is home to a twenty-team league with three divisions, with more than two thousand players. When two amateur football teams merged—the Cowboys and Rebels—Gyula Nemeth was hired to create the new logo. "The name Cowbells was decided by team management. I liked it from the beginning," Nemeth says. "Football is a very serious sport, and I tend to like when a team, especially on the semipro level, doesn't take itself too seriously."

Nemeth, who has been working as a designer since 1999, has recently been focusing a lot of his logo work on illustrative faces and heads. When he ventures out, he tends to memorize interesting faces so he can sketch them when he returns home. "I love to capture characters and the variety of it. It's just such a waste not to put an interesting face on paper," he notes. "I've done hundreds of simple vector head illustrations over the last couple of years. It's always fun to capture the likeness of somebody while simplifying the facial features until it's just a few lines and shapes."

His challenge with the Cowbell mascot was to convey something masculine and strong with a name that, quite frankly, doesn't exude those characteristics. "The name itself is kind of neutral, but also funny because of the famous *Saturday Night Live* skit with the cowbell. I had to think about a mascot that conveys the basic characteristics of the sport—aggression, energy and power," he explains.

> "It's always fun to design a logo for a team that doesn't have a cliché name like Lions or Bears. The more abstract the name, the more fun to figure out how to communicate it in a logo."
>
> —Gyula Nemeth

Nemeth designed three logo designs for the Cowbells to use for different purposes. "The bull was an easy solution, so that became the primary logo, while the little cowbell with the C/R (for Cowboys/Rebels) became the secondary icon. The third one is a demon-like character who will serve as the mascot for the Cowbells fans," he explains.

Nemeth did a series of sketches for the logo, experimenting with faces, forms and a bull. The previous Rebels logo was a profile of a man, shown left, so Nemeth wanted to include a man's face in his sketches. "The long-haired guy was the first sketch, and it looked a bit like the comic book character Lobo," he says. "The management didn't really like that version, so I changed the composition and the hairstyle and it went through immediately."

Since the previous names were Cowboys and Rebels, Nemeth wanted to incorporate characteristics from both in the new logo, but as he sketched, he realized it wouldn't be that simple. "I thought it could be a guy in a cowboy hat with a handlebar moustache, similar to the old Rebels mascot that was based on György Dózsa, a Hungarian historical figure. But for new fans it would read only as a cowboy without any 'rebel' in it, so I decided to do two characters."

He started by drawing different concepts for each character. The bull with a bell around its neck became the primary mascot, while a fierce-looking man holding a cowbell became a secondary icon. "The guy is a bit demonic but still human. I knew that even if I create a scary face, the cowbell will tone it down. It is a ridiculously peaceful object," he says. The Cowbells typeface, Okie, designed by Kris Bazen, perfectly complements the edginess of the logo designs.

The new Cowbells logos have a strong presence in the league, compared to the competition. "Most of the team logos are designed by a player or a friend of the management, so they are pretty amateurish, which is common in smaller leagues around the globe, not just in Budapest," Nemeth says.

WORDS FROM GYULA NEMETH

NESTING DOLL

I made two versions of this character for Ironhead, an apparel company in Canada. This head icon and a full-body nesting doll with a little boxing glove on her hand. Cute twist.

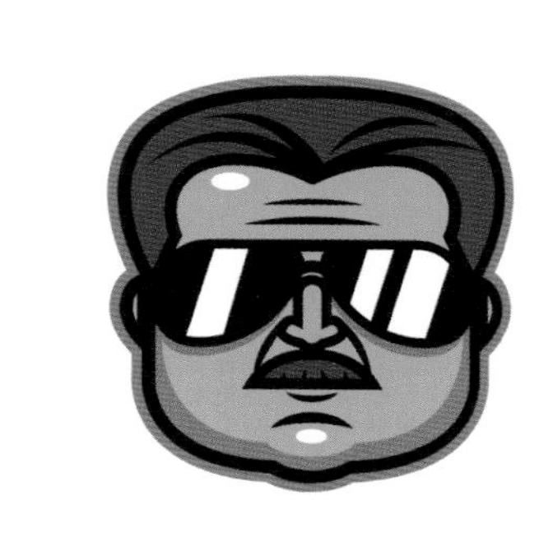

MIKE DITKA

A T-shirt company contacted me with the idea of producing merchandise with Ditka's iconic 1980s-style head on it. I guess licensing problems got in their way eventually, but I did some other head designs for the same company later on.

JOHN LENNON

This illustration was made for a music magazine in Budapest called *New Noise* (it has since folded). I did several John Lennon heads with different hairstyles. This was one of my favorites.

LANDSHUT CANNIBALS

The German hockey team Landshut Cannibals was playing with the idea of changing their identity a few years ago. Unfortunately, they changed their mind after I designed a few options for them—a sad story of a potentially successful logo not used. This is still one of my favorite head designs, and several future clients worked with me because of this particular piece.

SPIKE LEE

This is a personal piece. I have always liked the works of Spike Lee, and after watching some old Nike commercials with his character Mars Blackmon, I suddenly felt the urge to draw him.

A B C D

CATEGORY ///

HEADS

1

2

3

4

5

1C D Mmplus Creative C Fruit Ministry Indonesia **1D** D Double A Creative C Deep Blue
2A D J Fletcher Design C The Farmbar **2B** D Glitschka Studios C Jena **2C** D Sabingrafik, Inc. C King's Shops **2D** D Type08 C NWCS
3A D Tortoiseshell Black C Kings **3B** D Rickabaugh Graphics C Bethel College **3C** D 144design Inc C North American Hockey League **3D** D Gyula Nemeth C David Ortiz
4A D 12 points C Coccinelle **4B** D Just Creative Design C Spice Sage **4C** D Greyta C Royal Beard **4D** D Varick Rosete Studio C Florida State College of Jacksonville
5A D Keith Davis Young C Paul Octavious **5B** D Noe Araujo C Maya Media Studio **5C** D Gardner Design C Irish Dance Competition **5D** D Double A Creative C N/A

A B C D

1

2

3

4

5

1A D Independent graphic designer C N/A **1B** D Stevan Rodic C Sir Leon **1C** D Kreativbuero Jonas Soeder C Personal **1D** D Tribe C Odin Crossfit
2A D Tamer Koseli C rifki.co **2B** D Luke Bott Design & Illustration C O'Swell **2C** D Bryan Butler C Bryan Butler **2D** D Gyula Nemeth C Gefig
3A D Type08 C Rhino Store **3B** D Pix-l Graphx C Stay Ready **3C** D J Fletcher Design C Fatty's Brewing Co. **3D** D The Logoist C Unused
4A D Larry Levine C The Andy Warhol Museum **4B** D Josh Carnley C Josh Carnley Design & Illustration **4C** D Chad Michael Studio C Bluff City Film Company **4D** D smARTer C St. Croix Sensory
5A D smARTer C Gentlemen's Gazette **5B** D studio sudar d.o.o. C Audacis **5C** D Todytod C Booking.com **5D** D Marakasdesign C PAPA FILM Production

	A	B	C	D
1	 			
2				
3	 	 	 	
4	 	 		
5				

1A D Tactix Creative C Rivalry Rage **1B** D Glitschka Studios C Stay Hungry **1C** D Glitschka Studios C InkDot **1D** D Traction Partners C Menna's Joint
2A D Signals Design Group Inc C St Paul's Hospital **2B** D Gardner Design C Justin McClure Creative **2C** D Jerron Ames C Arteis **2D** D Jerron Ames C Arteis
3A D M3 Advertising Design C Chronos / M3AD.com **3B** D Fuszion C Emma's Espresso and Wine Bar **3C** D Chris Rooney Illustration/Design C Minerva Foundation **3D** D MKJ Creative C Performing Arts
4A D Jeremiah Britton Design Co. C Nutritional Wisdom **4B** D Jerron Ames C Fivestar Branding Agency **4C** D idgroup C N/A **4D** D Saputo Design C Pacific Lodge Youth Services
5A D Gardner Design C Justin McClure Creative **5B** D Doublenaut C Grayson Matthews **5C** D brandclay C Seer **5D** D Xander C Freedman

	A	B	C	D
1				
2		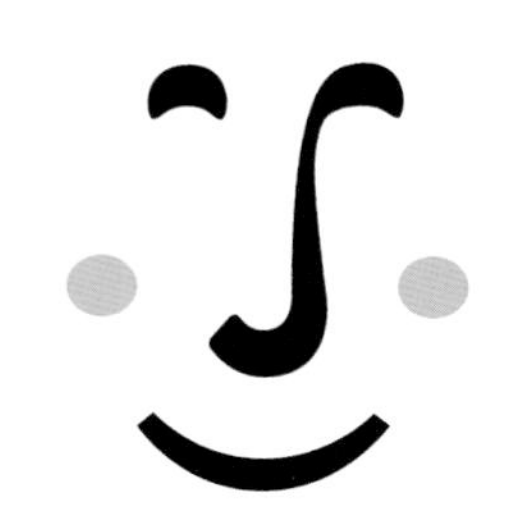		
3				
4	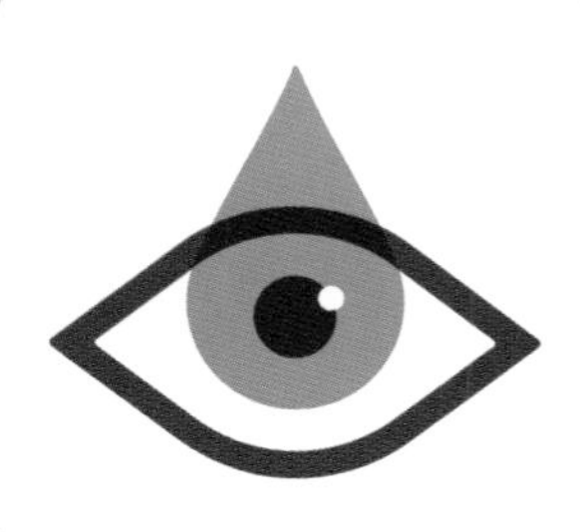			
5				

1A Ⓓ Jerron Ames Ⓒ Arteis **1B** Ⓓ Kantorwassink Ⓒ Sabo PR **1C** Ⓓ smARTer Ⓒ Randall Herrera **1D** Ⓓ Chadomoto / Dimiter Petrov Ⓒ BlackBird Agency / Sankt Petersburg, Russia
2A Ⓓ 01d Ⓒ Tube production **2B** Ⓓ o5 Design Ⓒ Praxis fur Zahnheilkunde Dr. Jahnke **2C** Ⓓ Jeff Phillips Design Ⓒ York Region Emergency Service **2D** Ⓓ Apus Agency Ⓒ N/A
3A Ⓓ Jeff Ames Creative Ⓒ infosurv **3B** Ⓓ Denis Aristov Ⓒ Concept Vision **3C** Ⓓ Alphabet Arm Design Ⓒ Panoptes **3D** Ⓓ Parallele gestion de marques Ⓒ Commission scolaire des Decouvreurs
4A Ⓓ The Quiet Society Ⓒ Designer Drinks **4B** Ⓓ NO-BAD Ⓒ N/A **4C** Ⓓ Gardner Design Ⓒ Harvesters FBKC **4D** Ⓓ Frontline Technologies Ⓒ Frontline Technologies
5A Ⓓ Tarsha Rockowitz Design Ⓒ thinking brain ARTS **5B** Ⓓ Type08 Ⓒ Think Fiend **5C** Ⓓ Dotzero Design Ⓒ Make Out **5D** Ⓓ Yury Akulin | Logodiver Ⓒ Speakerson

	A	B	C	D
1	CATEGORY /// PEOPLE 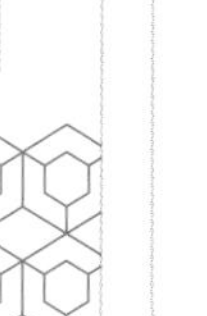			
2				
3				
4				
5		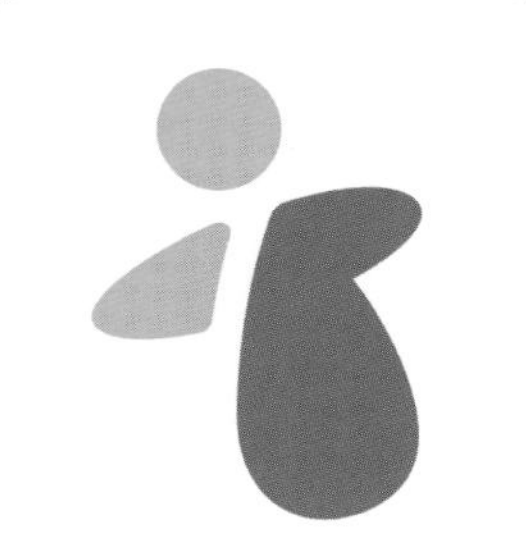		

1C D Tom Hough Design C Richardson Wildflower Festival **1D** D smARTer C Freshwater Community Church
2A D smARTer C Holding Court **2B** D AcrobatAnt C Block Party **2C** D R&R Partners C Baldlab **2D** D Luke Bott Design & Illustration C O'Swell
3A D Gizwiz Studio C Jon Buford **3B** D Color 9 Creative, Inc. C Black Belt Movers **3C** D 01d C Galamedia **3D** D 01d C Tuda Tuda
4A D smARTer C Bader-Rutter **4B** D Akhmatov Studio C Learning league **4C** D Niedermeier Design C Netrunner **4D** D Rebrander C Hiking
5A D Jerron Ames C Arties **5B** D Type08 C Beginnings **5C** D Denys Kotliarov C Brick technology **5D** D ANFILOV C http://www.atlas-ag.cz

A B C D

1

2

3

4

5

1A Ⓓ Glitschka Studios Ⓒ Deveney **1B** Ⓓ Andrey Kruglov Ⓒ NEPCOHAX **1C** Ⓓ 01d Ⓒ Tochka dostupa **1D** Ⓓ Akhmatov Studio Ⓒ Karate AKF Champion Cup Astana 2013
2A Ⓓ Parallele gestion de marques Ⓒ Centre Hospitalier Universitaire de Montreal **2B** Ⓓ Type08 Ⓒ ViVu **2C** Ⓓ Oven Design Workshop Ⓒ Maxiahorro **2D** Ⓓ Karl Design Vienna Ⓒ Sunponto / S. Kerber
3A Ⓓ Univisual S.r.l. Ⓒ Axitea **3B** Ⓓ eggnerd Ⓒ Shining Examples **3C** Ⓓ Fernandez Studio Ⓒ Dell **3D** Ⓓ KW43 BRANDDESIGN Ⓒ N/A
4A Ⓓ smARTer Ⓒ Cultivate Church Planting **4B** Ⓓ smARTer Ⓒ Macleod & Co **4C** Ⓓ lunabrand design group Ⓒ Foundation for Exceptional Kids **4D** Ⓓ Pix-I Graphx Ⓒ Ayur
5A Ⓓ Funnel Ⓒ Indiana Carton **5B** Ⓓ Karl Design Vienna Ⓒ Human Rights Logo Contest **5C** Ⓓ brandclay Ⓒ Mifii **5D** Ⓓ 1dea Design + Media Inc. Ⓒ SparkTalk

A B C D

1

2

3

4

5

STAFFIM

1A Ⓓ Steven Schroeder Ⓒ N/A **1B** Ⓓ smARTer Ⓒ The Father's House **1C** Ⓓ Tokshok Ⓒ Matreshki **1D** Ⓓ Tokshok Ⓒ MATRESHKI
2A Ⓓ Logo Planet Laboratory Ⓒ Lawn Genie **2B** Ⓓ 360ideas Ⓒ PINNACLE **2C** Ⓓ Tortugastudio Ⓒ N/A **2D** Ⓓ smARTer Ⓒ LD Sund Construction
3A Ⓓ Keyword Design Ⓒ South Shore Arts **3B** Ⓓ Dotzero Design Ⓒ Human Access Project **3C** Ⓓ Agency MABU Ⓒ Sacred Pipe Resource Center **3D** Ⓓ Square Feet Design Ⓒ Meringue Queen
4A Ⓓ Shierly Design Creative Ⓒ The Tavern **4B** Ⓓ Gizwiz Studio Ⓒ Joshua Fletcher **4C** Ⓓ H√°rsu √ñke Ⓒ Cihat Askin ve Küçük Arkadaslari (CAKA) **4D** Ⓓ Braizen Ⓒ Drew Newman
5A Ⓓ OCD | Original Champions of Design Ⓒ WNBA **5B** Ⓓ James Michael Design Ⓒ Knuckle Basher Ice Climbing Festival **5C** Ⓓ Jerron Ames Ⓒ Swansea Publishing **5D** Ⓓ Dmitry Zelinskiy Ⓒ Staffim

	A	B	C	D
1				
2				
3				
4				
5				

1A Ⓓ smARTer Ⓒ Randall Herrera **1B** Ⓓ DNKSTUDIO Ⓒ people 2 people **1C** Ⓓ Voov Ltd. Ⓒ Miitt **1D** Ⓓ Type08 Ⓒ Teammo
2A Ⓓ Gizwiz Studio Ⓒ Liz Tobin **2B** Ⓓ Gizwiz Studio Ⓒ Hector Simoudis **2C** Ⓓ Romulo Moya Peralta / Trama Ⓒ CMG Psicologia **2D** Ⓓ Jerron Ames Ⓒ Arteis
3A Ⓓ Karl Design Vienna Ⓒ Sunponto **3B** Ⓓ Tokshok Ⓒ Ufanet **3C** Ⓓ Design Film, LLC Ⓒ Making Champions **3D** Ⓓ Nox Creative Ⓒ Tapigo, LLC
4A Ⓓ Noe Araujo Ⓒ Juan Reyes **4B** Ⓓ Rebrander Ⓒ N/A **4C** Ⓓ Ryan Bosse Ⓒ Zero Food Print **4D** Ⓓ Dangerdom Studios Ⓒ Kenton Hansen
5A Ⓓ Chadomoto / Dimiter Petrov Ⓒ Vzemy.com **5B** Ⓓ The Quiet Society Ⓒ WorkCare **5C** Ⓓ Sean Heisler Design Ⓒ Plant Catching **5D** Ⓓ Lukedesign Ⓒ N/A

A B C D

1

2

3

4

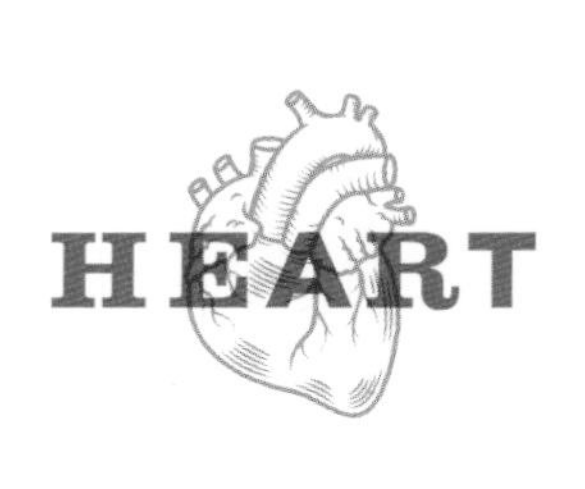

5

1A Ⓓ CNDC Ⓒ Chisholm Trail Casino **1B** Ⓓ Chris Rooney Illustration/Design Ⓒ Wiener **1C** Ⓓ LONI DBS Ⓒ Guru Cue Inc. **1D** Ⓓ Mart√≠n Azambuja Ⓒ The Production Factory
2A Ⓓ Doublenaut Ⓒ Grayson Matthews **2B** Ⓓ WIRON Ⓒ TESORI EDUCATION **2C** Ⓓ brandclay Ⓒ Can For Coffee **2D** Ⓓ Gyula Nemeth Ⓒ N/A
3A Ⓓ Gardner Design Ⓒ Sasnak, Carlos O'Kelly's **3B** Ⓓ Riordon Design Ⓒ Coup Capital Management **3C** Ⓓ 1 or Billion design Ⓒ Helan Chateau **3D** Ⓓ Flying Gorilla Studio Ⓒ Tribe Wear
4A Ⓓ Vitamin Group Ⓒ Solikamsk City Administration **4B** Ⓓ Juicebox Interactive Ⓒ Folk Hero **4C** Ⓓ Denis Aristov Ⓒ Ironconn **4D** Ⓓ Alphabet Arm Design Ⓒ Heart
5A Ⓓ Small Dog Design Ⓒ Grampians Podiatry Clinic **5B** Ⓓ Pavel Saksin Ⓒ Fastclick **5C** Ⓓ Karl Design Vienna Ⓒ Maratona d'Italia **5D** Ⓓ Independent graphic designer Ⓒ Gogobot

DESIGN /// VON GLITSCHKA

CLIENT /// THE WICKED WHEEL BAR & GRILL

CATEGORY /// MYTHOLOGY

The Wicked Wheel Bar & Grill in Panama City, Florida, needed a logo that reflected their passion for cars and bikes, and one that their patrons would appreciate. Enter Von Glitschka. His handcrafted sensibility was key to this project, just as classic car and bike enthusiasts don't mind getting their hands dirty when it comes to their rides.

"With the name 'The Wicked Wheel,' the type needed to be sinister of sorts, regarding its letterform styling. So instead of using existing typefaces, I hand-lettered the design," he says. "Choppers and classic cars are carefully built from scratch, so I felt the name should be treated the same way."

Once he got the type right, he began adding other elements to the design. "Those who enjoy bikes and classic cars also like nefarious themes like skulls and hot-rod oriented visual props like pickelhaube helmets. So I mashed those together and threw in a pair of wings to represent their free-spirited approach to their hard-core passions," he notes.

Because he didn't want the design to look too clean and perfect, he created a black-textured background to house the logo, giving it a lived-in look. Although Glitschka considers himself a digital designer, he likes things to be a little rough around the edges. "Digital design can look too clean, so everything I do first exists in analog. I draw out my shape and form before I build it in Illustrator," he notes.

Before Glitschka begins working digitally, he thoroughly explores the drawing phase. "Lots of sketches and drawn experiments lead to what I call my refined sketch. I'll use this as my road map for building my vector art in Illustrator," he says.

> "I may build it precisely, but the style I try to achieve is aesthetically handcrafted of sorts since it was worked through in analog."
> —Von Glitschka

Glitschka further refines his sketch and experiments with other design elements. He decided against using the banner or the cog in the final development.

Sometimes Glitschka creates specific motifs, like this textured nesting shape, to house the overall design so it works well in the specific context of use.

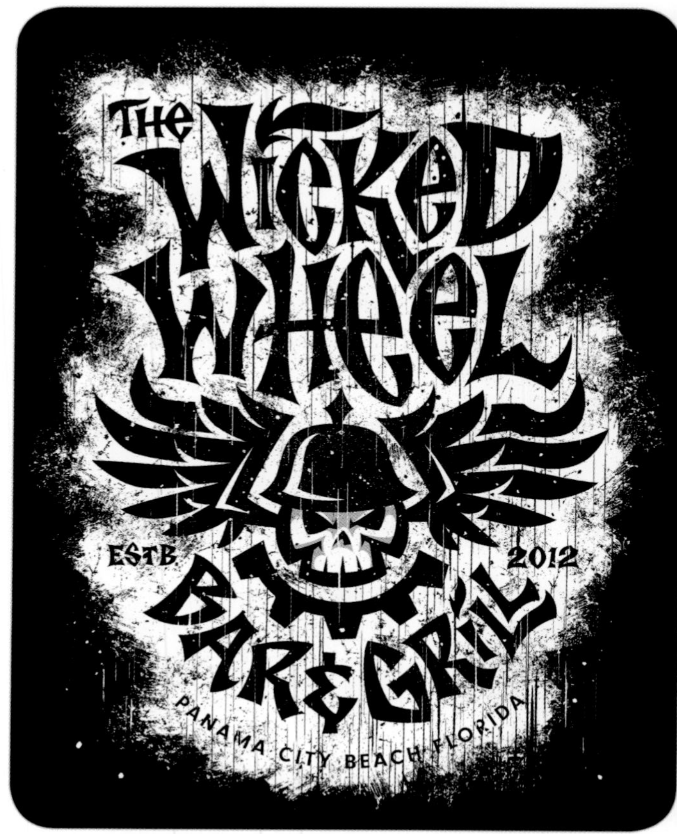

The final design utilizes real-world textures from splattered paint and cracks from an old painted door in order to encapsulate the design with an authentic look and feel. "The design isn't perfectly symmetric so I wanted the textures to make the forms imperfect too," Glitschka notes.

Glitschka did this variation to be printed on a black T-shirt.

WORDS FROM VON GLITSCHKA

The Wicked Wheel logo hit the right notes for his client and their customers.

MYTHOLOGY AND THE SUPERNATURAL

Almost every culture around the world has an established mythos related to its own history and lore. Ironically, when you get to the United States, our own history has a distinct lack of that same type of mythology and the visuals that go with it. I've always gravitated toward symbolism whether overt or subtle in context of design.

Growing up, I enjoyed learning about Greek or Egyptian gods and legends. I just found the imagery very intriguing. The closest we get to that level of mystery in American culture is the symbolism surrounding the Masonic Order, and those who set forward the whole Manifest Destiny ideal that is still reflected in our monuments and even the money we use. Many of these images were derived from other established mythologies such as Egyptian. One example is the obelisk, like the Washington Monument. Another is the all-seeing eye.

The world is far more global now than ever before, and I think people like supernatural topics in general. Mythology is squarely derived from a supernatural mindset, whether it's ancient or more modern like Bigfoot, Loch Ness Monster, Mothman, or UFOs for that matter.

I grew up in the Pacific Northwest, so from the time I was a kid I had heard of and followed everything mentioned about Bigfoot. I've known people who swear to have seen one, and they'd debate labeling the phenomenon mythological. I like playing with the concept though.

DESIGN /// STEVAN RODIC

CLIENT /// PERSONAL PROJECT

CATEGORY /// MYTHOLOGY

Stevan Rodic is heavily steeped in mythological origins when it comes to his designs, and he says living in Belgrade, Serbia, is a big factor. "Serbs are part of old Slavs ethnic group," he explains. "Recently I read that after Japan, we have the highest numbers of deities, legends and beliefs; hence the inexhaustible source of inspiration."

So it's no surprise that these characters creep into his logo designs. He did a personal series called Dark Side, which features logos inspired by zombie and voodoo culture. "These secret and dark moments tickle my imagination. I've always been fascinated by horror movies and books, so naturally I've extended this mythology into my design work," he notes.

Rodic, who designs logos for a variety of clients, says searching for the right inspiration a logo can be challenging. "You need to be able to visualize different characteristics that make up the theme of the design you're after. Then that has to be threaded and realized in a subtle way through a symbol or character," he says. As he draws, it all starts to come together. "I do a continuous dance with the pen until it's all transformed into an eye-candy mark. I find inspiration in the people I love, as well as animals, nature and delicious music beats."

This skull whistle logo was inspired by the ancient Aztec's death whistle, which was a tiny whistle resembling a human skull. Rodic did a literal interpretation of a skull on a modern day whistle.

Rodic sketched his zombie using negative space and kept refining it until he achieved just the right movement.

A B C D

CATEGORY ///

MYTHOLOGY

1

2

3

4

5

1C D Tortoiseshell Black C Geeky Jerseys **1D** D Torch Creative C Disney
2A D BE SIBLE C BLOCK ROCKI'N BEASTS **2B** D Dustin Commer C Runwell **2C** D 903 Creative, LLC C 903 Creative **2D** D Hubbell Design Works C Gearhead
3A D Wray Ward C Brandon Scharr / Patrick McLean **3B** D Second Shift Design C Black Creek Brewing Co. **3C** D Patrick Carter Design, Inc. C Wicked Barley **3D** D Alex Tass C Beast Media
4A D Swanson Russell C N/A **4B** D Sabingrafik, Inc. C Project Justice **4C** D smARTer C Macleod & Co **4D** D McGuire Design C Heavenly Sitters
5A D McGuire Design C Angelique Skin Care & Massage **5B** D 144design Inc C North American Hockey League **5C** D 144design Inc C North American Hockey League **5D** D Gyula Nemeth C Fanskrit

	A	B	C	D
1				
2				
3				
4				
5				

1A D Gardner Design C Justin McClure Creative **1B** D Unipen C Unicorn **1C** D Karl Design Vienna C Yunikon Switzerland **1D** D Squid Ink Creative C Pegasus Health Systems
2A D Karl Design Vienna C Casa Nova **2B** D Nox Creative C Dutch Army Co. **2C** D Karl Design Vienna C Karl Design Vienna **2D** D DEI Creative C Hellbent Brewing Co.
3A D Fernandez Studio C Lamassu **3B** D eggnerd C Dragons Soccer **3C** D Kovach Studio C Dragon - China trade market **3D** D Elevator C Martinis Marchi
4A D Braizen C One Eleven Photography **4B** D Braizen C Penny James **4C** D Raineri Design Srl C Braga **4D** D Miriad C Salvaguardia
5A D Exhibit A: Design Group C Udoo Planet Ltd. **5B** D Levogrin C Superium Games **5C** D Rebrander C Monster King **5D** D Sarah Rusin Design C The Ghosthouse

DESIGN /// TETHER

CLIENT /// AWAKE CHOCOLATE

CATEGORY /// BIRDS

When Matt Schnarr, Dan Tzotzis and Adam Deremo of Ontario, Canada, wanted to launch a new kind of product, they turned to the branding experts at Tether in Seattle to help them get it off the ground. Their product, Awake, is caffeinated chocolate—each bar contains the equivalent of a cup of coffee. "We loved the product, and everybody here wanted some," says Stanley Hainsworth, Tether's chief creative officer.

Tether did more than take them on as a client—they became an equity partner in exchange for the branding, packaging and promotion of Awake. What better way to ensure a product gets the best brand representation than being part owner of the product? Hainsworth and his new partners agreed that the branding should be approachable and gender neutral, unlike testosterone-fueled energy drink brands. It also needed to live in the chocolate aisle.

Tether design director, Ryan Meline, explored three different logo directions, but he was most excited about one in particular. "I asked myself the somewhat cliché question: If Awake were an animal, what would it be? The owl was such a fitting icon. The initial sketches were intentionally loose and meant to capture some of the fun of the category. We wanted a less polished aesthetic, not typical of what you find in the candy aisle," he notes.

> "Awake chocolate wanted to zig where other chocolate companies were zagging, and for that reason the owl was our recommended concept."
>
> —Ryan Melanie

"The other directions we proposed were a little more expected, promoting high-energy, but we felt the owl was the best direction," Hainsworth notes. "We wanted to be disruptive in the marketplace, so we talked about other successful companies with iconic logos, like Nike and Apple. Then we showed them how useful this icon would be at retail, and how it would look on merchandise. We demonstrated how we could build a successful brand personality around the owl." Nevil, as the owl was lovingly named by the Tether team, was an immediate hit with the partners.

The "Nevilution," as it's regarded in-house, went from sketchbook to digital refinements pretty quickly. "Part of the charm of this concept is that nothing was overthought or too refined," says Meline. The bright color palette was chosen to contrast against the chocolatey brown wrapper and pop off the shelf. "Knowing we would be printing with a limited number of colors, we simplified the palette and created a visual link between the eyes and the logotype. These glowing eyes are arresting on the shelf, especially on the larger bags," he explains.

When the founders of Awake initially approached Tether to help with branding, they had this prototype packaging. Hainsworth looked at it and asked them where they wanted to sell this. "They said in the chocolate aisle, but their package looked like an energy drink," he says. So the Tether team scratched this concept and started over.

Besides the typical challenges associated with launching a new brand, the team had to move at an exceptional pace because the Awake founders were invited to appear on CBC's *Dragons' Den*, the Canadian equivalent of *Shark Tank*, where entrepreneurs present their products to a panel of investors on television in hopes of getting someone to back it. Tether quickly designed prototype packaging, T-shirts and presentation materials for the event. Hainsworth took part in the televised presentation, which happily concluded with a bidding war between the investors—they all wanted a piece of Awake.

"The show allowed us to launch with a built-in infomercial shown to nearly two million people," recalls partner Matt Schnarr. "It has become part of our brand backstory, and it's certainly a main topic of conversation with Canadians familiar with our product."

Awake is, not surprisingly, the top chocolate bar on college campuses, and Nevil is more popular than ever, boasting more than ten thousand Twitter followers, and forty-six thousand "likes" on Facebook. "The response to Nevil has been owl-standing!" Schnarr says. "He is a game changer for our business and industry. Unlike traditional packaged goods companies, where consumers receive communication from corporate affairs or customer service in a very sterile environment, Nevil allows us to create a two-way dialogue in a very fun and friendly manner."

This simple character has taken on a life of his own, inserting himself into conversations on popular culture, mixing with celebrities and fans, and proving he's much more than a logo.

Tether designers worked up these concepts for Awake, along with promotion materials, but they had a favorite in mind. Hainsworth says, "What's better to stand for Awake than an owl?"

Meline did several variations of Nevil the owl. The "Nevilution" progressed quickly, through several iterations, then into color development. A simple, bright palette was chosen to contrast the brown wrapper.

The different Awake flavors dictate the color of Nevil on the packaging, although his eyes never change. In-store end caps also prominently feature Nevil.

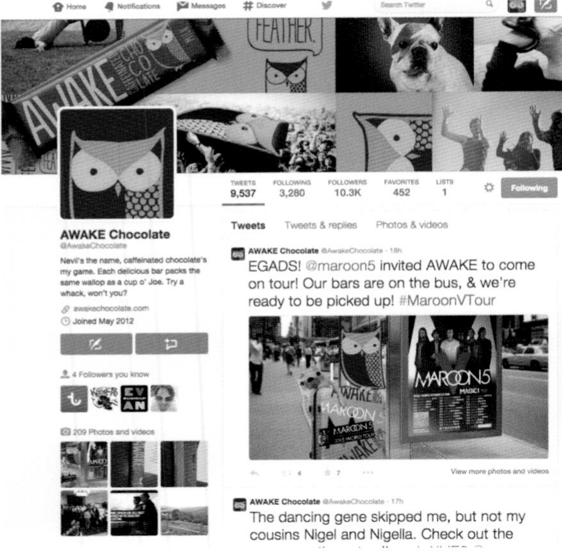

After the product launch, Nevil took on a life of his own. He visits college campuses and has a profound Twitter following.

A B C D

CATEGORY ///

BIRDS

1

2

3

4

5

1C D Glitschka Studios C Gallo **1D** D Glitschka Studios C Fidelis Farm & Vineyard
2A D Alexander Wende C Invictus Racing **2B** D SMOKE SIGNAL DSGN C Black Hammer Eagle **2C** D Levogrin C DC Trust Co. **2D** D Odney C N/A
3A D Odney C MBTs **3B** D Gearbox C Valor + Forge **3C** D Sunday Lounge C Salida Chamber of Commerce **3D** D Keith Davis Young C Transpecos
4A D Sunday Lounge C Wanderlust Road **4B** D Sudduth Design Co. C Teo **4C** D Glitschka Studios C Creative Con **4D** D Lucas Marc Design C Tribute Energy
5A D DMH C Rockhurst High School **5B** D Rickabaugh Graphics C University of Southern Indiana **5C** D Karl Design Vienna C Momentum **5D** D Art'Performance C Traektoria Logistics company

A B C D

1

Avianca

2

3

4

5

1A D Lippincott C Avianca **1B** D Type08 C GoldenEagle **1C** D Pix-I Graphx C Razyn **1D** D 1 or Billion design C Blackbird
2A D sodesign C Anna Illarionova **2B** D Jackson Spalding C Essence Music **2C** D Airtype Studio C Hoots Beer Co. **2D** D Glitschka Studios C Night Owl Society
3A D Daren Guillory Design C Yes Prep Public Schools **3B** D J Fletcher Design C Charleston Parliament **3C** D Levogrin C Smartbook **3D** D Frontline Technologies C Frontline Technologies
4A D Stephan Smith C N/A **4B** D Sean Heisler Design C Zendesk **4C** D Steve Bullock Design C Cura **4D** D Luke Bott Design & Illustration C Studyblue
5A D Sabingrafik, Inc. C Pearson Education Inc. **5B** D Type08 C Rhino Store **5C** D KOSMA Design Studio C www.tonikstudio.pl **5D** D Type08 C My Coop

	A	B	C	D
1				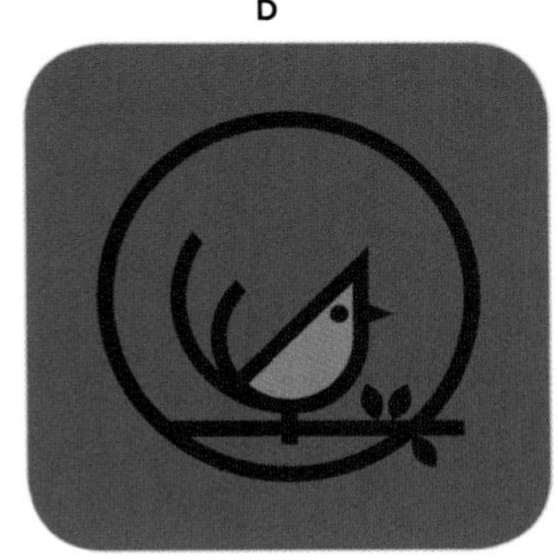
2				
3				
4				
5				

1A Ⓓ Cayenne Creative Ⓒ Harris Doyle Homes **1B** Ⓓ Keith Davis Young Ⓒ N/A **1C** Ⓓ 1 or Billion design Ⓒ Qitian Media **1D** Ⓓ QUIQUE OLLERVIDES Ⓒ Quique Ollervides **2A** Ⓓ DNKSTUDIO Ⓒ Baby Exclusive **2B** Ⓓ Jarrett Johnston Ⓒ Johnny's Place **2C** Ⓓ Buzzbomb Creative Ⓒ Memories & Moves **2D** Ⓓ Dmitry Zelinskiy Ⓒ Sparrow Inc. **3A** Ⓓ Luke Bott Design & Illustration Ⓒ N/A **3B** Ⓓ Bryan Butler Ⓒ 8-Bit Duck **3C** Ⓓ Oxide Design Co. Ⓒ Nebraska Craft Brewers Guild **3D** Ⓓ ParkerWhite Ⓒ Do Good Benefit **4A** Ⓓ Sabingrafik, Inc. Ⓒ Rancho Mission Viejo **4B** Ⓓ Dmitry Zelinskiy Ⓒ N/A **4C** Ⓓ Luke Bott Design & Illustration Ⓒ N/A **4D** Ⓓ QUIQUE OLLERVIDES Ⓒ Quique Ollervides **5A** Ⓓ David Gramblin Ⓒ Chicken Box **5B** Ⓓ Steven Schroeder Ⓒ N/A **5C** Ⓓ M@OH! Ⓒ Locally Laid Egg Company **5D** Ⓓ Oxide Design Co. Ⓒ Tamar

	A	B	C	D
1				
2				
3				
4				
5				

1A Ⓓ Besapiens Ⓒ Krasnokamsk Municipal Administration 1B Ⓓ J Fletcher Design Ⓒ Cardinal Chocolates 1C Ⓓ Independent graphic designer Ⓒ Inspire Metamarketing 1D Ⓓ Bloom Communication SRL Ⓒ Eurolenguas
2A Ⓓ Ortega Graphics Ⓒ Toucan Travel & Tourism 2B Ⓓ Karl Design Vienna Ⓒ Tucan Cafébar 2C Ⓓ Ninet6 Ltd Ⓒ Toucan 2D Ⓓ Slagle Design Ⓒ Teodora's Kitchen
3A Ⓓ Gardner Design Ⓒ Magic Talent 3B Ⓓ Bryan Couchman Design Ⓒ Wild Bird Recording 3C Ⓓ Bryan Butler Ⓒ Grant Woody 3D Ⓓ Steven Schroeder Ⓒ N/A
4A Ⓓ Kneadle, Inc. Ⓒ Crane 4B Ⓓ AcrobatAnt Ⓒ Santa Rosa Medical Center 4C Ⓓ Brian Rodenberg Design Ⓒ For Sale | Unused proposal 4D Ⓓ J Fletcher Design Ⓒ North Inlet
5A Ⓓ J Fletcher Design Ⓒ Dockhop 5B Ⓓ J Fletcher Design Ⓒ American Funship 5C Ⓓ Fernandez Studio Ⓒ TrueAbility 5D Ⓓ Tortugastudio Ⓒ PingWin

A B C D

1

CATEGORY ///

FISH, BUGS, REPTILES

2

3

BEE & BLOOM

4

5

1C D eggnerd C Beez Bagels **1D** D Roger Strunk C Apis Remote Sensing Systems
2A D Jerron Ames C N/A **2B** D Dessein C Dad & Daves Honey **2C** D Michael Lashford Creative C Tamalpais Honey Co. **2D** D Tamer Koseli C imhush.com
3A D Courtney Windham Design C Rockhurst Farm, Wilsonville, Alabama **3B** D Burocratik C Beesweet Honey **3C** D Yondr Studio C Bee & Bloom **3D** D Link Creative C JRM Hornets
4A D Tortoiseshell Black C Stingers Hockey **4B** D Sabingrafik, Inc. C Dermarché Labs **4C** D Josh Carnley C Riverfly Farms **4D** D Stevan Rodic C Mantis
5A D Sabingrafik, Inc. C Beltierra **5B** D Budanov. Branding & Identity C CRG **5C** D Norfolk Southern Corp. C Palatka Fish Camp **5D** D Jerron Ames C Arteis

	A	B	C	D
1	BRANDfish			
2		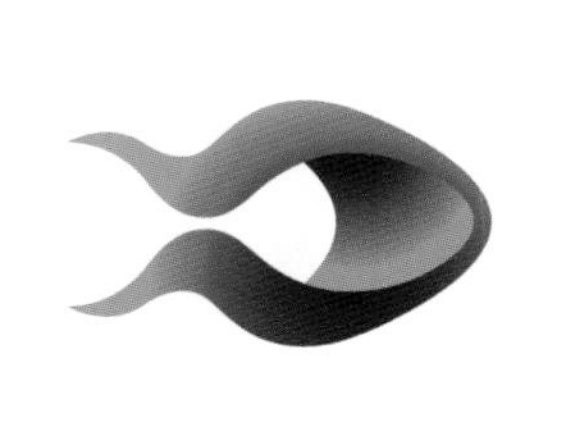		
3		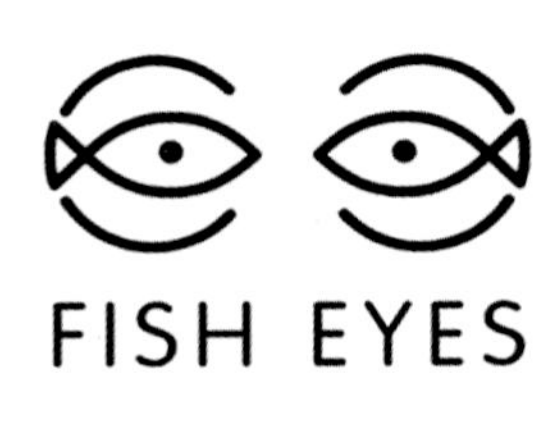		
4				
5				

1A D RetroMetro Designs C Unused Concept **1B** D arndtteunissen GmbH C Royal Fishing Kinderhilfe e.V. **1C** D Exhibit A: Design Group C Udoo Planet Ltd. **1D** D Ideogram C Oxlot 9
2A D Greyta C Allmaria Fishing Company **2B** D Graphic design studio by Yurko Gutsulyak C UEFC Ltd **2C** D Botond V√∂r√∂s C FishingPlace.com **2D** D Luka Balic C Kursiljo, Christian movement
3A D Luka Balic C Kursiljo, Christian movement **3B** D Just Creative Design C Cherokee Charters **3C** D Fuzzco C N/A **3D** D Dept of Energy C TinyPurpleFishes
4A D Pavel Saksin C N/A **4B** D Denis Aristov C Bauformat **4C** D Peppermill Projects C House of Bern Collections **4D** D Reghardt C N/A
5A D Dalton Agency C Ponte Vedra High School **5B** D Fernandez Studio C TrueAbility **5C** D Tom Hough Design C Sea World San Antonio **5D** D TYPE AND SIGNS C Ocean Care

	A	B	C	D
1				
2				
3				
4				
5				

1A D Luke Despatie & The Design Firm C William Street Beer Co. **1B** D Raineri Design Srl C CAMPO D'OGLIO **1C** D Kamayi C Wellindo Lintas Masa, PT **1D** D Jon Kay Design C
2A D Maskon Brands C Indian Octopus **2B** D Gardner Design C Justin McClure Creative **2C** D Karl Design Vienna C Karl Design - Marken fuer Morgen **2D** D TYPE AND SIGNS C OCTO'S GARDEN
3A D Freelance C Plush Design, Barcelona **3B** D Fraser Davidson C Cambridge Pythons **3C** D Visual Lure, LLC C NewtiTee **3D** D Tortoiseshell Black C N/A
4A D Rickabaugh Graphics C San Francisco State **4B** D 01d C Galamedia **4C** D Graphics Factory CC C LEN **4D** D Jerron Ames C PinLeap
5A D Josh Carnley C Jay Landings Marina & RV Park **5B** D Type08 C Speedette **5C** D Design Ranch C Boltwell **5D** D emedia creative C Select Vacations

DESIGN /// TRACY SABIN

CLIENT /// SAN DIEGO ZOO

CATEGORY /// ANIMALS

To celebrate the San Diego Zoo's one hundredth anniversary in 2016, art director Kambiz Mehrafshani wanted a commemorative logo. He hired prolific logo designer Tracy Sabin for the project. Sabin has been a designer and illustrator since 1973, doing packaging, book illustrations and most notably, logo designs.

The project's concept started with the very beginning of the zoo. "We like to say the Zoo began with a roar," Mehrafshani says, "when our founder, Dr. Harry Wegeforth, heard the roar of caged lions that were part of the 1915-16 Panama-California Exposition in Balboa Park. Dr. Harry decided then and there that San Diego was ready for a zoo and later convinced the city to follow his lead."

Because the zoo's history started with the roar of a lion, Mehrafshani wanted to explore logo concepts based on a lion, but with bright, celebratory colors. He imagined working with an image of a lion's head and mane depicted as a color wheel.

> "This concept originated from a beautiful visual of an abstract color wheel I found online. I asked Tracy to imagine the color wheel growing teeth, ears, mouth and a mane, thus transforming it into our centennial lion,"
> — Kambiz Mehrafshani

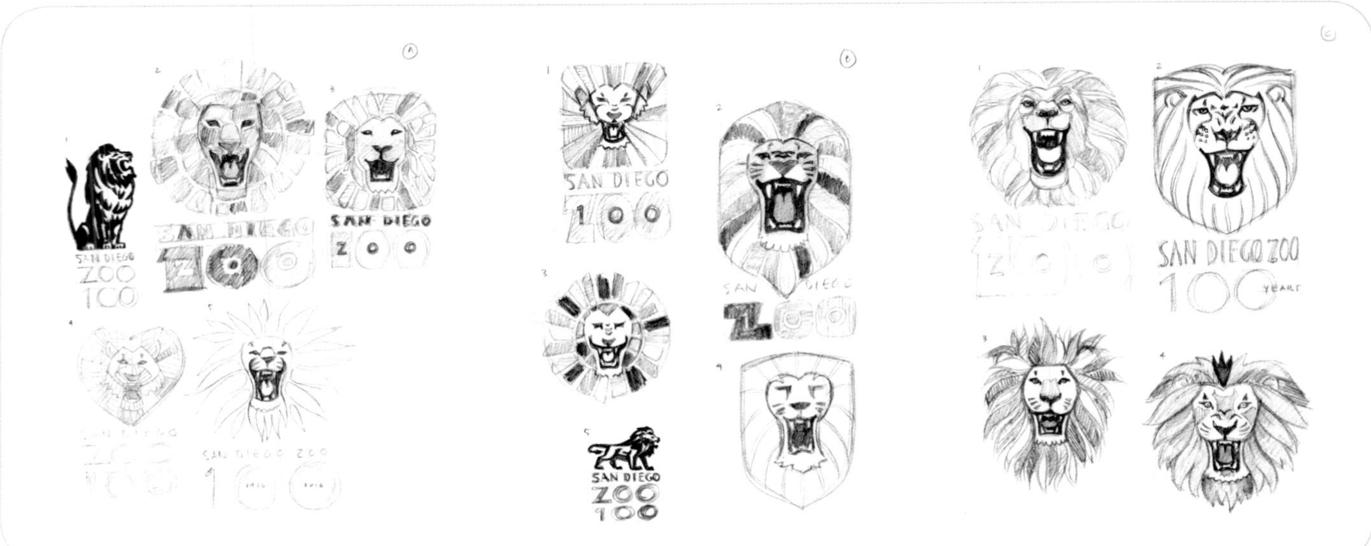

Sabin's initial sketches mostly focused on the directive given to him by Mehrafshani, which was to draw a lion's head similar to an abstract color wheel.

The first and most essential stage in Sabin's logo development process is research. "I looked at photos of lions in various positions: roaring, mouth closed, looking up or down, lit from different angles. I also explored the many ways that artists have depicted a lion from stylized to realistic, from modern to ethnic. I looked at color wheels, quilts, engravings and woodcuts," he explains. "It's only after I've steeped myself in these visual details that I am able to get pencil ideas to flow."

Sabin sketched a few color wheel variations, along with other lion head styles and a full-body version. "Although my first efforts at illustrating this color wheel idea were interesting, they were too literal and abstract. They didn't foster the personal connection Kambiz was hoping for," Sabin notes. The Zoo's design review team chose two directions for color explorations. Sabin refined and colored these concepts using warm colors typically associated with a lion's mane.

Unfortunately, the colors weren't working with the images. The color wheel concept looked more like a mosaic pattern at first glance and less like a lion, and the mane in the other concept created something different altogether, according to Mehrafshani. "It looked like a lion designed for a Brazilian Carnival mask, and the mane overpowered the face. Sadly, the vibrant color palette didn't work on either of the concepts."

Mehrafshani and his team stepped back and evaluated all of Sabin's efforts and realized their mistake. "Instead of testing one-color compatibility first, we had gone straight to full-color treatments. It was an oversight that came purely from our eagerness to see the final product. This was a revealing moment for us. We pressed the reset button, gathered the best pieces of what we'd already created, and started with some fresh ideas," he says.

Sabin revisited his earlier concepts, taking the best qualities from each concept, and simplified and combined them. He also felt the lion needed to look more regal and less ferocious. At this stage, Mehrafshani also requested type explorations. "We wanted something clean and modern, but that also subtly acknowledged a sense of history and celebration," he says.

The logo that was ultimately selected fit the best of both worlds—it was beautiful and powerful in both one-color and four-color applications, and it was easy to identify as a lion.

"When we landed on the final mark, it was a moment of pure elation. From the start we wanted a logo that spoke to the San Diego Zoo's remarkable past and its exciting future," Mehrafshani says. "Because Tracy learned so much through the ups and downs of the project, he was able to bring all that knowledge together into a beautiful representation of our history. I'm confident no one else could have created something so incredible and appropriate for our organization."

In a quick glance it's obvious both marks totally fail the one-color test, so Mehrafshani and his team evaluated the merits of each logo and determined several things: Although they liked the graphic separations in the first concept, they favored the plumage in the second concept, but it would need some graphic separations so it would work in one color. "We wanted the face to land somewhere between concept one and two—not realistic, but also not so stylized that it was lost as a lion." They also nixed the calligraphic type.

Sabin modified the lion's face, making it more regal, and separated the plume, ranging from tame to wild. Each type treatment was slightly modified so the design review team could explore different options. Ultimately, they were drawn to the third concept for the logo and type.

The final logo design works well as one color or with several colors. The design is crisp and contains all the elements the zoo required.

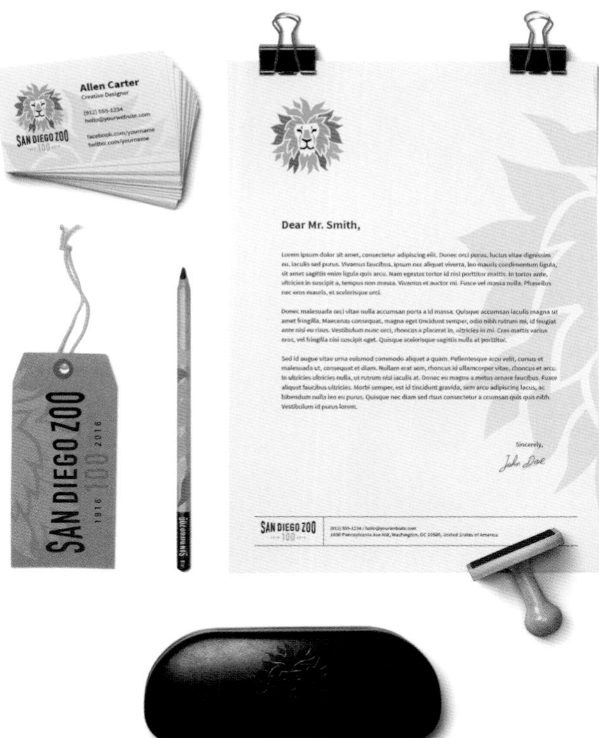

The logo has been adapted to stationery and online communications, as well to merchandise and T-shirts.

A B C D

1

CATEGORY ///

ANIMALS

2

3

4

5

1C D AcrobatAnt C N/A **1D** D Funnel C Sara Jones
2A D brandclay C Job Dog **2B** D Jerron Ames C Arteis **2C** D Chris Rooney Illustration/Design C San Francisco International Airport **2D** D Banowetz + Company, Inc. C Frenkel & Frenkel Attorneys and Counselors
3A D Funnel C Darin Bahl **3B** D brandclay C Dig File **3C** D Type08 C Petpartners **3D** D 36creative C Cavaletto Canine
4A D Doublenaut C Our Noble Companions **4B** D Trevor Rogers C The Beagle Freedom Project **4C** D Type08 C ToyBit **4D** D McGuire Design C Yard Dog BBQ Company
5A D Just Creative Design C Boarding&Beyond **5B** D Jon Eslinger / Design C Dog Haus **5C** D Gardner Design C City The Kitty **5D** D Almanac C Boo Cat Club

	A	B	C	D
1				
2				
3				
4				
5				

1A D Haffelder Studios C Brand Horse **1B** D Varick Rosete Studio C Friends of Jacksonville Animals **1C** D Exhibit A: Design Group C Udoo Planet Ltd. **1D** D Hubbell Design Works C VPI Pet insurance
2A D Just Creative Design C Boarding&Beyond **2B** D idgroup C Pensacola Humane Society **2C** D Jarrett Johnston C Los Gatos Christian School **2D** D J Fletcher Design C Saint Philip's Preschool
3A D Unipen C Open Chat **3B** D Graphics Factory CC C Gefest Europe **3C** D Akhmatov Studio C Aristan EPC **3D** D Emilio Correa C King Media
4A D Salvador Anguiano C Grupo Cachorro **4B** D Jackson Spalding C Monster Children **4C** D Torch Creative C Louisiana State University **4D** D Rickabaugh Graphics C Northwest Missouri State University
5A D Rickabaugh Graphics C Mountain View Wildcats **5B** D The Logoist C Unused **5C** D Odney C Southside Christian School **5D** D Gardner Design C Urban Prevue

A B C D

1

CHOKLAD
BUDET
SEDAN 2010

2

3

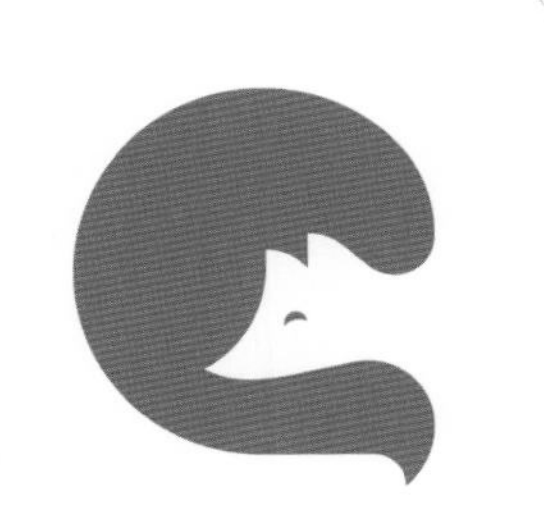

4

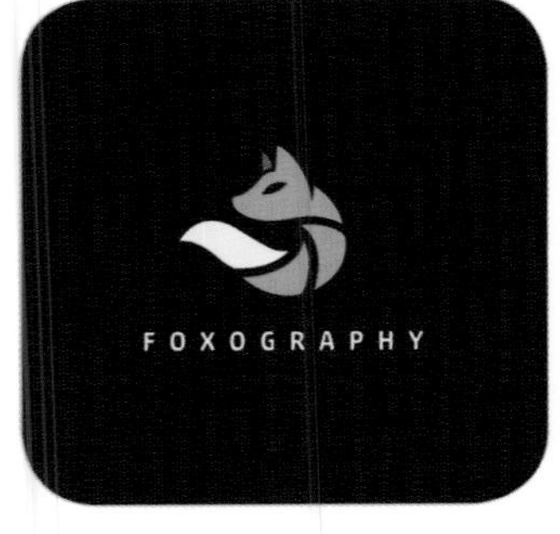

5

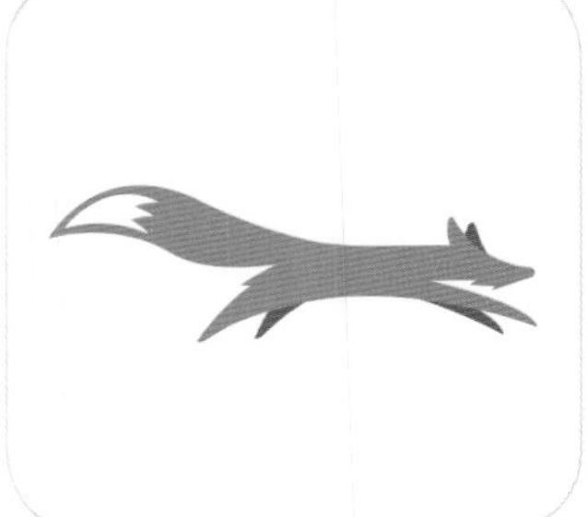

1A D TYPE AND SIGNS C Choklad Budet, Sweden **1B** D petervasvari.com C Brandpride **1C** D Akhmatov Studio C Park of Ideas **1D** D Plenum Brand Consultancy C Briant Privat banking
2A D Think Topography C Primitive Pursuits **2B** D Stevan Rodic C Solvreven **2C** D Emilio Correa C Emiliographics **2D** D Jeremiah Britton Design Co. C The Sly Mr. Fox Blog
3A D Sabingrafik, Inc. C Pearson Education Inc. **3B** D Grain C Grain Inc. **3C** D Pavel Saksin C Follow Foxy **3D** D Pavel Saksin C N/A
4A D Stevan Rodic C Foxography **4B** D Odney C MBTs **4C** D Roy Smith Design C The Fox **4D** D Independent graphic designer C Fitfox
5A D Artsmith Communications C Red Fox Communications **5B** D Independent graphic designer C N/A **5C** D Roy Smith Design C The Fox **5D** D Odney C MBTs

	A	B	C	D
1				
2				
3				
4				
5				

1A Ⓓ KW43 BRANDDESIGN Ⓒ Hanna Köhl **1B** Ⓓ Designbull Ⓒ Moose Coffee House **1C** Ⓓ brandclay Ⓒ Flying Moose **1D** Ⓓ Odney Ⓒ Hartman Ranch Meats
2A Ⓓ Gustav Holtz Design Ⓒ Wildfire Interactive **2B** Ⓓ Stevan Rodic Ⓒ Camo King **2C** Ⓓ THINKMULE Ⓒ Summer House Films **2D** Ⓓ 01d Ⓒ ZIMA
3A Ⓓ Odney Ⓒ Red Stag Ale **3B** Ⓓ BluesCue Designs Ⓒ Active Outfit **3C** Ⓓ Coleman Design Ⓒ 23 Mayfield, Boutique Guest House **3D** Ⓓ BluesCue Designs Ⓒ Impala
4A Ⓓ Rickabaugh Graphics Ⓒ Virginia Commonwealth University **4B** Ⓓ Sophia Georgopoulou I Design Ⓒ Aeolikos Dairy Products **4C** Ⓓ Exhibit A: Design Group Ⓒ Go Goat Biscotti **4D** Ⓓ midgar.eu Ⓒ Asun Asyar
5A Ⓓ Clark & Co. Ⓒ BLE **5B** Ⓓ smARTer Ⓒ Big Ass Fans **5C** Ⓓ Independent graphic designer Ⓒ Megazebra **5D** Ⓓ Luke Bott Design & Illustration Ⓒ Soquili Designs

A B C D

1

2

3

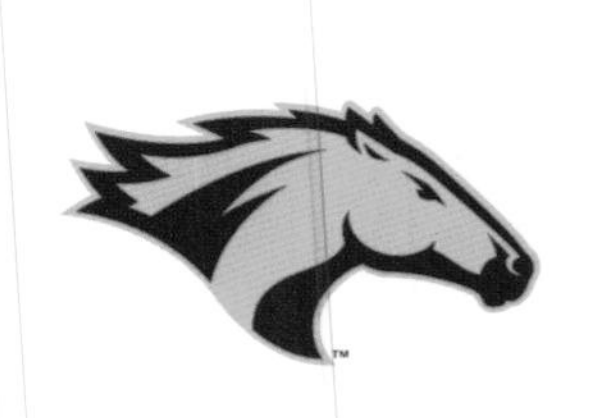

4

5

1A D Gardner Design C Krystal Bus **1B** D Odney C MBTs **1C** D INNERPRIDE C Elements Behavioral Health **1D** D Tactical Magic C Running Pony
2A D Fernandez Studio C Texas Lottery **2B** D 01d C Lordberg **2C** D Blue Taco Design C Cary Colt Payne, CHTD. **2D** D Glitschka Studios C Stallion Breeders
3A D Torch Creative C Cal Poly Pomona **3B** D Freelance C San Miguel Land Grant **3C** D Steven Schroeder C N/A **3D** D Jibe C TOGS
4A D Gardner Design C Willow Creek Ranch **4B** D THINKMULE C Byre **4C** D Rule29 C 1871 Dairy **4D** D J Fletcher Design C Southern Craft Creamery
5A D Patrick Carter Design, Inc. C Leche **5B** D Bloom Communication SRL C Portas Com **5C** D J Fletcher Design C Espresso Bison **5D** D Odney C Hartman Meats

A B C D

1

2

3

4

5

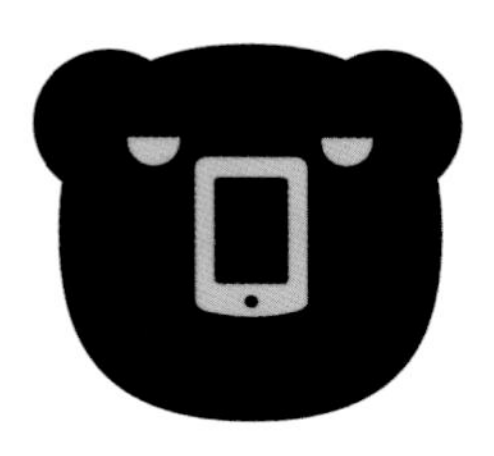

1A D Odney C MBTs **1B** D Grain C Millstone Weber **1C** D Bryan Couchman Design C Downtown OKC **1D** D Hiebing C A FIne Swine
2A D Jerron Ames C Yellowstone Half Marathon **2B** D Sabingrafik, Inc. C Monkey Films **2C** D BrandViva C Grizzly Peak Winery **2D** D smARTer C Macleod & Co
3A D Sabingrafik, Inc. C Pearson Education Inc. **3B** D Noriu Menulio C Artscape **3C** D Odney C Millers Homestead **3D** D Tortugastudio C Two Bears
4A D Sabingrafik, Inc. C Sycuan Casino **4B** D Torch Creative C Bloomfield College **4C** D Tin Bacic C Grimey League **4D** D studio sudar d.o.o. C MEdvescak PK
5A D Type08 C Rhino Store **5B** D Karl Design Vienna C Kodiac Kommunikation **5C** D R&R Partners C N/A **5D** D Type08 C Rhino Store

	A	B	C	D
1				
2				
3				
4				
5				

1A D J Fletcher Design C Downtown Toronto Pipe Club **1B** D Type08 C Giant Otter **1C** D Stevan Rodic C NearKat **1D** D Ulyanov Denis C Ristokraft
2A D Independent graphic designer C Spraf **2B** D Dustin Commer C Runwell **2C** D Kneadle, Inc. C Kneadle **2D** D Stevan Rodic C Flyyyer
3A D Karl Design Vienna C Karl Design Vienna **3B** D Hubbell Design Works C Introspex **3C** D Josh Carnley C Music City Magic Shop **3D** D Gardner Design C Magic Talent
4A D Gardner Design C Magic Talent **4B** D Stevan Rodic C N/A **4C** D Stevan Rodic C Shape Sense **4D** D Stephen Lee Ogden Design Co. C Runaway Rabbit
5A D R&R Partners C Run On Hudson Valley **5B** D J Fletcher Design C The Rarebit **5C** D J Fletcher Design C Folie A Deux **5D** D Logo Geek C Curious Alice

A B C D

1

2

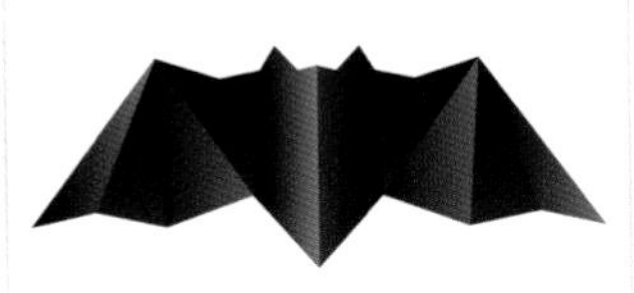

3

4

5

1A Ⓓ Gyula Nemeth Ⓒ Monkie Shop **1B** Ⓓ Kai-Co family of industries Ⓒ The Costa Rica Coffee Experience **1C** Ⓓ Maximo Gavete Ⓒ Recently **1D** Ⓓ Blackdog Creative Ⓒ Unkle Munkey's Brand
2A Ⓓ Logo Planet Laboratory Ⓒ Northside Locksmith **2B** Ⓓ Outdoor Cap Ⓒ Northside Locksmith **2C** Ⓓ Alex Tass Ⓒ Alex Tass / Nocturn **2D** Ⓓ Exhibit A: Design Group Ⓒ Kangaloop
3A Ⓓ Type08 Ⓒ Rhino Store **3B** Ⓓ Design Buddy Ⓒ RhinoFab **3C** Ⓓ Stevan Rodic Ⓒ Sneaky Elephant **3D** Ⓓ MeatStudio Ⓒ Oh Marvellous
4A Ⓓ Lucas Marc Design Ⓒ Archon Business Group **4B** Ⓓ Dangerdom Studios Ⓒ Personal **4C** Ⓓ Jerron Ames Ⓒ BiteSize **4D** Ⓓ Pavel Saksin Ⓒ N/A
5A Ⓓ created by South Ⓒ Elvis & Elephants **5B** Ⓓ M@OH! Ⓒ N/A **5C** Ⓓ Bounce Design Newcastle Pty Ltd Ⓒ Surfers Ally **5D** Ⓓ Heffley Creative Ⓒ Stoneybrook Farm

DESIGN /// JERRON AMES

CLIENT /// BLOOMINYOGA

CATEGORY /// NATURE

Jerron Ames, based in Farmington, Utah, has been designing logos for more than ten years. His organic, nature inspired style has gained him clients from as far away as South Africa and London. "I love nature and the outdoors, and I care about the environment, so if I get to design logos with plants, trees, and mountains, I am in heaven. Fortunately for me, people recognize that in my portfolio and then that generates more projects requiring nature themes," he says.

Of course, his yoga instructor client only had to look across the dinner table to find him. His wife, Tiffany Ames, is the founder of BloomInYoga, and she wanted to expand her business and polish her brand. "As someone of Irish decent, she had a desire for a hint of Celtic knot work combined with a Hindu mandala style design, but most importantly conveying a feeling of nature, organic growth and flowering," Ames explains. "A continuous line drawing was also suggested to convey no beginning and no end. The ultimate result for the logo was to resemble a flower or a bloom, while avoiding anything too feminine because of the variety of her students, both male and female."

He studied mandalas and knot work designs, noting the many possibilities, but he quickly realized it would be easy to get caught up in the myriad details associated with these symbols, so he reigned himself in, focusing on the flower aspect. Doodling on a piece of paper, Ames found a style he liked and shared with his wife, who had some minor tweaks.

Ames doesn't typically do a formal sketch phase, rather he doodles until he hits something he likes. Here he created doodles based on Irish mandalas and Celtic knot work designs he researched.

> "The desired colors were greens, but I ended up adding some gold for contrast and interest; I then picked a complementary typeface with slight customization, and we are both thrilled with the end result, which in and of itself is a beautiful thing."
>
> —Jerron Ames

WORDS FROM JERRON AMES

This early sketch wasn't quite hitting the right note for the client. "The leaves around the design were too detailed and unnecessary, taking focus away from the bloom. This type of design should eventually take your focus to the center, which in this early version was completely uninteresting, so I added a small flower shape to the center of the final version," he says.

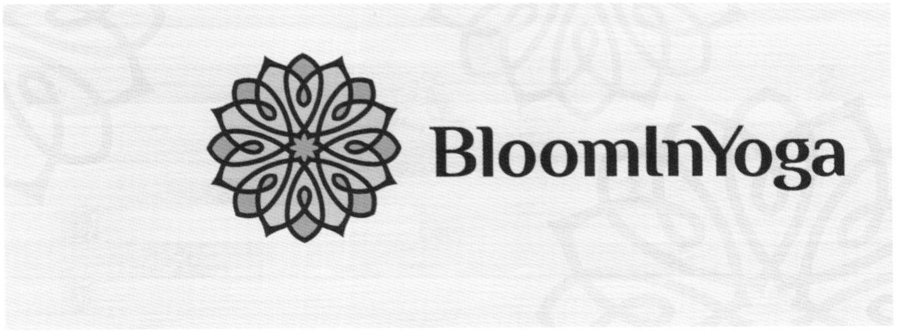

The final logo was an exercise in restraint. Ames was able to capture a flower in a mandala style that doesn't come off as too feminine, and the gold nicely complements the green, capturing just the right Celtic tone.

Sarah Peters, CMT

Sarah Peters is a massage therapist primarily working with children and infants. She wanted a logo with various colors, but not too colorful, as well as something a child may relate to. She wanted to avoid the typical abstract person giving or receiving a massage, and she was only interested in a hand or hands if it was done in a way that is original and relevant. I drew a palm and saw that I could incorporate a flower into the center. The client actually suggested the font style and it ended up looking very nice with the icon.

Montpellier Psychotherapy Practice

The Montpellier Psychotherapy Practice, located in London, provides high quality professional psychotherapy to its patients. This client came to me because of my organic, abstract and somewhat detailed design style. He specifically wanted to bring the calming and healing aspects of water and nature into the logo. I created a design of a flower being fed by water to show growth and development.

Coveted Seeds

Coveted Seeds sells ultrapremium cannabis seeds. The client wanted a high-end feel and was struggling with a way to show *coveted* in a logo. I suggested using a hand in the logo reaching for or holding up the seed as if it is something rare and very desirable. I also worked in an abundance of leaves and vines showing the potential of the seed.

Kukua

Kukuá is a learner placement organization in South Africa that helps qualified undergraduates and further education and training (FET) learners find internships or job placements in South Africa and abroad. They liked the idea of a tree to show growth, and we both liked the idea of a tree growing beyond a boundary to further it's potential.

Snohomish Running Company

Founded in 2012, this premiere event producer and promoter in the Snohomish County Washington region hosts scenic marathons such as the Snohomish River Run, Snohomish Women's Run, and the Everett Half. Wanting to promote the scenic routes, it was a must to have landscape elements incorporated into the logos such as the river, mountains and the sea.

Green Path Garden Supply

Although this didn't end up as the final logo for Green Path Garden Supply, this was my favorite. It's a very natural styled logo with a garden and path in the center that I think looks inviting. I then rolled up a few garden tools into the banner, making it unmistakably a garden supply store.

Nature Bag

Nature Bag is filled with tools, seeds, toys and other things designed to teach children about nature and make them excited about the environment. Although this logo wasn't ultimately picked, I think the fun style and concept was perfect—a plant growing out of a fun little bag without being too cartoony.

A B C D

1

2

3

4

5

1C D 1dea Design + Media Inc. C Watershed Canada **1D** D 1dea Design + Media Inc. C Watershed Canada
2A D Jeffhalmos C Canadian Photography **2B** D IndigoPark C Maple Lawn South **2C** D Rebrander C N/A **2D** D Rural City Creative C Hawaii Food and Wine Festival
3A D Estudio Mezanino C N/A **3B** D Patrick Carter Design, Inc. C New Leaf Vapor Co. **3C** D Lukedesign C N/A **3D** D Brandforma C N/A
4A D UNIT partners C Roya Spirit **4B** D Pavel Saksin C Green hope **4C** D Sean Heisler Design C Plant Catching **4D** D Bronson Ma Creative C Texas A&M College of Agriculture & Life Sciences
5A D Stephen Lee Ogden Design Co. C Citizen Crops **5B** D Sean Heisler Design C Bela Canela **5C** D Wheelhouse Collective C N/A **5D** D Pix-I Graphx C Bell Pharmacy

A B C D

1

bimbamboo

2

3

4

5

1A D Yury Akulin | Logodiver C Ecofole **1B** D smARTer C Ecossentials **1C** D Scott Oeschger Design C Star Group **1D** D Sunday Lounge C The Scottsdale Brewery
2A D Niedermeier Design C TERVIVA **2B** D AkarStudios C SALADFIX **2C** D Denys Kotliarov C Brick technology **2D** D Robert Finkel Design C Birch Hill
3A D Type08 C Type08 **3B** D MVC Agency C Manila Sky **3C** D Shierly Design Creative C Bayleaf Restaurant **3D** D CINDERBLOC INC. C Old Mill Inn + Spa
4A D LETR & Co. C Triscend **4B** D addicted2be C Noble Graphics/TBWA **4C** D Hasan Ali Akhtar C Al Madina International School **4D** D Unipen C Love Endless Knot
5A D bartodell.com C GearHost.com **5B** D Dept of Energy C Teadora **5C** D Mart√≠n Azambuja C Whole Foods **5D** D Julian Peck Creative C Lotus

	A	B	C	D
1				
2				
3				
4				
5				

1A D Jerron Ames C Randewoo **1B** D 36creative C SynapDx **1C** D Rise Design Branding Inc. C Aroma Paper **1D** D Karl Design Vienna C Hawaii.de
2A D Traction Partners C CocoaNilla **2B** D Jerron Ames C Rose Coil **2C** D 903 Creative, LLC C Rosalia Films **2D** D Denys Kotliarov C Brick technology
3A D Disciple Design C Lotos **3B** D grupo oxigeno C Grupo Nuestros Parques **3C** D Sunday Lounge C Salida Hydroponic Supply **3D** D Akhmatov Studio C Handmade soap
4A D Kairevicius C www.kairevicius.com **4B** D Jerron Ames C Sarah Peters CMT **4C** D Wheelhouse Collective C Moseley Photography **4D** D Pavel Saksin C Honey bee
5A D Stitch Design Co. C Sierra Steifman **5B** D Stitch Design Co. C Sara York Grimshaw and Saramel Evans **5C** D lunabrand design group C Sphinx Date Ranch **5D** D Sean Heisler Design C Bela Canela

	A	B	C	D
1				
2	 	 	 	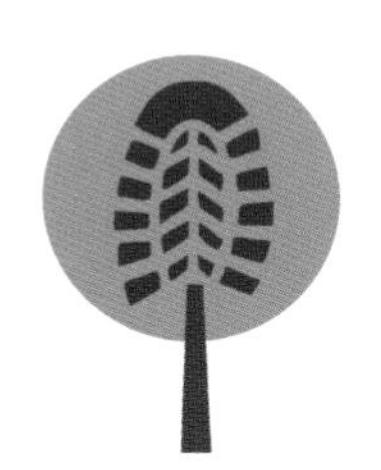
3		 		
4	 	 		
5	 	 	 	

1A D Jerron Ames C Arties **1B** D Mart√≠n Azambuja C El Horreo **1C** D Ideogram C Lagoya **1D** D Sean Heisler Design C Regeneration
2A D Sean Heisler Design C Amitree **2B** D Sean Heisler Design C Amitree **2C** D Logo Geek C Michaela Fitness **2D** D brandclay C Muddy Boots Landscaping
3A D Asgard C Oranienbaum State Local History Museum **3B** D Opacity Design Group C Woodbridge Properties Ltd. **3C** D Sophia Georgopoulou I Design C olive Forever **3D** D Visual Lure, LLC C da Vinci Tree
4A D TYPE AND SIGNS C OLIVITA **4B** D TYPE AND SIGNS C BANSHEE Cinema **4C** D Pavel Saksin C N/A **4D** D Noe Araujo C Funky Cinema
5A D Jerron Ames C Timberline Adventures **5B** D The Quiet Society C N/A **5C** D Rebrander C Plants Online **5D** D ZEBRA design branding C Valentina Mokina

A B C D

1

The Scottsdale Brewery

2

3

4

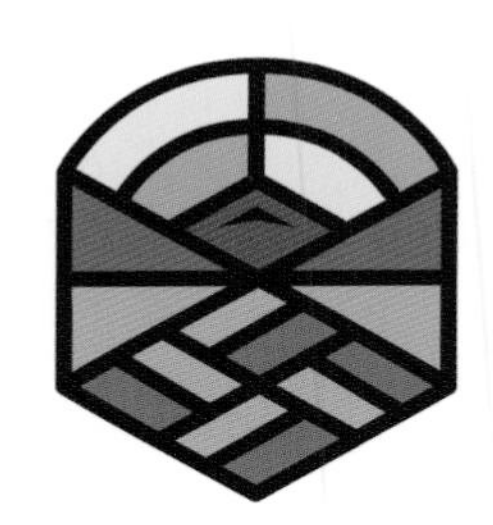

5

1A D Sunday Lounge C The Scottsdale Brewery **1B** D Visual Dialogue C Root **1C** D Misign - Visual Communication C Verginer Holzprofi **1D** D Hubbell Design Works C Acorn Tiny Homes **2A** D London Dewey C Acorn Kids **2B** D IDEAS C Brian Nutt **2C** D Refinery 43 C Cindy Giovagnoli **2D** D Webster C Nebraska City Tourism and Commerce **3A** D Roger Strunk C Kansas Skin - Skin and Laser Center **3B** D Oxide Design Co. C Nebraska Craft Brewers Guild **3C** D AkarStudios C Barley Bean **3D** D createTWO C South Alabama Woodworks **4A** D idgroup C Everman Cooperative Grocery & Cafe **4B** D Rainy Day Designs C Home Waters **4C** D A.D. Creative Group C Montana Rural HIT **4D** D Sean Heisler Design C Redemption **5A** D 903 Creative, LLC C NatureServe **5B** D Oronoz Brandesign C N/A **5C** D Tran Creative C Pacific Coast Triathlon **5D** D Rayat Brands C JDURC

	A	B	C	D
1				
2				
3				
4				
5				

1A D Rainy Day Designs C Electric Mountain Lodge **1B** D Jerron Ames C Fivestar Branding Agency **1C** D Parallele gestion de marques C Avalanche Skiwear **1D** D The Quiet Society C Tehachapi
2A D BluesCue Designs C Glacier Films **2B** D Alsobrook Creative C Daybreak **2C** D Jerron Ames C Arteis **2D** D Fernandez Studio C Summit Path
3A D Fernandez Studio C Summit Path **3B** D 903 Creative, LLC C yogg **3C** D Gizwiz Studio C Arianna Turnquest **3D** D A.D. Creative Group C Montana Rural HIT
4A D Visual Lure, LLC C Flower Mountain Weddings & Receptions **4B** D Anagraphic C MATT **4C** D Juicebox Designs C The Riverstone Development Group **4D** D Type08 C Zen Nail Spa
5A D smARTer C McGinley Associates **5B** D Rebrander C Mainstream **5C** D Type08 C Arkiive **5D** D Paul Wronski Graphic Design, LLC C Best Rest Baby, Brooklyn

A B C D

1

SAM

2

3

4

5

1A D Oronoz Brandesign C SAM **1B** D Miller Meiers Communication Arts Agency C City of Lawrence Kansas **1C** D Swanson Russell C FMC **1D** D Hayes Image C Eclipse
2A D Ye Olde Studio C Aman Organics **2B** D Red Studio Inc C Wells Fargo Center, Portland OR **2C** D Nox Creative C Texas Capital Partners, LLC **2D** D Creation C Plane Guard
3A D Jordahl Design C Beacon Summit **3B** D Jerron Ames C Arties **3C** D Fuzzco C ITZ'ANA **3D** D Quique Ollervides C Sarahí & René
4A D Brandon Harrison C Luis Godinez Photography **4B** D Luke Bott Design & Illustration C Wink **4C** D Chris Rooney Illustration/Design C Celltick **4D** D Luke Bott Design & Illustration C O'Swell 3
5A D Creation C The Novus Trust **5B** D Ye Olde Studio C 32 Sonatas **5C** D Jerron Ames C Pepper Advertising **5D** D BrandHand C Mars branding

DESIGN /// GARDNER DESIGN

CLIENT /// REDGUARD

CATEGORY /// SHAPES

RedGuard, which manufactures blast-resistant buildings and storage containers, approached Gardner Design several years ago to help them with their marketing and branding efforts. Then called A Box 4 U, it was immediately apparent to the Gardner team that the name, which had become synonymous with storage containers, no longer applied and actually diminished the value of these high-quality, sturdy buildings.

"The first step of this relationship was dealing with a name that had not matured with the product they were offering in their industry," explains Brian Wiens, art director at Gardner Design. "It also placed a limitation on the expanding product lines that were being developed enabling them to grow into other industries of safety and protection dealing with modular space." Since the company's brand color was already determined, the Gardner team recommended the name RedGuard, which firmly establishes the brand in its category.

The previous logo was a dimensional box, so Gardner's team took cues from this to retain some of the brand equity. "This demonstration of space evoked RedGuard's primary product of trade, which is space," explains Bill Gardner, president and founder of Gardner Design.

"I explored a few concepts revolving around protection: a building, shield and human ribs. I found it interesting that these buildings have a rib-like structure that creates strength and protection," Wiens says. "Ultimately I think the whole conceptual process led me to a simple form that lends itself to a building, a shield, and a rib-like outer structure that is protective."

The geometric shapes work together to create a box that unfolds itself, revealing a safe, secure space inside, just like RedGuard's products. By introducing a darker red to the logo palette, it creates depth and sophistication. Ultimately, this logo readily demonstrates the characteristics that make RedGuard unique, and it immediately garnered more recognition for the brand in its industry.

The old logo had a dimensional, hexagonal look that felt dated and wasn't memorable.

The Gardner team wanted to retain the box feeling of the original logo, but they explored different concepts focused on the structure and its protective elements. Wiens played with different shapes and dimensions.

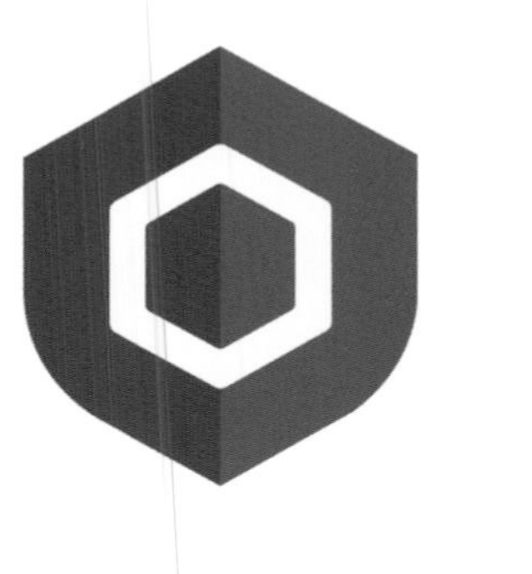

Other concepts included a shield and rib-like renderings. "Our rib cage protects our insides, so I played with these concepts as they relate to a building," Wiens notes.

After several explorations, the red box-like structure emerged as the winning concept.

DESIGN /// GARDNER DESIGN

CLIENT /// GREY-COLLAR SOLUTIONS

CATEGORY /// SHAPES

Grey-Collar Solutions provides software to utility infrastructure companies that streamlines communications and information across all platforms, from the people working in the field to upper management. The *grey collar* is a hybrid between non-technical user groups (blue collar) and technically advanced user groups (white collar), so Gardner Design had a unique opportunity to develop an identity system that integrates these concepts.

"This is a case where the client doesn't have a tangible product, so coming up with a visual solution can be tricky," notes Bill Gardner, president and founder of Gardner Design.

Designer Adam Anderson's early concepts revolved around two shapes: a collar and a circle. "Since *collar* is part of the name, we took a literal approach, using two different ideas. One has lines running through it that symbolize the pipes and moving parts and components that go on behind the scenes, and the other is more high-tech, using color tones that resemble pixels," he explains.

The round logos take on a global representation. "A large part of what their clients do is go into the ground to lay lines, so we wanted to portray the earth, with the lines symbolizing the pipes beneath the ground," Anderson explains. Each circle tells a slightly different story about Grey-Collar's services and clients.

Ultimately, they chose the circle that has an uneven split with different lines on each side. "The lines on the left are uneven and a bit disjointed and the lines on the right are clean and straight. This represents the streamlined flow of information, with the smooth straight lines and different layers," Anderson says.

The white and blue come together to form the gray solution. "The yellow paired nicely with the rest of the colors creating a fresh, modern palette," he notes. A customized sans serif in gray pairs nicely with the logo, lending an authoritative quality to the high-tech start-up.

> "In this case, the clients' product isn't easily associated with a noun or a thing. These are the most challenging to convey in a logo because you are forced to convey visual information in a conceptual manner."
>
> —Bill Gardner

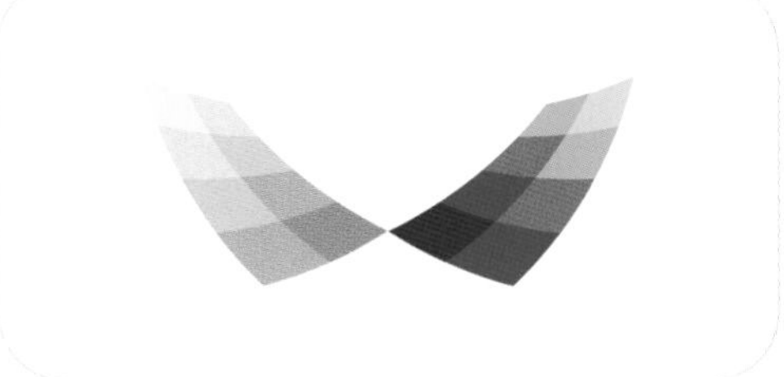

"We explored a number of different areas, and since the word *collar* is in the name we went through a more literal approach," Anderson says.

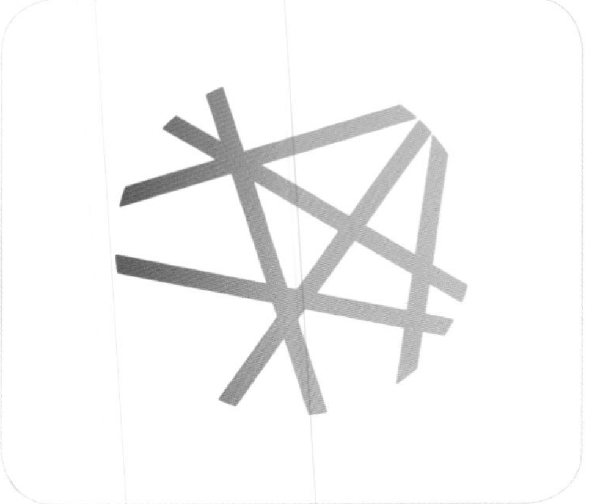

Anderson also designed circular concepts that symbolize the earth. The lines represent the underground pipes that Grey-Collar's clients install. The two intersecting circles are the two groups of people—blue collar and white collar—communicating and working together.

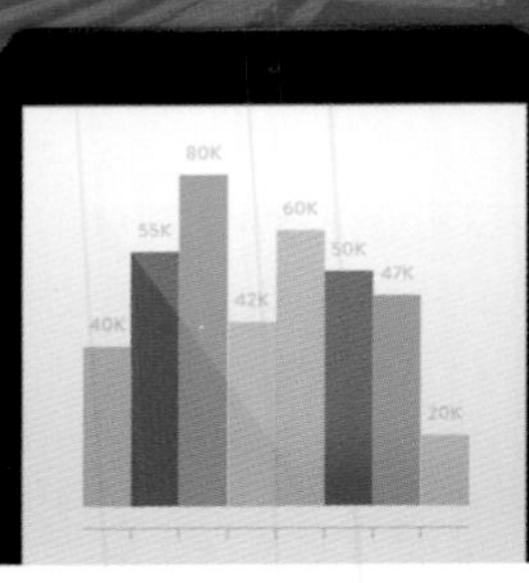

from the
GROUND UP.
WE.
Grey-Collar Solutions helps mine your data and turns it into business intelligence. Our analytic tools, technology, and industry expertise lead to better decisions, process improvement, and greater efficiency for your business.
More about us and what we do.

Ultimately, the client chose the circle with the uneven bands on the left migrating to the smooth, orderly bands on the right. The designers also introduced a clean, custom sans serif typeface in light gray.

	A	B	C	D
1	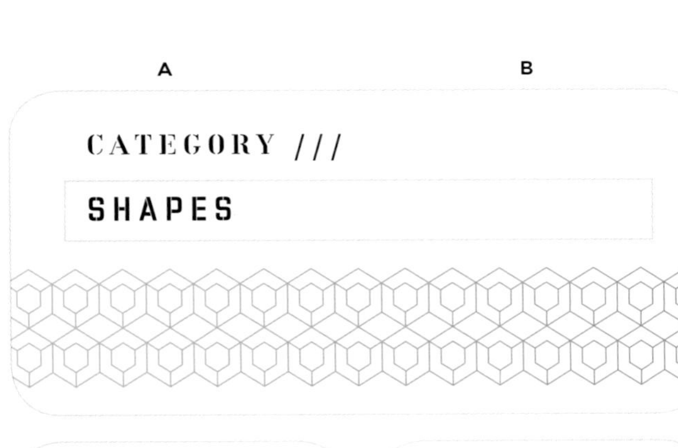			
2			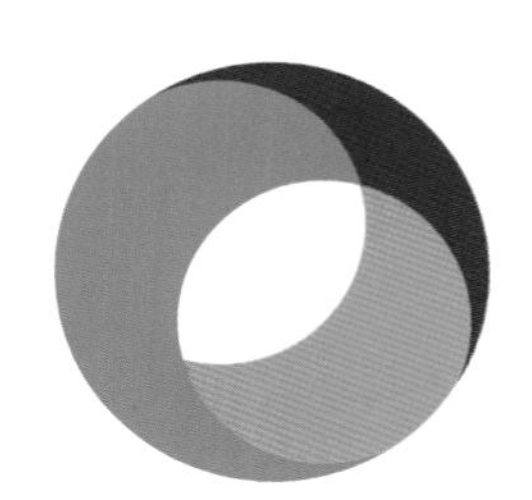	
3	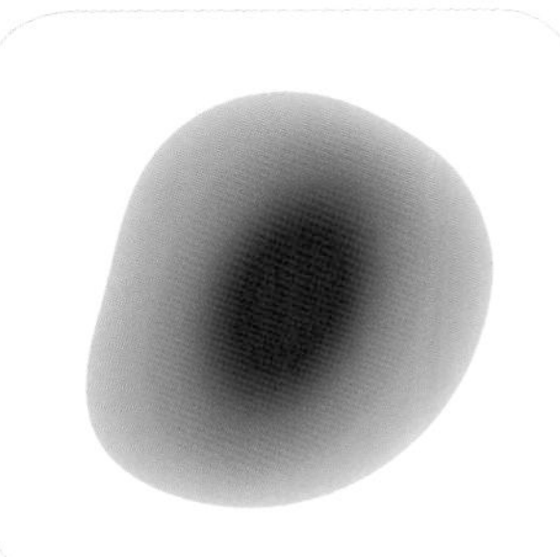		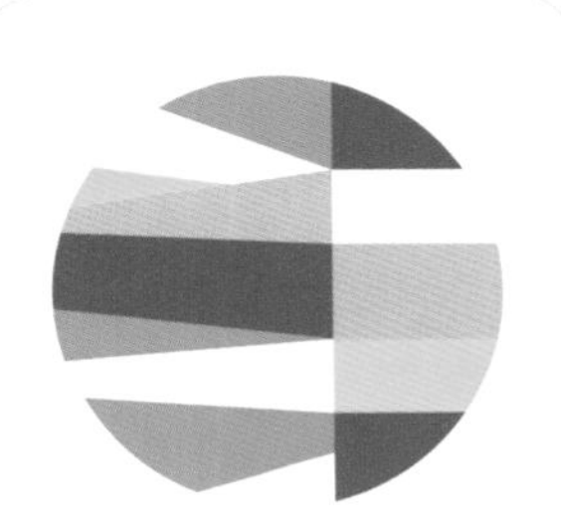	
4				
5				

1C D Karl Design Vienna C Human Rights Logo Contest **1D** D Gardner Design C OpenRoadBrands
2A D Eder Saos C SOS Total **2B** D Brandforma C N/A **2C** D Roy Smith Design C enviro **2D** D LONI DBS C University of Ljubljana, Faculty of Computer and Information Science
3A D ONY C Organic Vodka Group **3B** D ONY C Mango Telecom **3C** D Gardner Design C Grey-Collar Solutions **3D** D Sean Heisler Design C Bela Canela
4A D Almosh82 C Global Liquidity Solutions **4B** D Roy Smith Design C ennviro **4C** D Banowetz + Company, Inc. C Bragalone Conroy PC **4D** D Brandforma C RTM
5A D bartodell.com C Texas Heat Management **5B** D FRED+ERIC C Cup O' **5C** D Clutch Creative Company C Outpost24 **5D** D ANFILOV C http://perfectia.cz

	A	B	C	D
1	米			
2	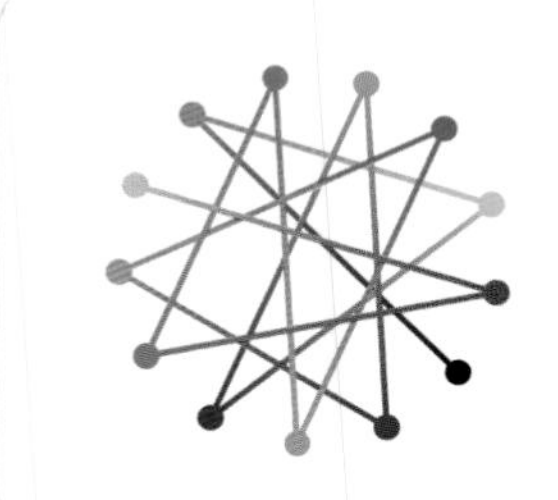	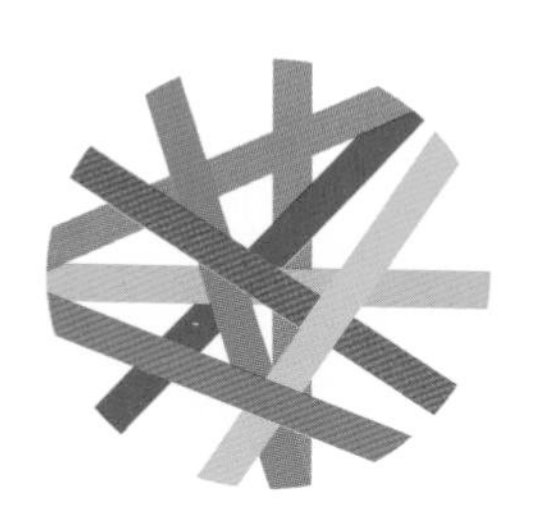		
3				
4				
5				

1A D Xplaye C Sushi Kava **1B** D Essex Two C Grothman Clinic **1C** D CAPSULE C Minnesota Orchestra **1D** D Niedermeier Design C omnificiency
2A D Pavel Saksin C ABC Interlingua **2B** D Gizwiz Studio C Wesley Miletello **2C** D SUMO C Newcastle University **2D** D Visual Dialogue C Nucleus
3A D Visual Lure, LLC C Vik Sharma Photography **3B** D Hayes Image C Entwine **3C** D idgroup C N/A **3D** D bartodell.com C livneypartners.com
4A D Pavel Saksin C Nomway global **4B** D Unipen C Triple A **4C** D Chris Rooney Illustration/Design C RiskIQ **4D** D Kreativbuero Jonas Soeder C ICWE GmbH
5A D Chris Rooney Illustration/Design C Celltick **5B** D Fernandez Studio C Institute for Healthy Living **5C** D R&R Partners C One Team **5D** D Gardner Design C HealthCore Clinic

	A	B	C	D
1				
2	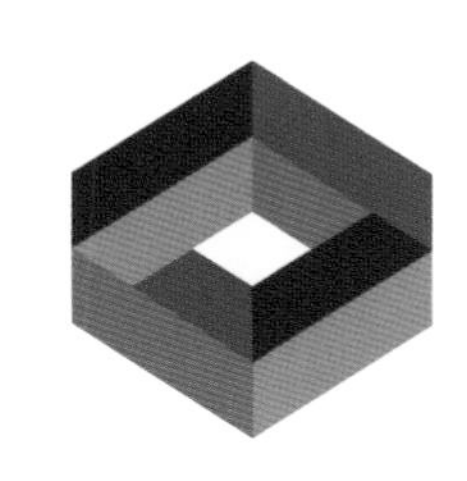		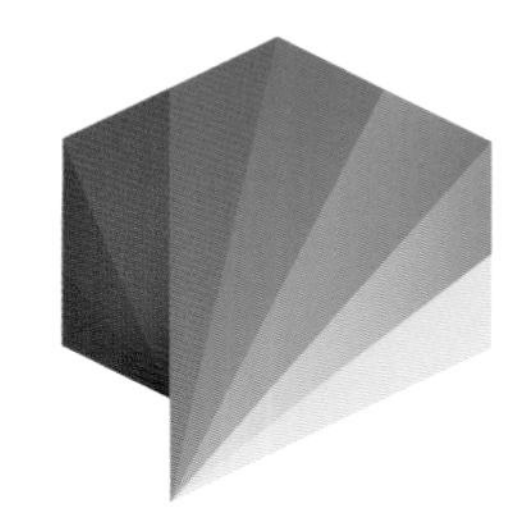	
3				
4	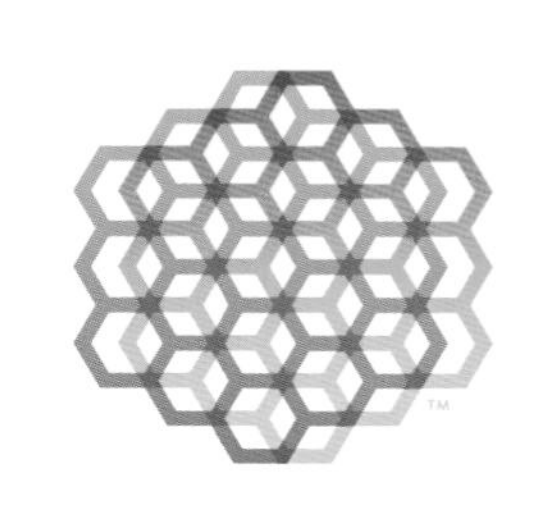			
5				

1A Ⓓ Besapiens Ⓒ Polevoy Group of Companies **1B** Ⓓ Paradox Box Ⓒ Paradox Box **1C** Ⓓ Sophia Georgopoulou | Design Ⓒ Glowbox **1D** Ⓓ Pavel Saksin Ⓒ Before box office
2A Ⓓ Unipen Ⓒ Theme Fusion **2B** Ⓓ bartodell.com Ⓒ livneypartners.com **2C** Ⓓ Independent graphic designer Ⓒ Livecube **2D** Ⓓ Buzzbomb Creative Ⓒ Simpli.fi
3A Ⓓ bartodell.com Ⓒ Hive Agency Los Angeles **3B** Ⓓ CNDC Ⓒ The Chickasaw Nation **3C** Ⓓ Sean Heisler Design Ⓒ Yesh **3D** Ⓓ Fabio Okamoto Design Ⓒ Creta
4A Ⓓ bartodell.com Ⓒ Claritrics **4B** Ⓓ eggnerd Ⓒ Beez Bagels **4C** Ⓓ Ideogram Ⓒ Binc **4D** Ⓓ Brandforma Ⓒ Unixar
5A Ⓓ Liquid Agency Ⓒ Portland Energy Consulting (PECI) **5B** Ⓓ Rebrander Ⓒ Content is King **5C** Ⓓ Pavel Saksin Ⓒ Mini toy factory **5D** Ⓓ M@OH! Ⓒ Photo

	A	B	C	D
1				
2				
3				
4		320 CAP		
5			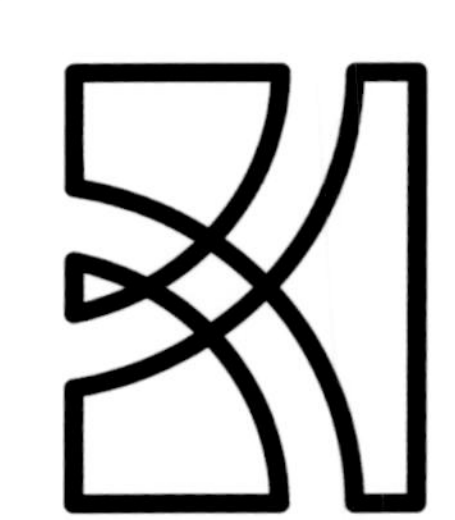	

1A D Oven Design Workshop C Aliancon S.A. **1B** D Eder Saos C Igloo App **1C** D Jerron Ames C Arteis **1D** D Pix-I Graphx C Vollers
2A D Studio Science C AuditFile **2B** D RedEffect C Belux **2C** D Besapiens C Polevoy Group of Companies **2D** D Grain C Millstone Weber
3A D Amy McAdams Design C VSA Indianapolis **3B** D Webster C Dundee Presbyterian Church **3C** D Meir Billet Ltd. C Nahala Real Estate **3D** D Blue Blazes, LLC C Ginn Realty Group
4A D Amy McAdams Design C VSA Indianapolis **4B** D BLVR C 320 Capital **4C** D DEI Creative C Red Propeller **4D** D Just Creative Design C MaxSquare
5A D Erwin Bindeman C Brendon Voogt **5B** D Gizwiz Studio C SAMER HABAIBEH **5C** D RedEffect C LimeCreative / Karistianis **5D** D Gardner Design C Southeastern Community College

	A	B	C	D
1				
2				
3				
4	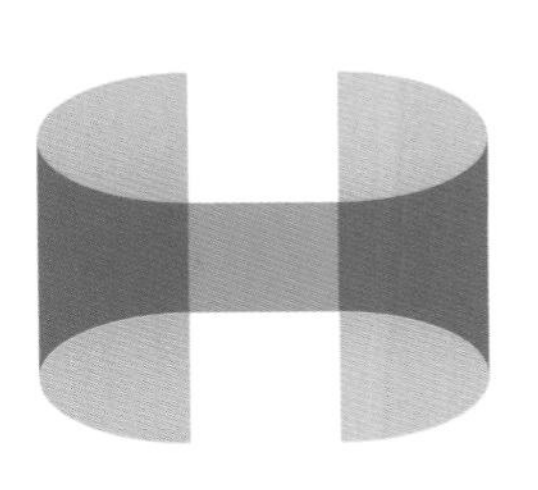		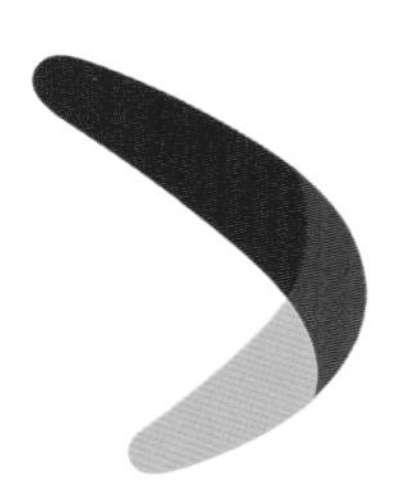	School of Hospitality and Tourism Split
5				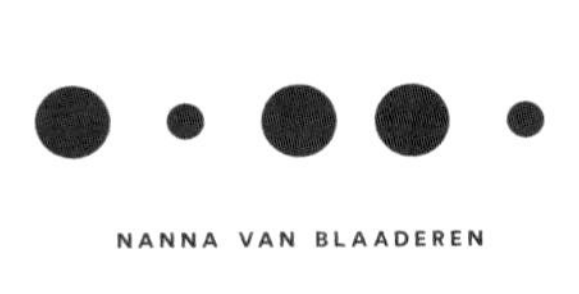

1A D Pavel Saksin C Stone garant **1B** D Luka Balic C Lux Aeterna Association **1C** D Besapiens C Smart Security **1D** D Nox Creative C Dutch Army Co.
2A D Xplaye C MNA de Mexico **2B** D Sebastiany Branding & Design C Monsanto **2C** D Dara Creative C Further Learning Academy **2D** D Dara Creative C Further Learning Academy
3A D JACK C Owen + Alchemy Juice Apothecary **3B** D Kairevicius C Bay Cloud Partners **3C** D Pavel Saksin C N/A **3D** D Buzzbomb Creative C N/A
4A D Greteman Group C Hutton Construction **4B** D ZEBRA design branding C Dimitrovgradsky zavod vkladyshey **4C** D KW43 BRANDDESIGN C Germanwings **4D** D Elevator C N/A
5A D Lippincott C Houghton Mifflin Harcourt **5B** D Visual Dialogue C Broad Institute **5C** D Envision Creative Group C Finance Genius **5D** D KW43 BRANDDESIGN C Nanna van Blaaderen

A B C D

1

2

3

ARDURA

4

5

1A Ⓓ Akhmatov Studio Ⓒ Geyser media & communications **1B** Ⓓ Kairevicius Ⓒ www.radity.com **1C** Ⓓ DEI Creative Ⓒ Red Propeller/Holland Residential **1D** Ⓓ Sachs Media Group Ⓒ Plaza Tower
2A Ⓓ Neuronalics Ltd. Ⓒ Afrolink **2B** Ⓓ Pavel Saksin Ⓒ Englex **2C** Ⓓ Type08 Ⓒ Splitit **2D** Ⓓ Open Door Design Studio (ODDS) Ⓒ John Geci Glass
3A Ⓓ Kreativbuero Jonas Soeder Ⓒ ARCA Records **3B** Ⓓ Asgard Ⓒ International Scientific Conference Science of the Future St. Petersburg 2014
3C Ⓓ DELICATESY Elzbieta Zaczek Ⓒ Ardura **3D** Ⓓ Oluzen Ⓒ CENTRO DE ATENCION INTEGRAL PARA LA DISCAPASIDAD
4A Ⓓ Denis Aristov Ⓒ N/A **4B** Ⓓ MKJ Creative Ⓒ Dance **4C** Ⓓ Elevator Ⓒ L'Aroma **4D** Ⓓ DesignByLefty Ⓒ can't reveal now
5A Ⓓ Chadomoto / Dimiter Petrov Ⓒ Antoaneta Yordanova **5B** Ⓓ Karl Design Vienna Ⓒ Momentum **5C** Ⓓ MKJ Creative Ⓒ Pennsylvania Bio **5D** Ⓓ Lippincott Ⓒ Eteris

DESIGN /// LIPPINCOTT

CLIENT /// SOUTHWEST AIRLINES

CATEGORY /// SYMBOLS

Southwest Airlines has always been the brightest airline carrier in the United States, literally, with its blue, red and yellow aircrafts. Its colorful personality has served the brand well over the years as the largest domestic low-cost carrier, with a loyal customer base. However, in recent years, competing low-cost airlines with new attitudes have gained traction in an already crowded marketplace, so Southwest hired Lippincott to refresh the brand identity and help the airline get back to its roots.

"Southwest had already taken a very careful look across the brand and they realized that they were presenting themselves in a fragmented way," says Rodney Abbot, senior design partner on the project. Southwest had two logos that were being used for separate purposes. One logo was a drawing of a plane ascending over the Southwest name that was used in marketing communications, while the other logo, a heart with wings, was utilized throughout the customer experience.

"They were supporting two different identities and not getting great traction from a pure branding standpoint," Abbot says. The bright colors of the brand were also disjointed when used as an identifier. The advertising, for example, tended to be predominantly yellow, whereas the planes themselves were primarily blue and red.

Abbot and his team at Lippincott took a close look at the brand to come up with a strategy that would align the visual assets with the mission of the company. "It was really about getting potential customers to take a first look at Southwest, as well as maintaining the loyalists they already have. There are many customers who are passionate about Southwest, and we wanted them engaged and excited about where the company was headed. We wanted to make the identity fresh and modern without losing its heart, so to speak," he explains.

Old Southwest logos.

> "So from the very first meeting we said the heart would be the centerpiece—the one truly iconic symbol and story that only Southwest could own and deliver on."
>
> —Rodney Abbot

The design team explored many different ways to present the heart, including a heart in motion. Abbot says, "The *a-ha* moment for us was when we started to explore the balance between the tricolored stripes—which is a core element in the Southwest visual identity system—with the heart. When we brought these two elements together, everything fell into place."

Of course, you can't just plop a heart on a plane and expect people to love it. Lippincott learned that the red belly of the plane was really symbolic to Southwest employees. It represented a warrior spirit that has been in the brand's DNA since the beginning, when the founders had to fight for the right to start the airline carrier in the early 1970s. "Because the red was about passion, we didn't want to lose the story, so putting the heart on the belly of the plane was an important part of maintaining that story. To keep the potency and fly with heart was part of the experience, and hopefully it means more to people now, because it has more clarity, and it's easy to understand," Abbot explains.

The heart is also present by the door as customers enter the plane. "Most airlines typically will put the symbol on the tail really big. We liked the idea of using the heart very small by the door," he says. "That idea of using the heart as a punctuation and discreet element was a very important part of the story. In the past, the heart was part of the iconography and came across as sentimental and cute. The new image is much more professional and polished, and it's used in a very deliberate way to communicate the unique qualities of the brand."

In addition to the heart, the planes were repainted in a glossier, more saturated finish, with blue as the primary color, and a new logotype was developed for the Southwest name, which now appears boldly on the fuselage across the windows, instead of on the tail. The visual characteristics of the heart and new logotype also informed the design of Southwest Sans, a custom typeface that is now used in all brand communications.

The iconic heart logo has been adapted to all materials including packaging, pins and digital and print materials. When the campaign was rolled out in the fall of 2014 at Dallas Love Field, Southwest's hub, it was well received, and the accompanying ad describes it best: "Without a heart, it's just a machine."

Early sketches of the logo take on many forms and even indicate movement. The Lippincott team eventually focused on the angle of the stripes on the plane tail and carried that into the heart symbol.

Once the heart logo was established, the Lippincott team worked with the colors, taking the stripes off the tail design and putting them into the heart.

Southwest®

Southwest Sans came from the heart, literally. It was crafted taking cues from the characteristics of the new logo, using the point and base of the heart and the rounded letterforms.

The new planes feature the Southwest name across the fuselage and feature deeper, more saturated paint colors.

The old planes maintained a red belly that indicated a warrior spirit, which was part of Southwest's legacy. The Lippincott team felt that replacing the red belly with the heart would have more impact symbolically. The heart was also placed next to the plane door, reinforcing Southwest's commitment to its customers.

The final identity rollout as seen on packaging, pins and in the Southwest terminal.

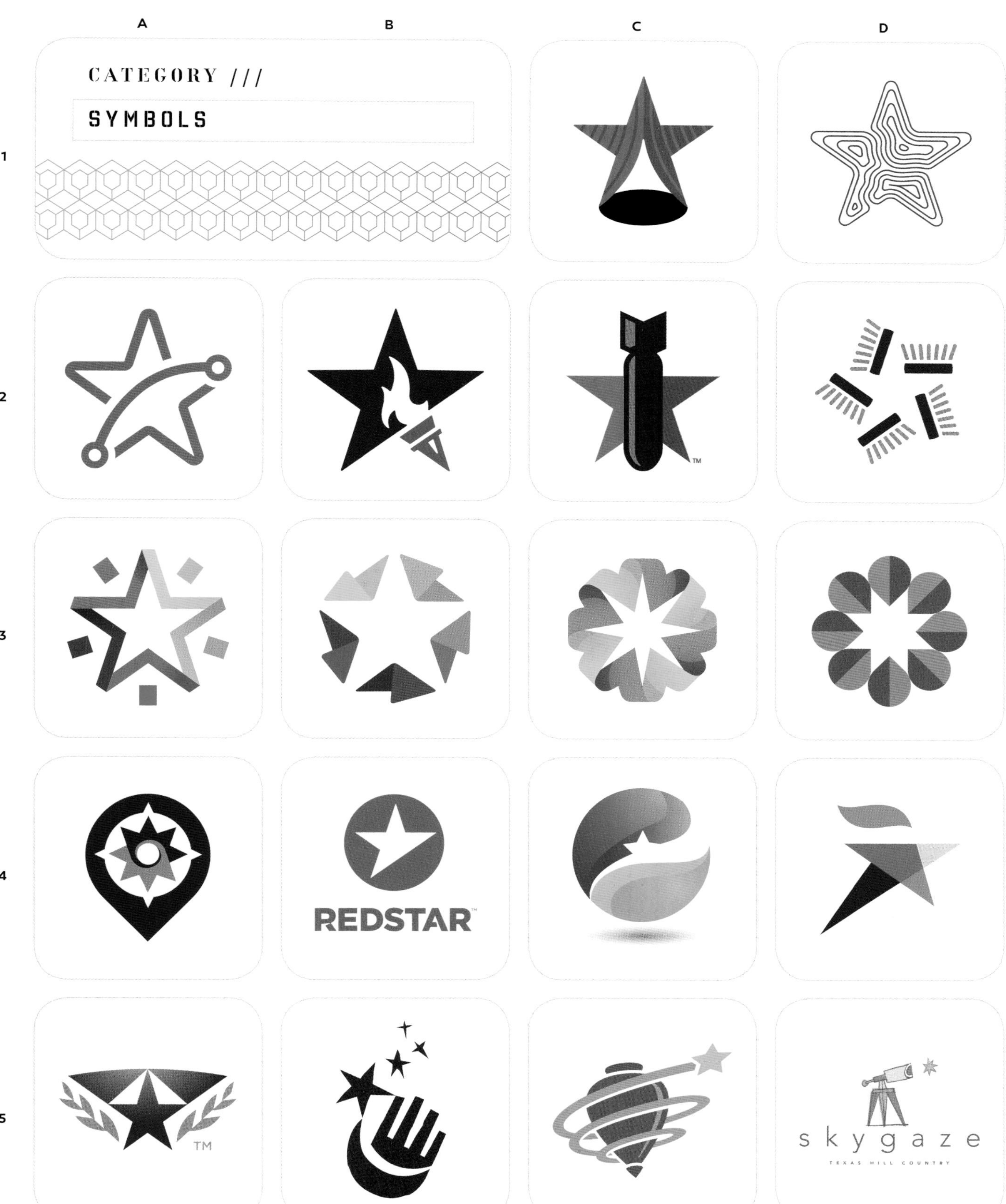

1C Ⓓ Gardner Design Ⓒ Magic Talent **1D** Ⓓ eggnerd Ⓒ North Texas Land Scholars
2A Ⓓ Prejean Creativen Ⓒ Bridgestar Logistics **2B** Ⓓ Tribe Ⓒ Institute for International Education **2C** Ⓓ bartodell.com Ⓒ Bomb City Supply Co. **2D** Ⓓ Fernandez Studio Ⓒ Groom Elite
3A Ⓓ 01d Ⓒ Zagorodnaya nedvizhimost **3B** Ⓓ Art'Performance Ⓒ Altea Group **3C** ⒹGardner Design Ⓒ HealthCore Clinic **3D** Ⓓ Chris Rooney Illustration/Design Ⓒ Flowers Community Initiatives
4A Ⓓ Todytod Ⓒ Booking.com **4B** Ⓓ Anthony Rees Ⓒ Redstar **4C** Ⓓ Gizwiz Studio Ⓒ Khaled Elsheref **4D** Ⓓ Fernandez Studio Ⓒ PAI
5A Ⓓ Gardner Design Ⓒ General Coach **5B** Ⓓ Sean Heisler Design Ⓒ Creedoo **5C** Ⓓ R&R Partners Ⓒ N/A **5D** Ⓓ Sabingrafik, Inc. Ⓒ skygaze

A B C D

1

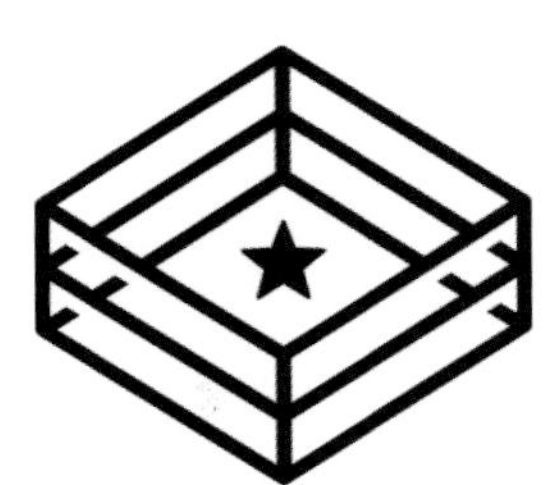

2

3

4

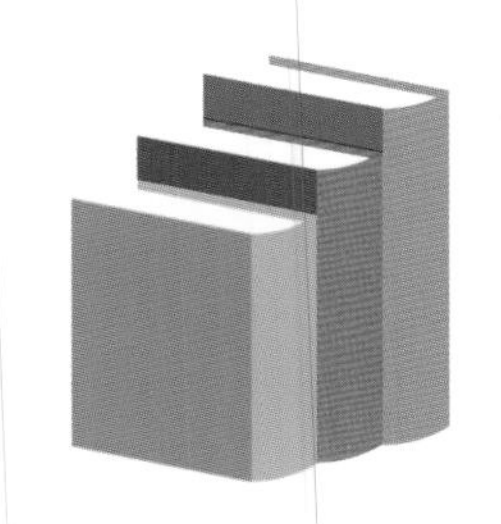

5

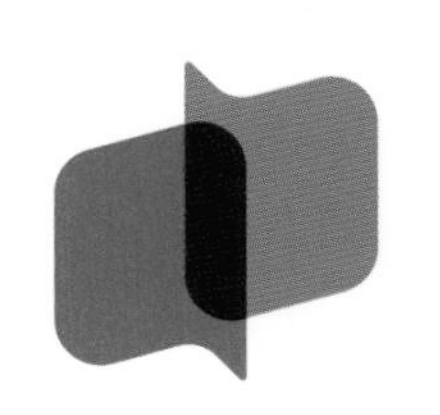

1A D Jerron Ames C Pepper Advertising **1B** D Bryan Butler C TypeFight **1C** D Sean Heisler Design C Children's Digital Library **1D** D Sean Heisler Design C Children's Digital Library
2A D Gizwiz Studio C Leslie Martin **2B** D Studio Absolute C Author Talk. **2C** D RolandRekeczki C Libri **2D** D idgroup C Episcopal Day School
3A D KOSMA Design Studio C www.jakubmichalski.pl **3B** D M@OH! C The Book House on University **3C** D TriLion Studios C Center for Educational Rights **3D** D Dangerdom Studios C Time to Time
4A D Pavel Saksin C Step education **4B** D Pavel Saksin C Booktalk **4C** D brandclay C News Quantified **4D** D Jibe C MedForums
5A D 5Seven C Pandora Sales Research **5B** D Jerron Ames C Arteis **5C** D emedia creative C CRC **5D** D Apus Agency C N/A

	A	B	C	D
1		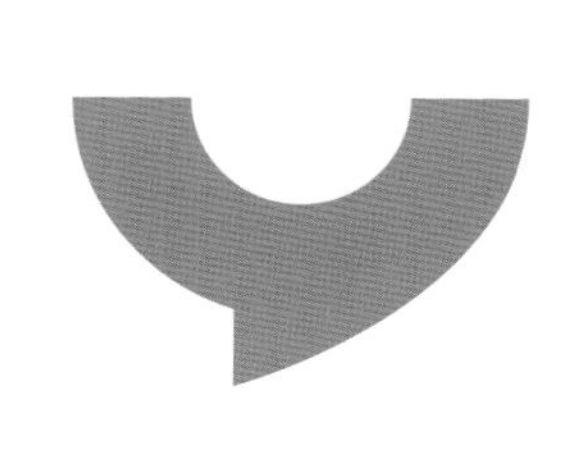		
2				
3				
4				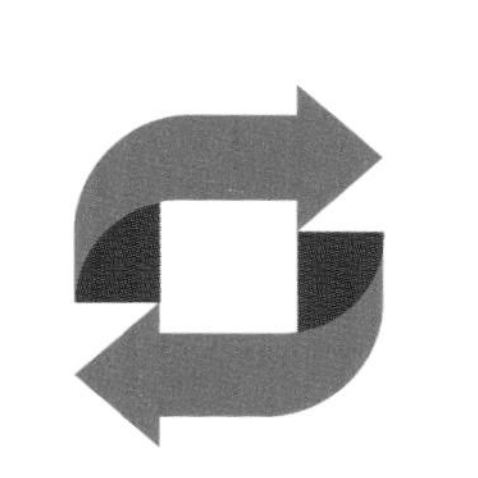
5				

1A D Shadia Design C Blah Blah Speech Pathology **1B** D brandclay C Yella **1C** D Optimacad C Tuner Media **1D** D Studio Science C Kore
2A D Paradigm New Media Group C Fleur Di Lis Group **2B** D Todytod C Booking.com **2C** D Type08 C DIYnot **2D** D Type08 C Renovate Forum
3A D Jibe C N/A **3B** D JonathanHowell.com C N/A **3C** D Effendy Design C ProsperousCopy **3D** D Lukedesign C N/A
4A D Cinq Partners C N/A **4B** D Independent graphic designer C 33degrees **4C** D Karl Design Vienna C Karl Design Vienna **4D** D Gardner Design C SiteBox
5A D Rebrander C Content Protection **5B** D Bohn Studio C Paragon Care **5C** D Creative Parc C Wildflour Bakery **5D** D Independent graphic designer C Kurochka i korochka

	A	B	C	D
1	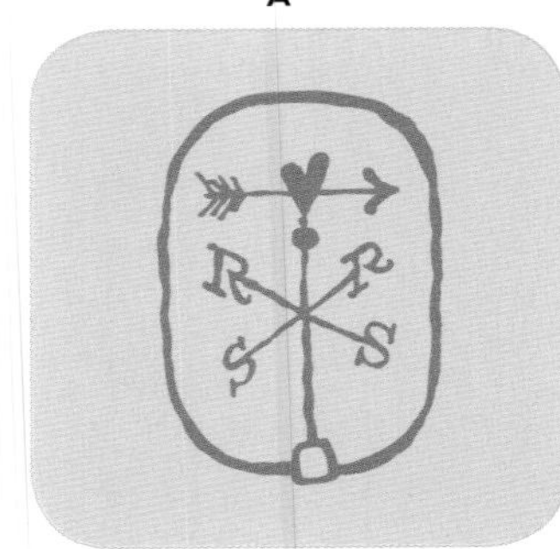			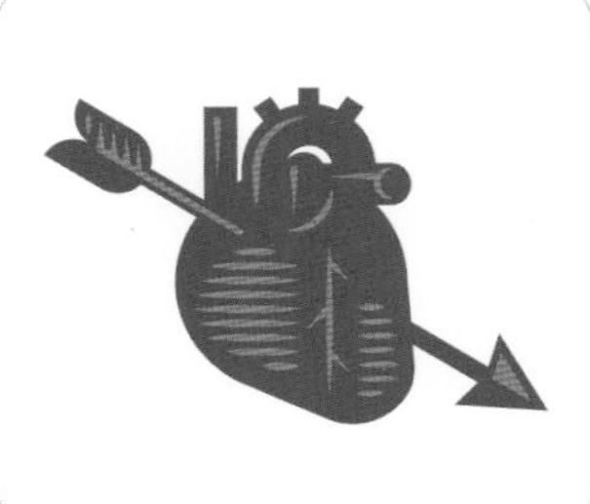
2				
3				
4				
5		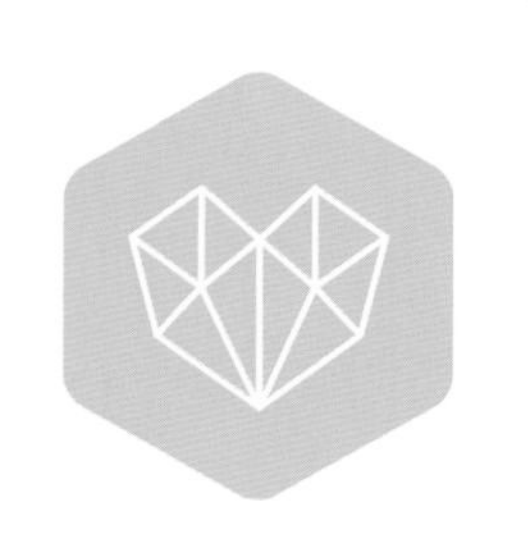		

1A Ⓓ Quique Ollervides Ⓒ Sarahí & René **1B** Ⓓ Odney Ⓒ N/A **1C** Ⓓ Funnel Ⓒ Lyon Distilling Co. **1D** Ⓓ J Fletcher Design Ⓒ GMMB
2A Ⓓ Just Creative Design Ⓒ Ireland Group Real Estate **2B** Ⓓ Juicebox Interactive Ⓒ Folk Hero **2C** Ⓓ Niedermeier Design Ⓒ Physicians United **2D** Ⓓ Kovach Studio Ⓒ Multi Love
3A Ⓓ Jon Kay Design Ⓒ Fangamer **3B** Ⓓ Stephen Lee Ogden Design Co. Ⓒ West Broad Church **3C** Ⓓ Just Creative Design Ⓒ Welcome Smiles **3D** Ⓓ Green Ink Studio Ⓒ N/A
4A Ⓓ Yury Akulin | Logodiver Ⓒ First Pharmacy **4B** Ⓓ Jason Durgin Design Ⓒ Rides for Lives **4C** Ⓓ Karl Design Vienna Ⓒ Neuherz Vienna **4D** Ⓓ Jon Kay Design Ⓒ Fangamer
5A Ⓓ Polypod Ⓒ Brave Heart Fund **5B** Ⓓ Pixler Designs Ⓒ Pixel Lovers **5C** Ⓓ Kay Loves Candy Ⓒ Creative Hearts Network **5D** Ⓓ Be!Five branding & identity Ⓒ Samara region

	A	B	C	D
1				
2				
3				
4				
5				

1A Ⓓ Ali Seylan Ⓒ Turkish Deaf Sports Federation **1B** Ⓓ Luke Bott Design & Illustration Ⓒ Wink **1C** Ⓓ Dangerdom Studios Ⓒ Motion Authors **1D** Ⓓ Visual Lure, LLC Ⓒ Hey Guys Comedy
2A Ⓓ MAD CONSORT Ⓒ Groupe LFE **2B** Ⓓ Scott McFadden Creative Ⓒ Scott McFadden Creative **2C** Ⓓ Plumb and Pixel Ⓒ Quest Church **2D** Ⓓ Absolu communication marketing Ⓒ Cimetière Saint-Michel
3A Ⓓ artslinger Ⓒ Athletes USA **3B** Ⓓ Dotzero Design Ⓒ Demand Engine **3C** Ⓓ Bethany Heck Ⓒ 34 Brand **3D** Ⓓ Ideogram Ⓒ Kulture City
4A Ⓓ The Quiet Society Ⓒ Sevenly **4B** Ⓓ More Branding+Communication Ⓒ STG Pizzeria **4C** Ⓓ Hubbell Design Works Ⓒ 98 Skulls **4D** Ⓓ Fuzzco Ⓒ BLCC
5A Ⓓ Oxide Design Co. Ⓒ Center for Civic Design **5B** Ⓓ BASIS Ⓒ The National Right to Read Foundation **5C** Ⓓ Niedermeier Design Ⓒ American Homestay Network **5D** Ⓓ Rule29 Ⓒ Team RWB

A B C D

1

2

LIGHTNING IN A BOTTLE
—COMPETITION—

3

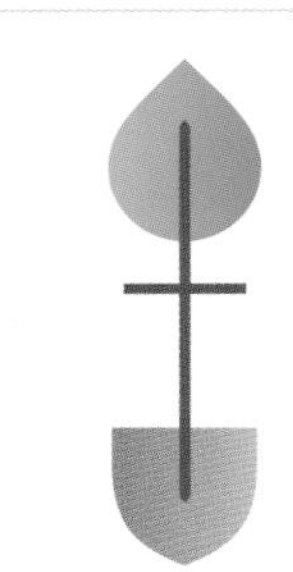

4

POSITIVE
ENERGY

5

HEALTH
FACILITIES
GROUP
architecture

1A D Varick Rosete Studio C One Spark **1B** D idgroup C McKenzie Law Firm **1C** D Sean Heisler Design C Aldor **1D** D Lippincott C Farmers Insurance
2A D Karl Design Vienna C Steerin AG **2B** D ab+c Creative Intelligence C ab+c Creative Intelligence **2C** D Airtype Studio C Big Happy Boot Camp **2D** D The Blksmith Design Co. C Personal
3A D Glitschka Studios C Glasgow Church **3B** D smARTer C Cultivate Church Planting **3C** D Sean Heisler Design C Warehouse Church **3D** D Fixer Creative Co. C Leadership Transformations
4A D MVC Agency C Manila Sky **4B** D Fuzzco C Positive Energy **4C** D Deksia C Rapid Response **4D** D Gardner Design C HealthSim United
5A D Gardner Design C Health Facilities Group **5B** D Tran Creative C Medical Practice Management Services **5C** D Gardner Design C Health Facilities Group **5D** D Gardner Design C Health Facilities Group

DESIGN /// JAY FLETCHER

CLIENT /// FURNITURE SERVICES INC.

CATEGORY /// ART/MISCELLANEOUS

Like many well-known logo designers, Jay Fletcher majored in illustration and started his career in that field working for publications. "I loved illustration, but a lot of my friends were getting jobs doing design work at agencies, and it seemed so much more interesting and challenging to me—the idea that you're communicating for somebody else and that your work has a much longer shelf life," he says. "The idea that graphic design is 'functional art' is what initially drew me to it."

Based in Charleston, South Carolina, Fletcher now primarily designs logos for clients, putting both his illustration and design skills to use. When Furniture Services Inc., came to him to redesign their logo, he came up with several design directions incorporating different artistic elements. "Something in the 'smart furniture' icon ballpark seemed the most interesting and challenging to me, but I wanted to give them a simple type solution as well, in case the more illustrative options weren't appealing," Fletcher says.

His simple, clean furniture executions create an interesting balance of lines and shapes. "I'm a big believer in simplicity and honesty in design. We live in a world where you're constantly being sold something, so I think there's a lot to be said for backing off and calmly saying, 'Here's this thing, take it or leave it,'" Fletcher explains.

Having a visual direction in mind when he begins most projects, Fletcher begins developing the concept directly on the desktop. "My work tends to be very boiled down and, I think, executed very geometrically, so it's usually quicker for me to jump right into Adobe Illustrator to see what's working and what isn't. I can draw basic ideas quicker with a computer than I can by hand, and then if something works, I'm already 20 percent into a final digital version," he notes. "So most of my 'sketches' are random assortments of shapes, lines and type within Illustrator that are usually long-gone or evolved by the time we hit the finish line."

The winning option, in this case, turned out to be an early contender in Fletcher's experiments. "This is typical of where my mind goes at the start of a logo project—trying to cleverly merge multiple ideas into a single icon," he says. The credenza, paired with the typeface Gotham creates an artful, iconic image that is subtle and ultimately stands out in a service category that is often shouting for consumers' attention.

"I tend to want everything to be extremely clean and simple, down to the number of angles or stroke widths used within a logo, because the end result looks more confident. There's often a fine line between something being boring or brilliant."

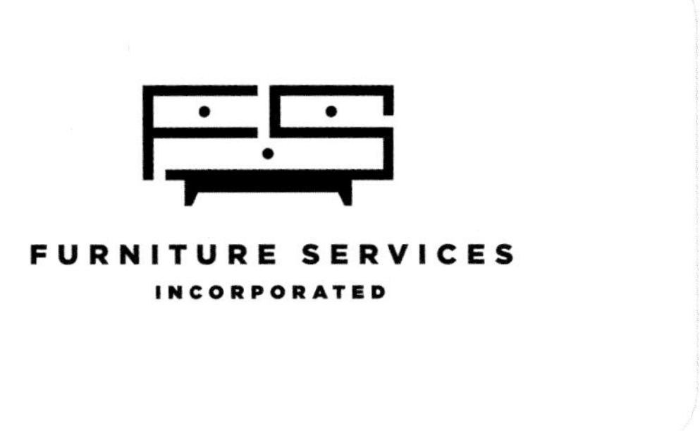

The final logo works well in color and black and white for different applications. Even though all the solutions were highly customized, the winning option felt the most tailor-made for the client.

"These 'furniture assembly' options were the coolest and most appropriate to me, since they hit more heavily on the idea that FSI can do it all and deliver package deals," Fletcher says. These marks, rooted in simple lines and geometry, are just as striking in black and white as they are in color.

FSI's old logo was kind of a monogram, so Fletcher presented an option that was a little closer to that. The stencil look is meant to lend an industrial vibe, but the monolinear execution keeps it feeling modern.

Fletcher explored different ways to execute chairs, tables, cabinets and more. "FSI can handle any aspect of an interior that you need handled, so I wanted the solutions to feel basic, almost elemental, like building blocks. The 'chair within a hexagon' option best exemplifies that approach," he says.

"I wish I could say there was a higher thought to this one, but the vintage coffee table shape just seemed pretty and also offered a chance to divide up the three letters," he says. "It's not my favorite of the bunch, but I thought it had enough merit to present as an option."

DESIGN /// ANAGRAMA

CLIENT /// BIOVIDEO

CATEGORY /// ART

Biovideo is a video service that captures the first precious moments of a baby's life from birth to first cuddles and kisses with parents and family members. Its founder, Carlos Villaseñor, founded the company after the birth of his first daughter, when he, himself was faced with the difficult choice of either videotaping his daughter's birth or holding his wife's hand. He decided that's a choice no parent should ever have to make, and thus, Biovideo was born.

He hired Anagrama, based in Mexico City, Mexico, to develop the brand identity for Biovideo. Anagrama is a multidisciplinary firm known for its adventurous use of color, typography and scale in its branding of several boutique shops in Monterrey. Anagrama cofounder, Sebastian Padilla, recalls, "The client was very clear about wanting an icon for the brand, so the first task was to sit down and think about the right way to approach this project."

Villaseñor wanted a symbol that could be placed on different products associated with Biovideo, such as diapers and baby toys. The designers came up with an obvious, albeit clever, visual concept.

> "The icon arose from the collision of two ideas: video and love," Padilla says. The resulting logo is a seamless merger of the two concepts—a pink heart and blue video camera. "There's no way you can miss these colors, which is why we decided to up the saturation on the pink and baby blue, and avoid a visually weak solution."
>
> —Sebastian Padilla

The logo mark was paired with the Biovideo name set in DIN Next Rounded Regular on a curved baseline.

CLIENT /// SMARTAS

Traditionally, branding for toilet tissue has focused on comfort and cuteness, until now. Smartas, pronounced "smart ass," produces lively and bold disposable articles sold in various colors and aromas.

Padilla says, "Each client sees his or her own window of opportunity, and this particular client realized that toilet tissue branding is quite standard, and no one had ever done anything exciting with it. Our goal was to design a visual idea that represents Smartas's fun and youthful spirit."

The solution combines a mortarboard and toilet tissue roll giving a conceptual wink at the brand's tongue-in-cheek name. The typeface rounds out the brand's friendly and honest personality.

A B C D

1

2

3

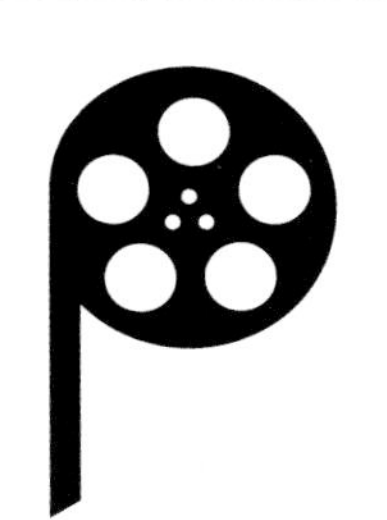

4

5

1C D Pavel Saksin C Scissors movie **1D** D Gardner Design C Justin McClure Creative
2A D Pavel Saksin C Video studio **2B** D Jerron Ames C Arteis **2C** D Sean Heisler Design C The Film Poets Wedding Videographers **2D** D Effendy Design C N/A
3A D Sean Heisler Design C GolfCam **3B** D QLi Design C Undercurrent **3C** D Gardner Design C Justin McClure Creative **3D** D DOXA C Fayetteville Public Library
4A D Gizwiz Studio C Pavitra Vadiveloo **4B** D McGuire Design C Globaltography **4C** D Type08 C 3 Boys Photography **4D** D Scott McFadden Creative C Maukel Photography
5A D Gardner Design C Authentus / Busch Gardens **5B** D Ninet6 Ltd C Le Bright Photography **5C** D TYPE AND SIGNS C picshooter **5D** D Rebrander C selfie

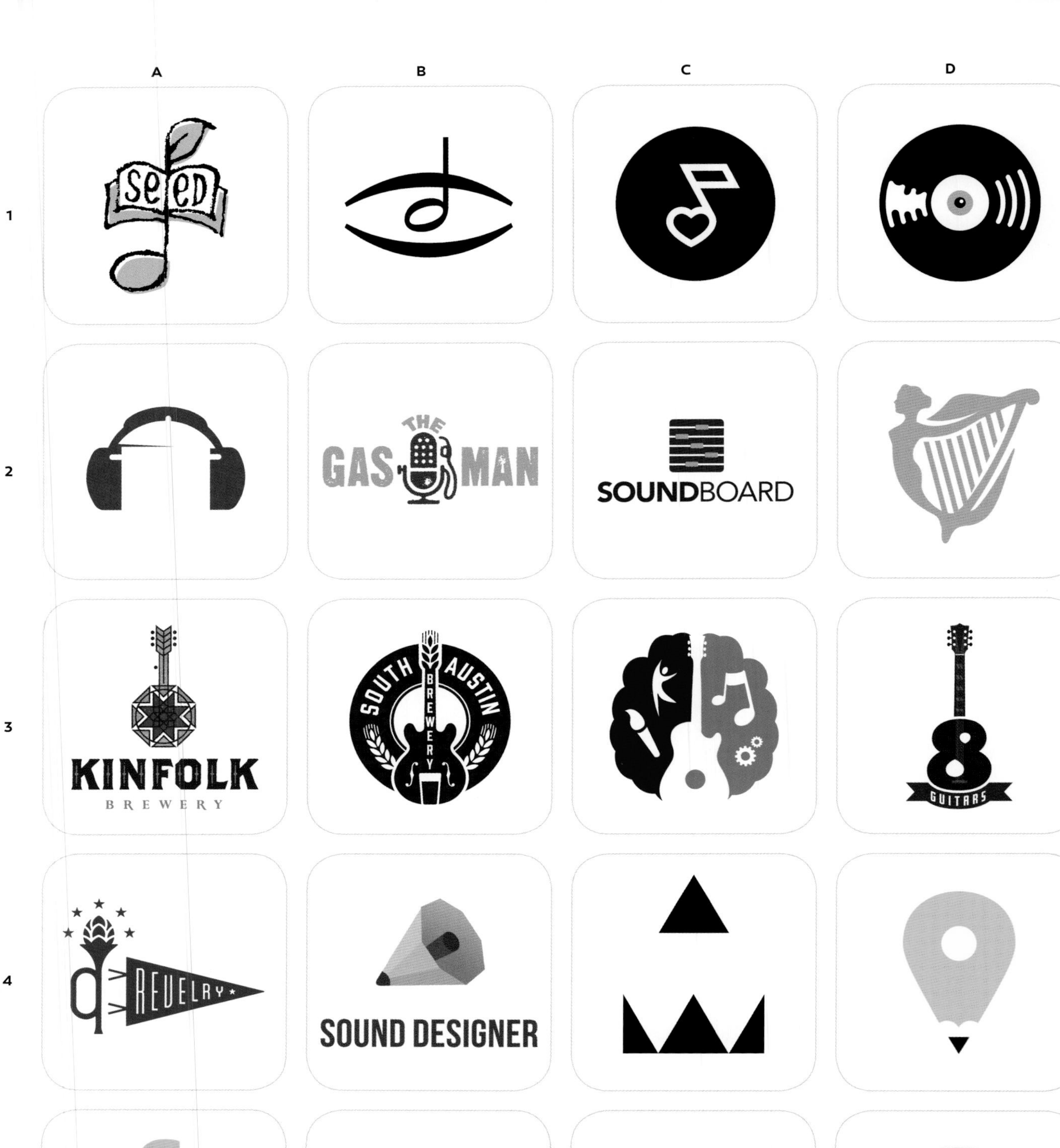

1A Ⓓ Dotzero Design Ⓒ Courtenay Hameister **1B** Ⓓ Design Studio Minin and Pozharsky Ⓒ Isaak Shvarts International Film Music Festival **1C** Ⓓ Quique Ollervides Ⓒ CoraSound **1D** Ⓓ Helms Workshop Ⓒ Visual Audio Productions
2A Ⓓ Pavlodar School of Design Ⓒ AudioCook **2B** Ⓓ Rhombus, Inc. Ⓒ Mike Gastineau **2C** Ⓓ 5Seven Ⓒ Pandora Sales Research **2D** Ⓓ Z&G Ⓒ N/A
3A Ⓓ Jackson Spalding Ⓒ Kinfolk Brewery **3B** Ⓓ Stiles Design Ⓒ South Austin Brewery **3C** Ⓓ Austin Logo Designs Ⓒ N/A **3D** Ⓓ Hubbell Design Works Ⓒ 8 Guitars
4A Ⓓ J Fletcher Design Ⓒ Revelry Brewing **4B** Ⓓ Rebrander Ⓒ Sound Designer **4C** Ⓓ Paul Wronski Graphic Design, LLC Ⓒ Paul Wronski, Creative Director **4D** Ⓓ rylander design Ⓒ MapWorks Learning
5A Ⓓ DOXA Ⓒ Fayetteville Public Education Foundation **5B** Ⓓ Dangerdom Studios Ⓒ Motion Authors **5C** Ⓓ Anthony Rees Ⓒ Art Class **5D** Ⓓ Trevor Rogers Ⓒ Kraemer Middle School

	A	B	C	D
1				
2				
3			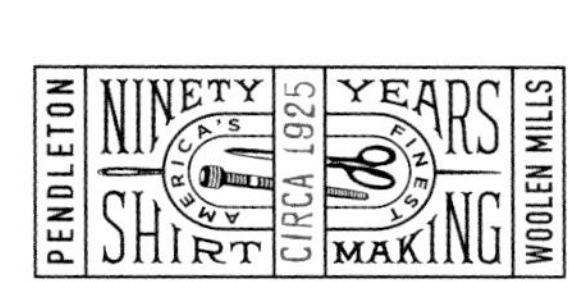	
4				
5				

1A D Jarrett Johnston C Phillips 66: Pipeline LLC **1B** D smARTer C Bader-Rutter **1C** D Sean Heisler Design C The Writer's Vantage **1D** D TYPE AND SIGNS C Royal Paint
2A D Sean Heisler Design C Toufold **2B** D Lippincott C Creative Art Works (CAW) **2C** D Rebrander C KIT CUT **2D** D Karl Design Vienna C Schneider Immobilien
3A D TYPE AND SIGNS C Curlscrewer **3B** D Flight Deck Creative C Barber Shots **3C** D Dotzero Design C Pendleton Woolen Mills **3D** D Ideogram C William Gray
4A D Taylor Goad C N/A **4B** D Yana Okoliyska C Patchwork **4C** D Stevan Rodic C severe leisure **4D** D MVC Agency C Seldens Designer Home Furnishings
5A D Steve Bullock Design C Cura **5B** D J Fletcher Design C Furniture Services Inc. **5C** D J Fletcher Design C Furniture Services Inc. **5D** D Mikhail Polivanov C I Am Home Interior Design Studio

	A	B	C	D
1	CATEGORY /// **MISCELLANEOUS**			
2				
3				
4		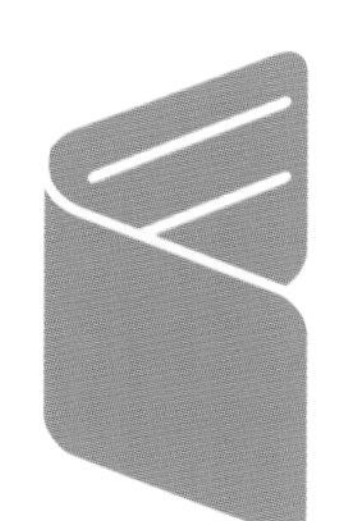		
5				

1C D Odney C N/A **1D** D 36creative C Boston Knucklehead
2A D Joce Creative C Mistral Communication / Distillerie fils du Roy **2B** D Chad Michael Studio C Empire Real Estate **2C** D Glad Head C Royal Courtyard **2D** D Bethany Heck C Cyberwoven
3A D Gardner Design C Magic Talent **3B** D brandclay C Teespring **3C** D Brand Agent C The Gatehouse at Grapevine **3D** D OneFish Creative C Grand Traverse Resort & Spa
4A D Studio Ink C Stylshare **4B** D brandclay C Billfold **4C** D Type08 C BLE **4D** D Dessein C Kabukiu
5A D Karla Portocarrero C Dry Manhattan Umbrellas **5B** D Double A Creative C Vo Jewelry **5C** D Fernandez Studio C TrueAbility **5D** D Fancy Creative C Peaceknots

A B C D

1

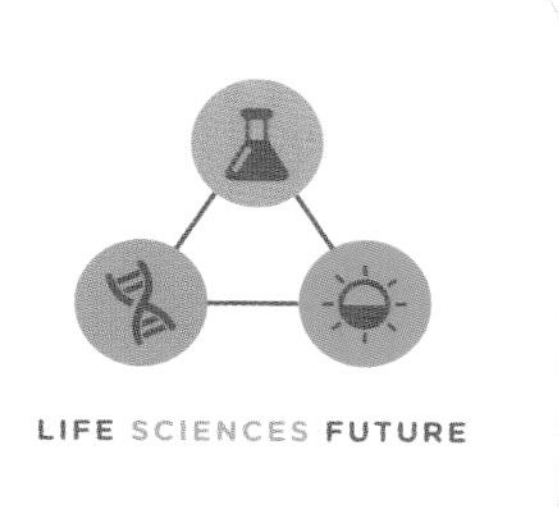

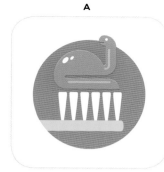

2

3

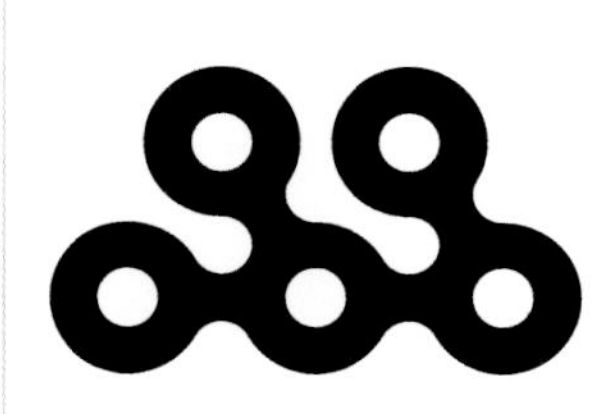

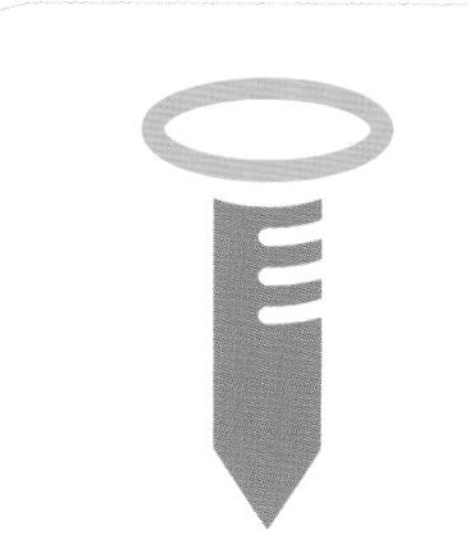

4

5

1A Ⓓ Logo Planet Laboratory Ⓒ Dino Dental (unused concept) **1B** Ⓓ Unipen Ⓒ Sport Press **1C** Ⓓ Akhmatov Studio Ⓒ appitube **1D** Ⓓ MKJ Creative Ⓒ Pennsylvania Bio
2A Ⓓ Pavel Saksin Ⓒ Code **2B** Ⓓ Paul Wronski Graphic Design, LLC Ⓒ EFS **2C** Ⓓ Hasan Ali Akhtar Ⓒ SecurityDo **2D** Ⓓ Type08 Ⓒ Kiall
3A Ⓓ Kairevicius Ⓒ Meister Bikes **3B** Ⓓ Odney Ⓒ MBTs **3C** Ⓓ DOXA Ⓒ Blessings Construction **3D** Ⓓ Rocksauce Studios Ⓒ FantasticFest
4A Ⓓ Type08 Ⓒ Sphone **4B** Ⓓ Kairevicius Ⓒ www.kairevicius.com **4C** Ⓓ Xcluesiv Cloud Technology Ⓒ iMobileApps **4D** Ⓓ Sean Heisler Design Ⓒ The Acvitivity Exchange
5A Ⓓ The Brandit Ⓒ Valiant Brewing Co. **5B** Ⓓ Gizwiz Studio Ⓒ Caroline Maunder **5C** Ⓓ 01d Ⓒ Mimisha.by **5D** Ⓓ Mikey Burton Ⓒ Money Magazine

DESIGN /// MATT STEVENS

CLIENT /// JJ'S RED HOTS

CATEGORY /// FOOD

Jonathan Luther grew up outside of Buffalo, New York, where eating Red Hots hot dogs was a rite of passage. So when he was looking to start a restaurant with his dad in his hometown of Charlotte, North Carolina, hot dogs were top of mind. "I couldn't find a good hot dog in town, so I decided to open my own place." He hit the road with a "camera and fork" going to all the major hot dog markets in the country, taking copious notes on the flavors and décor of every place he dined. When he returned from his travels, he was ready to get down to business, so he contacted designer Matt Stevens to discuss the brand direction for JJ's Red Hots.

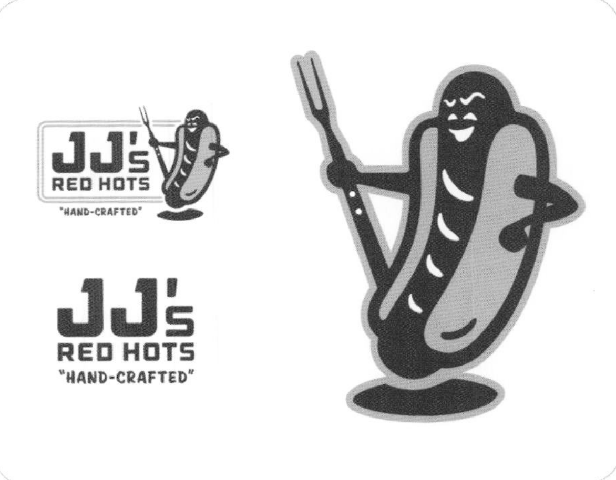

This logo design captures just the right personality of JJ's Red Hots, working in tandem with the typography.

Stevens has been a designer for twenty years, doing a mix of branding and identity work as well as illustration. Luther discovered Stevens's work on a website and really liked his style. He was even happier when he found out Stevens was local. "Jon had a lot of brand attributes already down on paper and had a working menu put together," Stevens says. "He had traveled the country taking photos of some of the most classic, revered and well-known hot dog joints. We spent a lot of time just reviewing that reference together. The mascot direction was something we knew we wanted to explore, but it was only one direction out of several presented."

Stevens's early iterations of the hot dog mascot had a devilish connotation—even holding a pitchfork. Luther liked the spirit and humor of the mark, but wanted to tone down the devilish qualities. "Getting the mischievous facial expression was key. It wasn't specifically in the brief, but that attitude was definitely there all along," Stevens notes. The pitchfork was replaced with a proper grill fork and grill marks on the body communicated how the product is prepared and what differentiates it from other hot dog restaurants. "Our Red Hots are always grilled, never boiled," Luther says.

The logo had to strike a balance between classic and modern influences. So he paired the logo with a modified version of the font Outage, which complements the hot dog's form and isn't too clean. Stevens says, "It looked like a face that has been around for a while, which is how Jon wanted JJ's portrayed." It has definite roadside appeal when used for signage on the exterior of the building.

> "We wanted the logo to have a bit of a diner feel, but not lose that roadside hot dog stand feeling as well. We also didn't want it to feel completely retro. We weren't trying to capture something in a time capsule, but wanted it to feel like it had been influenced by all these classic things."
> —Matt Stevens

JJ's Red Hots is a classic culmination of the best hot dogs from around the United States, featuring nine signature dogs. Each dog has its own logo featured on the menu. For instance, Joliet Jake, a Chicago-style hot dog, features the Windy City's skyline, and the Dirty Jerz has a distinct Jersey aesthetic. "Jon came up with the names and that's what inspired the graphics," Stevens says. JJ's patrons were encouraged to collect logo pins for their favorite dogs as part of a rewards program in the restaurant rollout.

Since opening its first store in Charlotte, JJ's has opened two new locations, and Stevens continues to collaborate with Luther. "Matt has been instrumental in helping us with the brand and everything associated with it. We have a great relationship that continues to this day," Luther says.

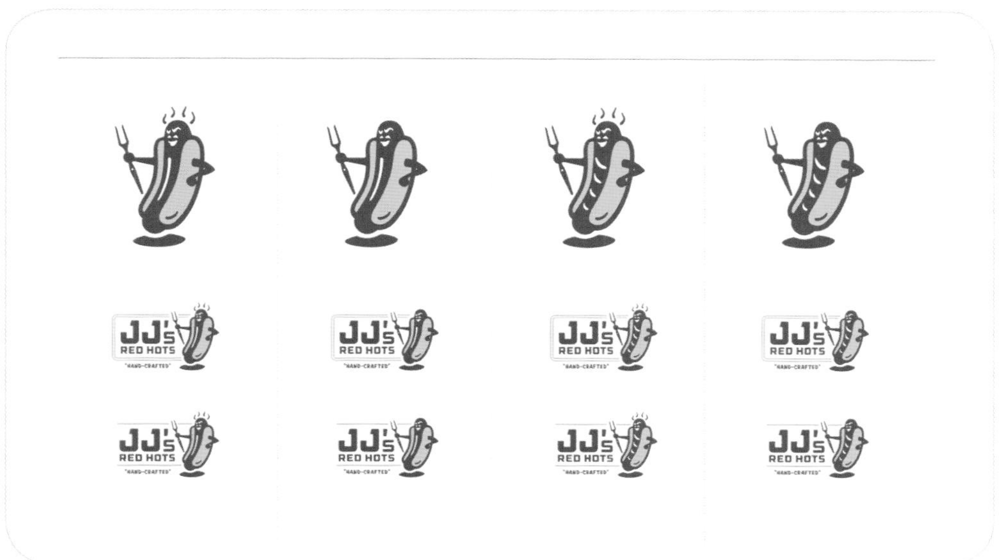

Early iterations of the JJ's mascot were devilish and didn't have grill marks. Stevens worked closely with Luther to achieve just the right personality for the character—fun and irreverent.

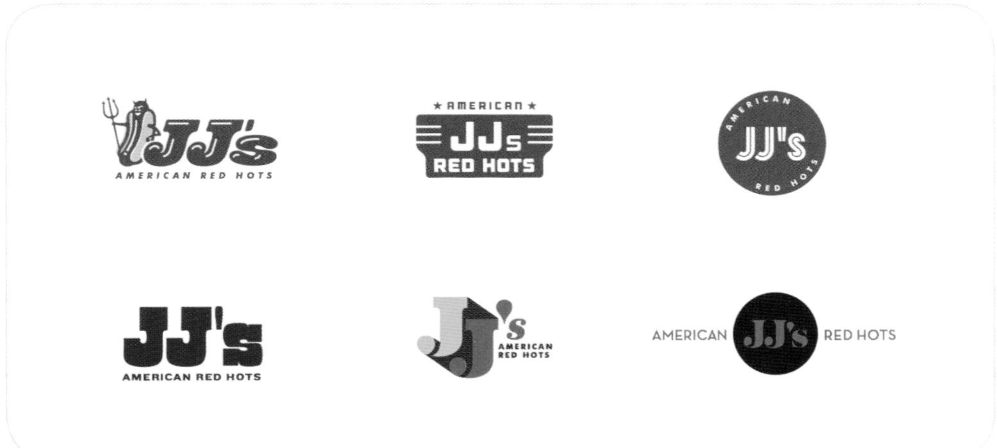

Early studies included more handmade looks, ranging to diner signage all the way to cleaner, more midcentury inspired designs. The final logo needed to be a combination of the clean diner look, yet retain the character of a mom-and-pop shop. The chosen type had that clean diner feel and the inclusion of the character kept the desried personality.

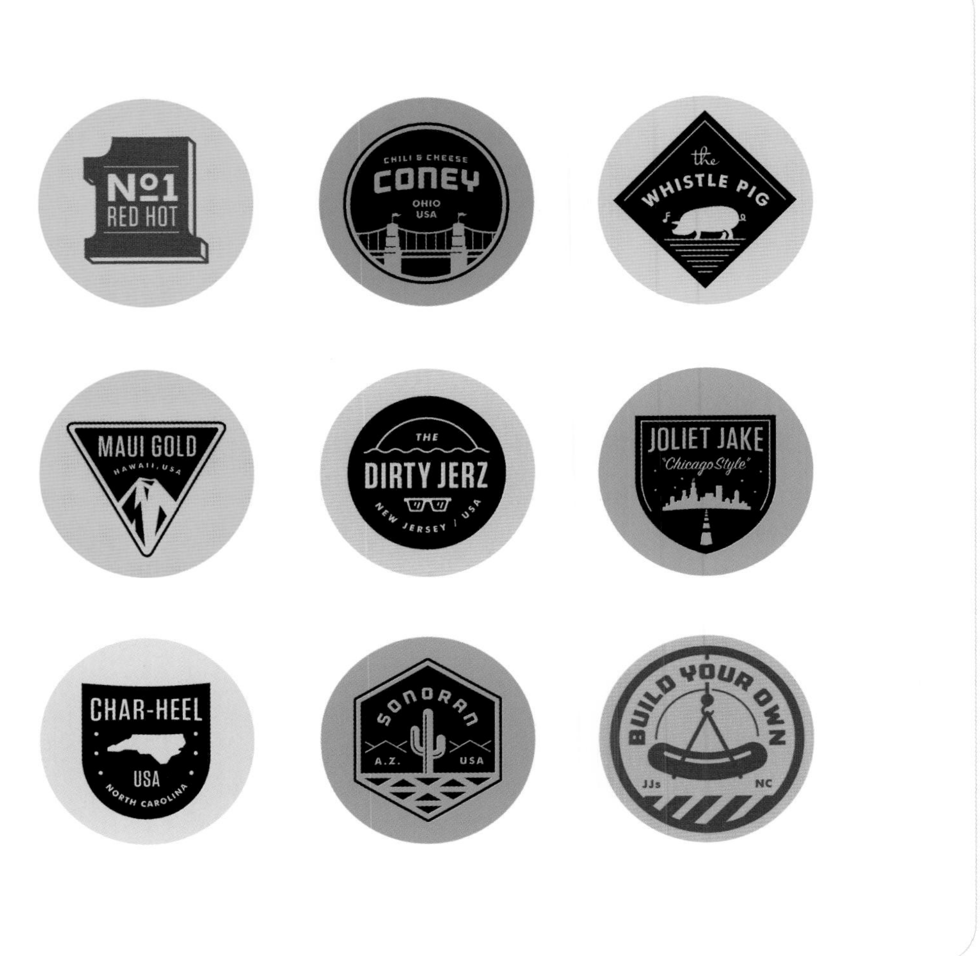

For each of JJ's nine signature hot dogs, Stevens designed a representative logo. These logos are featured in the menu and on pins that were given away to customers.

This fun pattern is featured on the food basket liners, working in concert with condiment drippings and all.

WORDS FROM MATT STEVENS

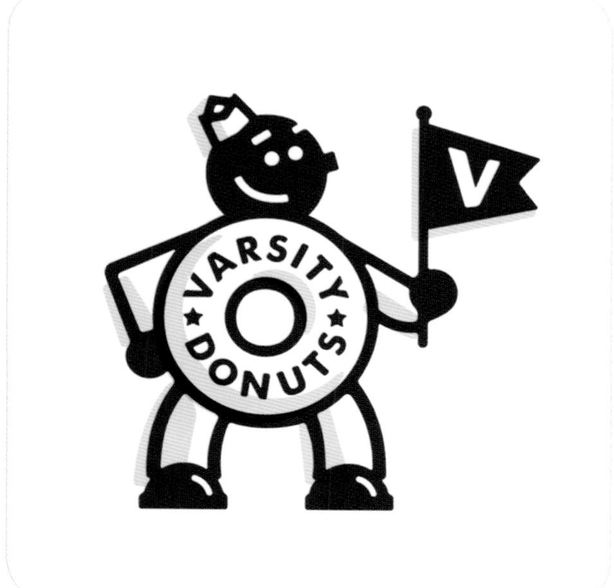

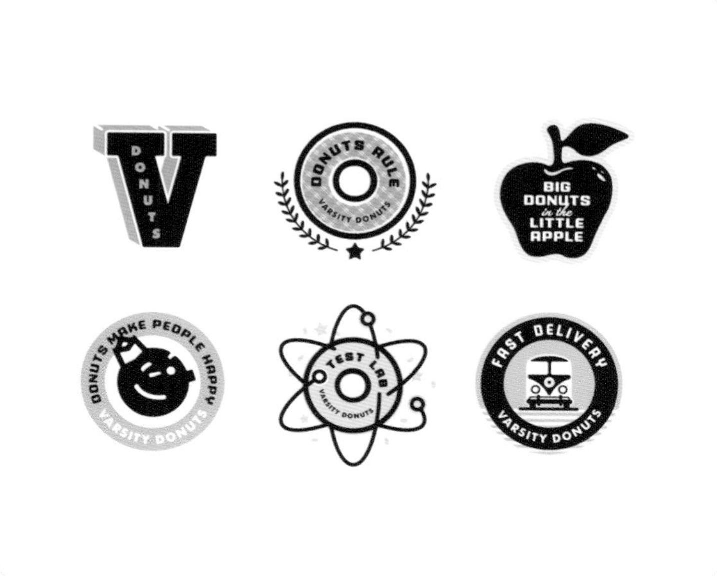

VARSITY DONUTS

I did a spoof on the Dunkin' Donuts logo for an April Fool's post on *Brand New* in 2011, with the help of Dunkin' Donuts's creative director. Later, I heard that my mascot, "Dunkie" was being used for Varsity Donuts in Manhattan, Kansas, without my permission. I contacted the owner, and it turns out she didn't know it was a copy, so she promised to stop using it. It was a strange gray area, because it was my design, but of a mascot I didn't even own. I spoke to the owner further, and we struck up an agreement for me to actually work on the project for her and come up with a new mascot. It was great that a bad situation had turned into a fun project.

The owner of Varsity Donuts wanted the mascot, which was named Otis, to feel classic. I was excited about the stuff I did early on and felt like it was the best work. We ended up doing lots of explorations later that did not get used, and came back to the early stuff. Sometimes you have to do that to prove the early stuff is better, but it's tough when you feel like you already nailed it.

A B C D

CATEGORY ///

FOOD

1

2

3

4

5

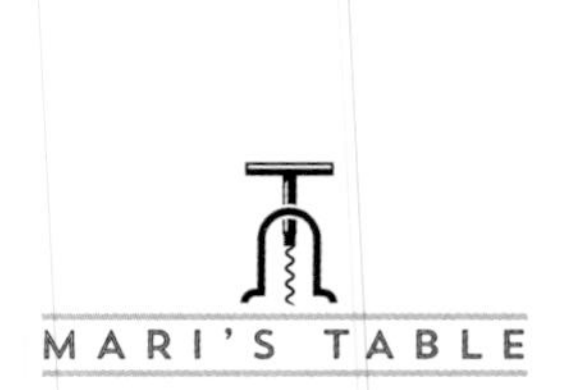

1C D Stevan Rodic C Cafe A Roma **1D** D Paul Tynes Design C Aperture
2A D FullFill C Koultoura **2B** D J Fletcher Design C Coffee Kind **2C** D Salih Kucukaga Design Studio C Function Coffee Roasters **2D** D Rebrander C N/A
3A D Helms Workshop C Austin Beerworks **3B** D Haffelder Studios C The Noble Pint **3C** D Dotzero Design C Portland Craft Beer Festival **3D** D Asgard C Alkon Group
4A D brandclay C Lounge Hounds **4B** D Sunday Lounge C Salida Chamber of Commerce **4C** D Scott Oeschger Design C DB, Inc. **4D** D Jerron Ames C N/A
5A D Hubbell Design Works C Mari's Table **5B** D Wray Ward C Central Piedmont Community College **5C** D Jerron Ames C Wine Broker **5D** D Flight Deck Creative C Jesper Jensen

	A	B	C	D
1				
2				
3				
4				
5				

1A Ⓓ Thomas Cook Designs Ⓒ D's Bottle Shop **1B** Ⓓ Helms Workshop Ⓒ Top Hops Beer Shop **1C** Ⓓ Johnson & Sekin Ⓒ On The Border **1D** Ⓓ Artini Bar Designs Ⓒ Spec
2A Ⓓ Gardner Design Ⓒ Basilio Buda Sausage Co **2B** Ⓓ Jody Worthington Graphic Design Ⓒ Kimberly Park Communications **2C** Ⓓ Roost Designs Ⓒ Panera Bread **2D** Ⓓ Cayenne Creative Ⓒ Cahaba River Society
3A Ⓓ RolandRekeczki Ⓒ NapiMenu **3B** Ⓓ Dustin Commer Ⓒ Seed To Plate **3C** Ⓓ Second Street Creative Ⓒ Indy Grown **3D** Ⓓ Scott Oeschger Design Ⓒ DB, Inc.
4A Ⓓ BLVR Ⓒ Relish **4B** Ⓓ brandclay Ⓒ Power Supply **4C** Ⓓ OCD | Original Champions of Design Ⓒ Marcus Samuelsson Group and Karlitz & Co. **4D** Ⓓ Mendiola Design Associates Ⓒ rasamasa.com
5A Ⓓ Jess Glebe Design Ⓒ Self **5B** Ⓓ J Fletcher Design Ⓒ The History Press **5C** Ⓓ Jonathan Schubert Ⓒ N/A **5D** Ⓓ Amy McAdams Design Ⓒ Pearings Cafe + Yogurt

	A	B	C	D
1				
2				
3				
4				
5				

1A D Asgard C Alkon Group **1B** D Oven Design Workshop C Producfrutas **1C** D Alexander Wende C Berrysys **1D** D Michael Lashford Creative C Quince
2A D BLVR C Kaliroy **2B** D Brooke Muckersie C Fruitalicious **2C** D Rhombus, Inc. C CHERRiSH **2D** D Maykel Nunes C Katyelle Nunes
3A D Proof Positive Brand Design C Leelanau Fruit Company **3B** D sk designworks C Children Achieving Challenge **3C** D Wheelhouse Collective C Nebraska Appleseed **3D** D Envision Creative Group C Juice Central
4A D KW43 BRANDDESIGN C KW43 BRANNDESIGN, Designerdock **4B** D mmplus creative C pf healthy juice **4C** D ONY C Lime **4D** D idgroup C N/A
5A D brandclay C Pinecone **5B** D Zenetic C www.iluminada.com **5C** D Noe Araujo C Monkey Films **5D** D Gizwiz Studio C Napoleon Cornejo

A B C D

1

2

3

4

5

1A D Chris Millspaugh Design C Douglas County, KS **1B** D eggnerd C Fuhrmann Sweet Corn **1C** D The Brandit C Barley's Greenville **1D** D MODA Collaborative C The Grizz Old Fashioned Bearded Hops
2A D PM Design / Restaurant Identity C Amici's Brick Oven **2B** D Justin Gammon | Design + Illustration C DHEC / Brains on Fire **2C** D Type08 C Playway AS **2D** D Stevan Rodic C Delisious Brains
3A D Chris Millspaugh Design C Limestone Pizza **3B** D Rebrander C Pizza Online **3C** D HanleyCreative C Smile Donut **3D** D eggnerd C Beez Bagels
4A D Glitschka Studios C PBJForGood.com **4B** D Haffelder Studios C Mad Batter **4C** D Funnel C Empire Cake **4D** D Odney C Burger Hot Spots
5A D 01d C Peasantville **5B** D TYPE AND SIGNS C Fish&Chips Shop **5C** D Marakasdesign C SUSHI GO! Food Delivery **5D** D Curb Crowser C General Mills

DESIGN FIRM /// TACTIX

CLIENT /// CORNERSTONE PROPERTY SERVICES

CATEGORY /// STRUCTURES

Cornerstone Property Services, based in Phoenix, Arizona, had no apparent brand identity, despite being in business for thirty years. The old logo was just a basic logotype comprised of Zapf Chancery and Trajan Bold and said nothing about the company or its services.

So when Cornerstone hired Tactix to design a new logo, they wanted it to focus on the people and their commitment to their clients' needs when maintaining their rental properties. Tactix, a full-service brand design studio in Mesa, Arizona, has churned out hundreds of successful, illustrative logos for its clients since opening shop in 2004. Paul Howalt, cofounder of Tactix, says, "We did a brand strategy for Cornerstone that focused on this directive of the people and staff, discussing their culture and mission." Ultimately, Cornerstone's mission is about responsiveness and efficiency in maintaining their clients' properties to ensure renters are happy.

So Howalt sketched some logos that included people and hands with buildings and other elements that reflected this community aspect that Cornerstone was known for. However, after reviewing these concepts, they veered away from that direction and instead wanted to see buildings as part of the strategy. "They basically said, 'Keep drawing until we see something we like,'" he explains. These are words no designer or illustrator ever wants to hear, but fortunately, Howalt had a lot of ideas in his bag. He created several concepts that included buildings, symbols and initials to see if any of these triggered a response from the client.

They homed in on a couple of the architectural drawings, in particular a logo that incorporates several structures including residential and commercial building types. "Once we hit on that building arrangement, we did some color sketches and bounced them off the client," Howalt notes. "I tried to push them into a more progressive and cheerful color palette, but they liked the more muted colors. I think in the end it sort of fits them and fits the area more appropriately than the bright jewel tones. It's pretty conservative around here."

With the color direction chosen, two logo marks were created, each featuring different elements that are representative of the area. "In Arizona, there are a lot of pools and palm trees and, of course, the desert landscape, so those were considerations. We also had to include both residential and commercial buildings," Howalt explains.

The conservative Trade Gothic typeface used for the company name pairs perfectly with the streamlined, overlapping graphic elements that make up the logo.

The old Cornerstone logo didn't say anything about the company or its offerings.

> "In the end we couldn't translate all those things in one mark so we broke those elements into two marks that could be interchanged for different collateral material. It also took the pressure off of having that one perfectly crafted mark."
>
> —Paul Howalt

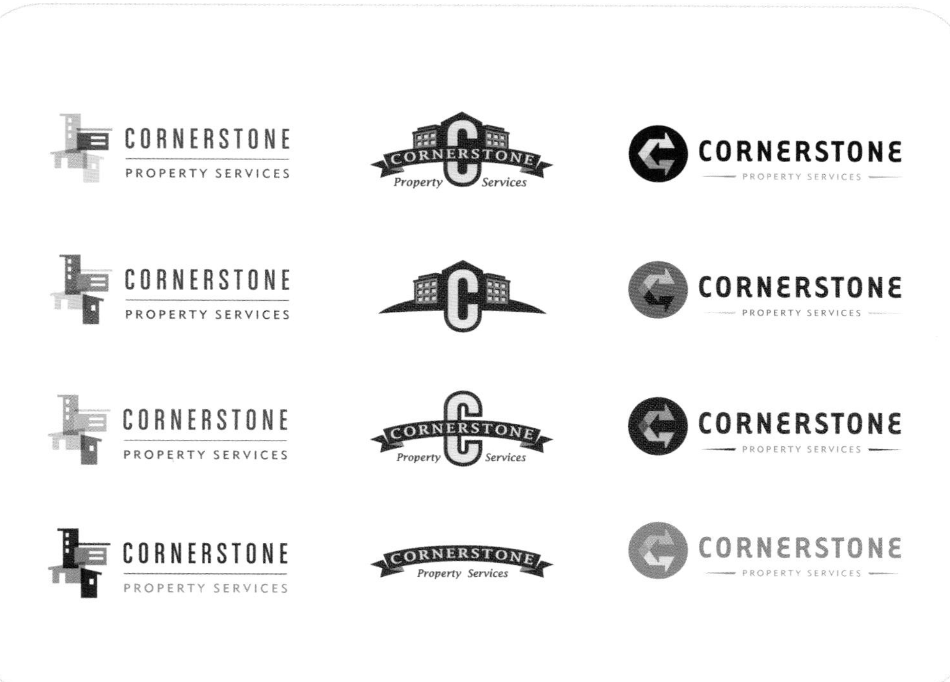

While developing different concepts, Howalt also came up with a range of color palettes to present to the client, from warm to cool.

Howalt sketched several concepts that focused on the people and the services Cornerstone provides, based on the brand strategy they developed with the client.

The client rejected the initial sketches and wanted something different, but they couldn't put their finger on it, so Howalt presented a range of designs that included structures, initials and symbols using a range of typefaces.

Two logos were developed for the final to fit all of Cornerstone's needs since they service both residential and commercial properties.

A B C D

1

2

3

4

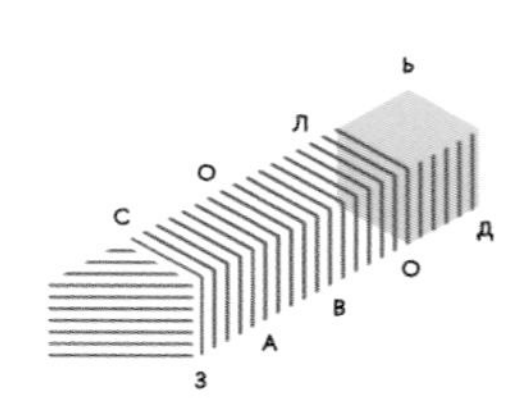

5

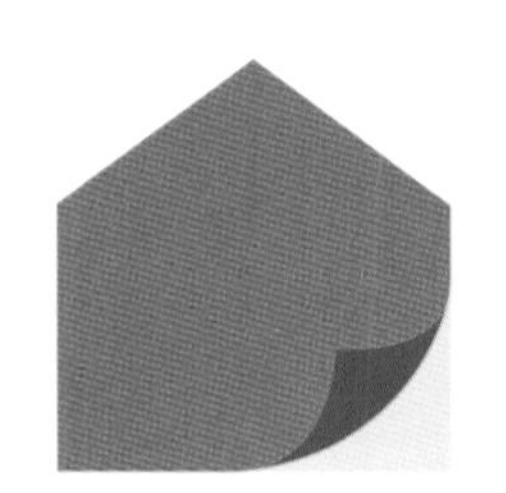

1C D David Cran Design C Oxford House **1D** D danielguillermo.com C SVA
2A D Sophia Georgopoulou | Design C Home by Nature Co. **2B** D Scott McFadden Creative C Pepsi **2C** D DARO Creative C SIDWELL Custom Homes + Landscaping **2D** D Start City Group C Start
3A D Jerron Ames C Fivestar Branding Agency **3B** D Type08 C Inhabiti **3C** D David Bieloh Design C The Run House, Benicia, California **3D** D KW43 BRANDDESIGN C Waymate
4A D Karlis Dovnorovics C N/A **4B** D Sean Heisler Design C Jessica Evans **4C** D Vitamin Group C The Museum of history of salt "Solzavod" **4D** D Gizwiz Studio C Kathy Ridge
5A D Jerron Ames C Arteis **5B** D Gizwiz Studio C Tarick Fouz **5C** D 01d C Zagorodnaya nedvizhimost **5D** D brandclay C RennoReady

	A	B	C	D
1	THE FARMER'S Daughter			
2	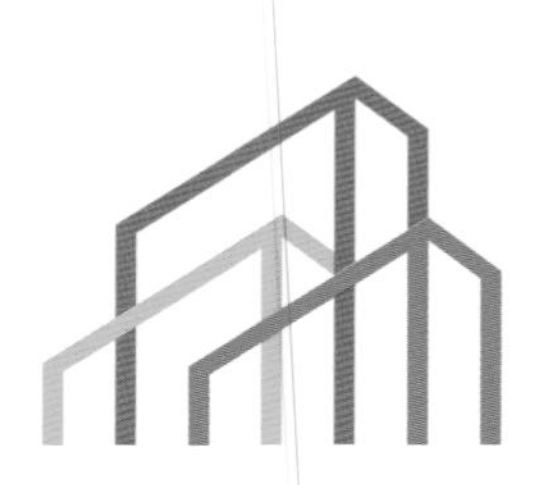			
3				
4				
5				

1A D TrioSigns,Inc. C The Farmer's Daughter Boutique **1B** D Type08 C eTop Real Estate **1C** D Fuzzco C N/A **1D** D Sabingrafik, Inc. C Boathouse housing development
2A D Brandberry C ZIM contest **2B** D Akhmatov Studio C Valent - architectural design **2C** D Levogrin C Nirman **2D** D grifter design C Loyola University Chicago
3A D Jerron Ames C Arteis **3B** D Sean Heisler Design C Warehouse Church **3C** D Timber Design Company C The Labor District Cafe **3D** D McMillianCo. C Greenpeace International
4A D Jerron Ames C Arteis **4B** D DOXA C NoMa **4C** D Pavel Saksin C Bodli **4D** D Jibe C Lehi City
5A D J.Wick Design C New York Genome Center **5B** D Banowetz + Company, Inc. C Hyatt Times Square **5C** D Yury Akulin | Logodiver C Urban Coffee **5D** D Tactix Creative C N/A

	A	B	C	D
1				
2				
3				
4				
5				

1A D Jerron Ames C Arties **1B** D Austin Logo Designs C The Property Co. **1C** D Type08 C Pollaro **1D** D Sabingrafik, Inc. C Half Door Brewing Co
2A D Parallele gestion de marques C Maison Gomin, services commemoratifs **2B** D A.D. Creative Group C Moss Mansion **2C** D TYPE AND SIGNS C Steeple, Estate Agents, South Africa **2D** D Fernandez Studio C Lincoln Park Zoo
3A D Fixer Creative Co. C Leadership Transformations **3B** D Visual Lure, LLC C Abiding Grace Chapel on the Creek **3C** D Sabingrafik, Inc. C Church of Jesus Christ of Latter Day Saints **3D** D gresus.com C N/A
4A D Dangerdom Studios C Time to Time **4B** D Torch Creative C Disney **4C** D Roy Smith Design C Hudson Heights **4D** D Alphabet Arm Design C Bridj
5A D Circuit 26 Design C Daniel Sockwell **5B** D Cezar Bianchi B+D C Crefimar **5C** D Sabingrafik, Inc. C Island Pools **5D** D Blackdog Creative C St. Louis Derby

DESIGN /// RANDY HEIL

CLIENT /// R&R PARTNERS

CATEGORY /// TRANSPORTATION

R&R Partners has offices in eight major cities in the United States, so when designer Randy Heil was given the opportunity to create a logo for an in-house mural for the Phoenix, Arizona office, where he works, he took a playful approach with the two leading consonants. "The *R*s originally stood for Rogich & Rogich, founders since departed. New clients are always asking what the *R*s stand for, and we like to make up various answers, like Rum & Ritalin and Rubes & Rebels," Heil says.

He worked out a few different robots before settling on this vintage, drop-jaw version.

In fact, over the years, employees have been logging alternatives for the *R*s. "My concept for the mural was to create fake logos for a few of the more amusing alternatives. I had a list of over one hundred such alternates to choose from," he notes. "I began with Road Trips & Robots, which I thought stood out from the rest. After sketching the first logo, I decided to forego any other R&R pairings and instead flesh out the road trip imagery for the mural."

Heil visually contemplated several robot variations before laying anything down. "I rarely sketch when brainstorming a logo concept. I've been paralyzed below my shoulders as a result of an auto accident as a teen, and I draw by holding a pencil in my mouth. For me, the sketching process takes quite a bit of time and effort, so I learned to compensate by mentally constructing ideas, then jumping to Adobe Illustrator to flesh out the most promising concepts. My mouth stick and trackball are much easier to work with than pencil and paper," Heil explains.

He traced over photos of old Corvettes he imported into Illustrator, and then altered the car's proportions to give it a cartoonish appearance. The retro-style robot and Golden Gate typeface, along with the vintage Corvette, give this logo a *Back to the Future*/Route 66 aesthetic mash-up that's both cool and classic.

This sort of midcentury modern aesthetic is pretty typical in much of Heil's logo work. "I try to use solid areas of color with clean, tense curves and the use of implied lines when possible. I enjoy the visual aesthetic of the 1940s and 1950s and that tends to show up in my work."

Roadtrips & Robots final logo and poster designs.

WORDS FROM RANDY HEIL

PACIFIC RETROLINER

This was created for a transit consultant who had a fondness for the golden age of train travel. The mark was reproduced on faux signage that he displayed in his "rail room," which houses his extensive model train collection.

THROTTLE

Throttle was going to be a large motorcycle-themed expo in Las Vegas. Throttle was actually a working title while organizers finalized the event name. Moto was another concept I created before the project was scrapped and the creative director started avoiding my calls and ignoring my invoices.

MOTORCOACH APPRECIATION WEEK

This is an event held in Laughlin, Nevada, as a way of saying thank you to the industry's dedicated businesses, employees, families, suppliers and partners for their continued support and commitment. The motorcoach business has been instrumental in Laughlin's success as a world-class tourist destination. This version of the logo featured an old-school motorhome, but the final version featured a modern, bus-like motorcoach.

TRAFFIC SAFETY ICONS

This was a personal project. I like the challenge of trying to visually tell a story while using minimal elements.

DESIGN /// 01D

CLIENT /// VELOIMPERIA

CATEGORY /// TRANSPORTATION

Veloimperia, which means bicycle empire, was founded in 1999 and is the oldest online bicycle store in Russia. It's also one of the most popular, ranking in the top ten online stores. The design firm 01D, based in Minsk, Belarus, was hired to redesign and modernize the logo to make it more appealing to its intended audience. Designer Dmitry Ulasen says, "The old logo was old-style and completely incomprehensible to consumers."

The design team studied the characteristics of Veloimperia to help guide them in the logo design. These attributes include honest service, fair prices, delivery to anywhere in Russia and partnerships with qualified sellers. Veloimperia is also the exclusive retailer for some Russian bicycle brands, so the designers had to consider that the new mark would need to work with these different logos on the website.

Within the frame of the project, 01D sketched several designs focused on bicycles, crowns, wings and gears. However, they quickly discovered that some of their concepts were already in use by competitive bike companies. "We liked the crown and bicycle chain concept, but it was confusingly similar to already existing logos," explains Ulasen.

Another concept, an eagle with gear-like wings, was determined to be too severe and aggressive. The designers also explored simple concepts based on different sporting categories such as off-road use, trail riding and city travel.

Ultimately, the client favored the design of the king riding a bicycle, firmly placing Veloimperia at the head of the online bike category in Russia. "It successfully plays on the store name and the goods it sells," Ulasen says.

Early sketches show a broad range of concepts for Veloimperia.

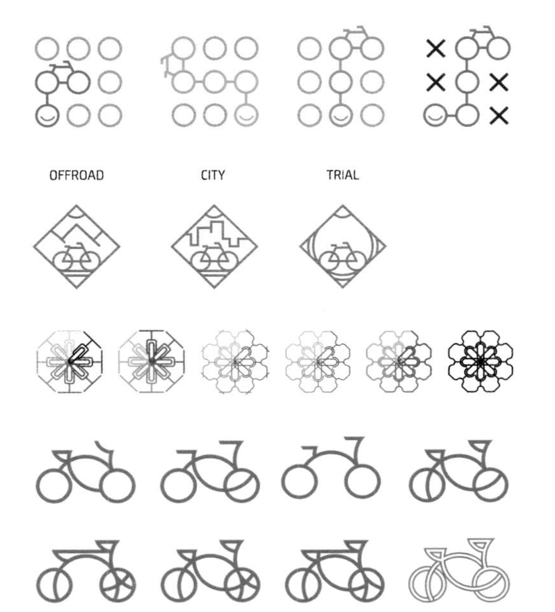

These concepts were presented, but ultimately the client either didn't like them or they too closely resembled competitive logos with the same characteristics.

The king logo concept eventually won the day. 01D created several variants, and the client is still considering which one to use as of this printing.

Leading Charter Technologies

This is a charter flight company that organizes flights on business jets for VIP clients. Their wealthy clients expect top-notch service and amenities when using this service, so it was important that the logo reflect these values.

Ulasen and the team at 01D did a lot of conceptual sketches that included logotypes with the company's initials, jets within stars, businessmen and several jets that appear to be flying. It was necessary to develop a logo containing a stylized aircraft or its parts. The final logo is sleek and sophisticated and elevates the brand in its category.

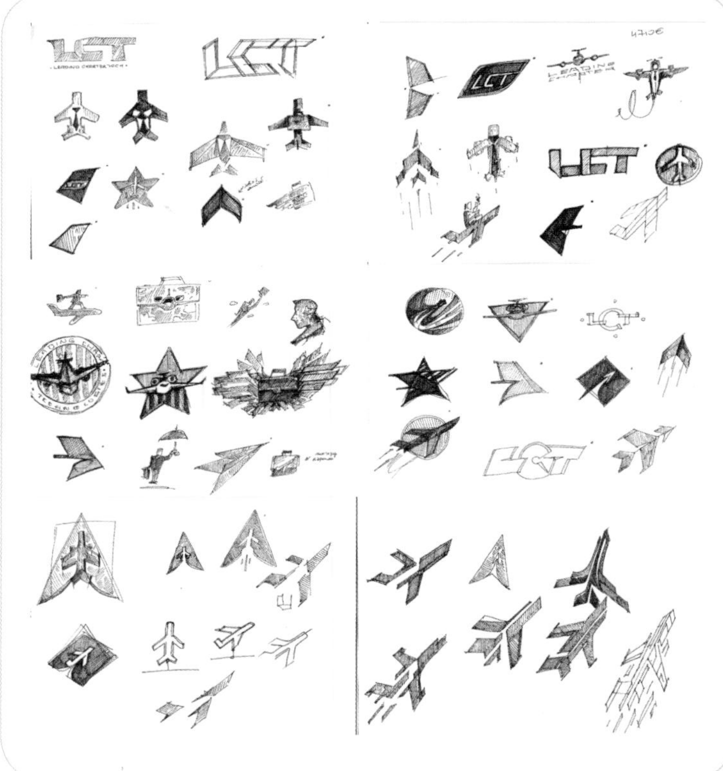

A B C D

1 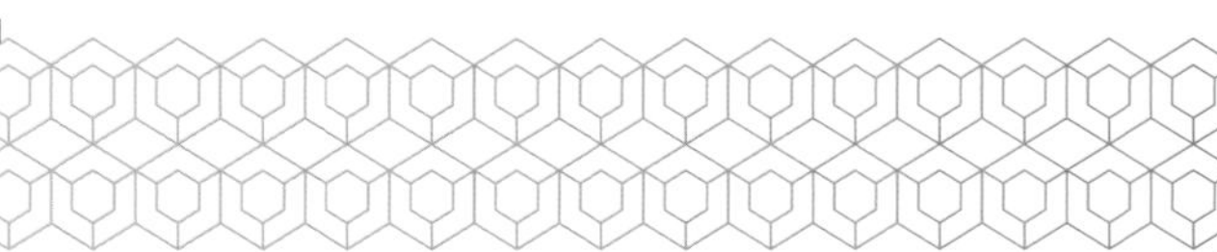

2 

3 

4 

5 

1C D Jerron Ames C Arties **1D** D R&R Partners C N/A
2A D Musab C Electrissimo **2B** D gresus.com C Reinex **2C** D David Cran Design C Elhot Metal Fabrication Seattle **2D** D David Cran Design C Autosport Seattle.
3A D Proof Positive Brand Design C Leelanau Fruit Company **3B** D Type08 C Atlantis Trading **3C** D 01d C Sovtes **3D** D Maximo Gavete C VanandGo
4A D Sparkfly Creative C MocoFoodtrucks.com **4B** D R&R Partners C Motorcoach Week **4C** D Slagle Design C Park Street Pizza **4D** D WestmorelandFlint C Kraus Anderson
5A D Slagle Design C EduGo **5B** D Karl Design Vienna C Green Biker **5C** D 01d C Bicycle empire **5D** D Yatta Yatta Yatta C Restore Hetch Hetchy

A B C D

1

2

3

4

5

1A D J Fletcher Design C Khi-Khi Milk Co. **1B** D Tim Frame Design C Cotton Bureau **1C** D Rick Carlson Design & Illustration C Tricycle Productions **1D** D mmplus creative C fruit ministry indonesia **2A** D Designer and Gentleman C Cinema Train **2B** D Fuzzco C N/A **2C** D Gardner Design C Wichita Union Station **2D** D Ulyanov Denis C Calipso **3A** D Mart√≠n Azambuja C Mundial **3B** D Mart√≠n Azambuja C MVD Roasters **3C** D Helms Workshop C Modest Mouse **3D** D notamedia C Maleta **4A** D baCreative C Aircraft Gastropub **4B** D Galambos + Associates C O'Hare International Airport **4C** D Deksia C Red Water Restaurant Group **4D** D Doublenaut C Spitfire Coffee Roasters **5A** D Karl Design Vienna C ECOJET **5B** D Vitamin Group C ClickandTravel **5C** D Be!Five branding & identity C Pit Palmer Studio **5D** D Yury Akulin I Logodiver C Diarfly

A B C D

1

2

3

4

5

1A D Jerron Ames C threedefined **1B** D Luke Despatie & The Design Firm C Atomic Beauty **1C** D Jon Kay Design C Fangamer **1D** D brandclay C Seer
2A D Jerron Ames C Arteis **2B** D Kairevicius C www.kairevicius.com **2C** D Luke Despatie & The Design Firm C Atomic Coffee Roasters **2D** D Gyula Nemeth C District 11 SCI-FI CLUB
3A D Jerron Ames C Arteis **3B** D Todytod C Greenzones **3C** D Sean Heisler Design C Reignite **3D** D Oronoz Brandesign C N/A
4A D Green Ink Studio C Spinnaker Oilfield Services **4B** D Anthony Rees C Maelstrom Lawyers **4C** D Jerron Ames C Fivestar Branding Agency **4D** D Clark & Co. C Sail Away
5A D Luke Bott Design & Illustration C O'Swell **5B** D Quiskal C Boutique L'Arrivage **5C** D DEI Creative C Pryde + Johnson **5D** D Julian Peck Creative C ShipYard

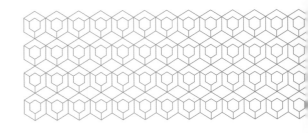

ABOUT THE AUTHORS

BILL GARDNER

Bill Gardner is president of Gardner Design, which has produced design and branding work for Cessna, Spirit AeroSystems, Coleman Outdoor, Kroger, Hallmark, Cargill Corporation, Busch Gardens, Wichita State University, RedGuard and many others. He is the founder of LogoLounge.com and the co-author of the affiliated book series. He also is the author of Logo Creed: The Mystery, Magic, and Method Behind Designing Great Logos, a foundation book for students, educators and professionals alike, and multiple Lynda.com courses about logo design. Bill recently became the first recipient of the Fellow Award from the AIGA Wichita chapter for his contributions to the local, national and global design community.

EMILY J. POTTS

Emily J. Potts has been a writer and editor in the design industry for more than 20 years. In that time she's managed a slew of publications, people, and events. Currently, she is a regular contributor to several design blogs, and consults and writes for a variety of clients. www.emilyjpotts.com

INDEX

DIRECTORY

01d
Belarus
www.01d.ru

1 or Billion design
China

12 points
Russian Federation
79030063152
www.12pt.ru

144design Inc
United States
www.144design.com

1dea Design + Media Inc.
Canada
(613) 384 7693
www.1dea.ca

3 Advertising LLC
United States
www.whois3.com

360ideas
United States
(316) 250 8182
www.kalenkubik.com

36creative
United States
www.36creative.com

3x4 Design Studio
Iran

5Seven
United States
(707) 266 1823
www.5seven.com

70kft
United States
(214) 653 1060
70kft.com

903 Creative, LLC
United States
(434) 774 5164
www.903creative.com

A.D. Creative Group
United States
(406) 248 7117
www.adcreativegroup.com

ab+c Creative Intelligence
United States
(302) 655 1552
a-b-c.com

Absolu communication marketing
Canada
www.absolu.ca

AcrobatAnt
United States
(918) 938 7905

addicted2be
Bulgaria
359 895 688 684
behance.net/addicted2be

Agency MABU
United States
(701) 250 0728
www.agencymabu.com

Airtype Studio
United States
(336) 422 7026
www.airtype.com

AkarStudios
United States
www.akarstudios.com

Akhmatov Studio
Kazakhstan
www.akhmatov.com

Alama Design
United Arab Emirates
971506251258
www.3alama.com

Alex Rinker
United States
www.rinker.co

Alex Tass
United States
(407) 423 6424
www.alextass.com

Alexander Wende
Germany
17663682882
www.alexwende.com

Ali Seylan
Turkey
90 532 4965896
aliseylan.com

Allen Creative
United States
www.allencreative.com

Almanac
United States
(314) 875 9411
www.brandalmanac.com

Almosh82
India
www.almosh82.com

Alphabet Arm Design
United States
(617) 451 9990
www.alphabetarm.com

Alsobrook Creative
United States

Amy McAdams Design
United States
(317) 727 6446

Anagrama
Mexico
anagrama.com

Anagraphic
Hungary
www.anagraphic.hu/en

Andrey Kruglov
Russian Federation
79206288113
www.motiondesign.ru

Andrius Vilbrantas
Lithuania
370 63322212
www.instudio.co

ANFILOV
Czech Republic
420 602 26 26 33
anfilov.cz/portfolio

Anthony Rees
United States

Apex Creative
United States
(480) 389 6229
apexcreative.net

Apus Agency
Russian Federation
89217565758
vladimirisaev.com

Arcane / HONEY
Canada
(519) 679 6755 x214
www.honeydesign.ca

arndtteunissen GmbH
Germany
492116355360
www.arndtteunissen.de

Artini Bar Designs
United States
www.artinibar.com

Art'Performance
Russian Federation
8 800 555 14 42
art-performance.ru

artslinger
Canada
www.artslinger.ca

Artsmith Communications
Canada
(178) 042 4262
www.artsmith.ca

Asgard
Russian Federation
www.asgard-design.com

Associated Integrated Marketing
United States
(316) 683 4691
www.meetassociated.com

ATOM Creative Agency
Russian Federation
79193330315

Atypic
United States
(704) 447 7190
www.atypiccraft.com

Austin Logo Designs
United States
(512) 705 1710
www.austinlogodesigns.com

baCreative
United States
www.billaitchison.com

Banowetz + Company, Inc.
United States
(214) 823 7300
www.banowetz.com

Barker
Brazil
55 11 996271969

bartodell.com
United States
(806) 392 6446
www.bartodell.com

BASIS
United States

BE SIBLE
United States
(210) 305 4939
infeccionvisual.com

Be!Five branding & identity
Russian Federation
www.befive.ru

Besapiens
Russian Federation
79686726098
www.besapiens.ru

Bethany Heck
United States
(334) 663 7385
heckhouse.com

Blackdog Creative
United States

Blackletter
United States
(614) 352 2603
blkltr.com

Blocq Studio
Serbia
381640730646
www.blocqstudio.com

Bloom Communication SRL
Romania
40762246300
www.designyourfuture.ro

Blue Blazes, LLC
United States
(360) 521 6054

Blue Taco Design
United States
(917) 385 8468

Blue Tongue Design Ltd
United Kingdom
07530 265360
www.bluetonguedesign.co.uk

BluesCue Designs
Philippines
639173262583
www.bluescue.com

BLVR
United States
(619) 501 3392
www.blvr.com

Bohn Studio
Australia
394290255

Botond Vörös
Hungary
36702285187
www.botondvoros.com

Bounce Design Newcastle Pty Ltd
Australia
61 2 4969 3334
www.bounce.net.au

Braizen
United States
(800) 664 1637
getbraizen.com

Braley Design
United States
(415) 706 2700
braleydesign.com

Brand Agent
United States
(214) 979 2050
www.brand-agent.com

Brandberry
Russian Federation
79279005155
www.brandberry.net

Brandburg
Poland
512693936
www.brandburg.pl

brandclay
United States
(734) 260 9771
www.brandclay.com

BrandFirst
United States
(908) 813 0855
brandfirstnj.com

Brandforma
Ukraine
dribbble.com/iox

BrandHand
Russian Federation
79207440404
mars-branding.ru

Brandiose
United States
(619) 463 5630
brandiose.com

Brandjamin
United States
(301) 275 2667
benjaminkauffman.com

brandon
Lebanon
9619545668
www.brandonideas.com

Brandon Harrison
United States
(612) 240 1229

BrandViva
United States
(541) 301 6185

Braue: Brand Design Experts
Germany
49 471 983820
www.braue.info

Brian Rodenberg Design
United States
(608) 438 2342
www.brianrodenberg.com

Brittany Phillips Design
United States
(479) 225 1001
www.brittanyphillipsdesign.com

Bronson Ma Creative
United States
(210) 767 3135
www.bronsonma.com

Brooke Muckersie
Australia
www.ianbrooke.com.au

Bryan Butler
United States
(417) 793 2210
www.whatbryan.com

Bryan Couchman Design
United States
(843) 817 3929

Budanov. Branding & Identity
Russian Federation
79057111112
budanov.ru

Burocratik
Portugal
www.burocratik.com

Buzzbomb Creative
United States
(972) 345 6168
thebuzzbomb.com

Camp5 Communications
Canada
(226) 791 0425
www.kaico.ca

CAPSULE
United States
www.capsule.us

Cayenne Creative
United States
(205) 322 4422
cayennecreative.com

Cezar Bianchi B+D
United States
(786) 477 2043
www.cezarbianchi.com.br

CF Napa Brand Design
United States
(707) 265 1891
cfnapa.com

Chad Michael Studio
United States
(972) 302 5198
www.chadmichaelstudio.com

Chadomoto / Dimiter Petrov
Bulgaria

359899877177
www.chadomoto.com

Charm Creative
United States
(704) 615 7719
www.charmcreative.com

Chris Millspaugh Design
United States
(785) 312 9101
www.chrismillspaugh.com

Chris Rooney Illustration/Design
United States
(415) 827 3729
www.looneyrooney.com

CINDERBLOC INC.
Canada
(416) 777 2562 x102
www.cinderbloc.com

Cinq Partners
United States
(860) 214 8663
cinqpartners.com

Circuit 26 Design
United States
(252) 717 1852
circuit26.com

Clark & Co.
United States
(350) 903 5954
clark-and-co.com

Clutch Creative Company
United States
(802) 373 4994
clutchcreativeco.com

CNDC
United States
(580) 421 9500 x 21605

Coleman Design
United Kingdom
44 798 463 4696
www.colemandesign.co.uk

Colleen Coolidge Lindner
United States
(706) 464 3129

Color 9 Creative, Inc.
United States
(402) 891 4233
www.color9creative.com

Courtney Windham Design
United States
(205) 902 3949
courtneywindhamdesign.com

CRE8 DESIGN
Taiwan
886 2 8797 5000
www.cre8-designstudio.com

created by South
Australia
419518730
www.createdbysouth.com.au

createTWO
United States

Creation
United Kingdom
07852 229 751
www.creationlondon.co.uk

Creative Parc
United States
www.creativeparc.com

Creativille
United States

Crooked Tree Creative
United States
(828) 424 7532
crookedtreecreative.com

Curb Crowser
United States
curbcrowser.com

CWP Design Studio
United States
(484) 429 9422
www.cwpdesignstudio.com

Dalton Agency
United States
(904) 398 5222
daltonagency.com

Dana Tanamachi
United States
danatanamachi.com

Dangerdom Studios
United States
(316) 558 1102
dangerdom.com

Daniel Eris
United Kingdom
www.danieleris.com

Daniel Fernandez
United States
(407) 221 5542
www.dffernandez.com

Daniel Schnitzer
Austria
6801126554
schnitzerdesign.carbonmade.com

danielguillermo.com
United States
danielguillermo.com

Dara Creative
Ireland
www.daracreative.ie

Daren Guillory Design
United States
(832) 465 4498
graphicbio.com

DARO Creative
United States
(206) 451 4989
www.darocreative.com

Dave Smith Artist
United Kingdom
01803 613753
www.davidadriansmith.com

David Bieloh Design
United States
(931) 933 3086
www.davidbieloh.com

David Cran Design
Canada
(604) 564 4121
www.davidcran.com

David Gramblin
United States
crankybeard.com

DDB Sydney
Australia

DEI Creative
United States
deicreative.com

Deksia
United States
(515) 318 7171
deksia.com

DELICATESY Elzbieta Zaczek
Poland
48605266432

Denis Aristov
Russian Federation
denisaristov.com

Denys Kotliarov
Ukraine
380667078277
kotliarov.com

Dept of Energy
United States
(206) 910 0288
www.deptofenergy.com

Design Buddy
United States
(615) 425 6851
designbuddy.com

Design Film, LLC
United States
(210) 773 1020
www.josuezapata.com

design ranch
United States
(816) 472 8668
www.design-ranch.com

Design Sense
Belgium
32 0 57 447 665
www.designsense.be

Design Studio Minin and Pozharsky
Russian Federation
7 921 3131059
studiomip.com

Designbull
United Kingdom
1225442566
designbull.co.uk

DesignByLefty
Switzerland
41 79 264 85 88
www.lefty.ch

Designer and Gentleman
United States
(219) 314 7744
www.designerandgentleman.com

Dessein
Australia
618 9228 0661
www.dessein.com.au

Deuxtone
United States
(210) 274 9674
deuxtone.com

Disciple Design
United States
www.discipledesign.com

DMH
United States
(816) 471 4364
www.dmhadv.com

Dmitry Zelinskiy
Russian Federation
7 908 71 70 850
dddzzz.ru

Dmitry Zhelnov
Russian Federation
7 916 722 41 00
behance.net/dimaje

DNKSTUDIO
Ukraine
dnkstudio.com.ua

Doc4
United States
(479) 879 7950
www.doc4design.com

Dotzero Design
United States
(503) 892 9262
www.dotzerodesign.com

Double A Creative
United States
(402) 960 6553
www.doubleacreative.com

Doublenaut
Canada
(416) 979 5933
www.doublenaut.com

DOXA
United States
(479) 582 2695

Dustin Commer
United States
www.dustincommer.com

Eder Saos
Canada
(905) 560 0725
edersaos.com

Effendy Design
Pakistan
92 3323093892
www.effendydesign.com

eggnerd
United States
(817) 368 8933
www.eggnerd.com

Elevator
Croatia
385 98 434556
www.elevator.hr

Eleven19
United States
(402) 408 3072
eleven19.com

EMC illustration & design
United States
(714) 293 6009
www.behance.net/ericchimenti

emedia creative
Australia

Emilio Correa
Mexico
www.emiliographics.com

Endless
United States
(509) 590 5691
dribbble.com/JohnnyXerox

Envision Creative Group
United States
(512) 628 0087
www.envision-creative.com

Erwin Bindeman
South Africa
27790982068
www.erwin.co.za

Essex Two
United States
(773) 489 1400
www.sx2.com

Estudio Brado
Brazil
www.estudiobrado.com.br

Estudio Mezanino
Brazil
11 31513727
www.estudiomezanino.com.br

Exhibit A: Design Group
Canada
(604) 873 1583
www.exhibitadesigngroup.com

Fabio Okamoto Design
Brazil
55 11 995154796
www.fabiookamoto.com.br/design

Fancy Creative
United States
(304) 550 4382

Farm Design
United States
(310) 828 1624
farmdesign.net

Farmboy
United States
(515) 314 1321
farmboyinc.com

Fernandez Studio
United States
(512) 619 4020
www.fernandezstudio.com

FiftyIFifty
Australia
430339464

Fixer Creative Co.
United States
fixercreative.com

Flat 6 Concepts
United States
(888) 796 8289
www.flat6concepts.com

Flight Deck Creative
United States
(214) 534 9468

Flying Gorilla Studio
United States
(817) 944 5437

Fraser Davidson
United Kingdom
fraserdavidson.co.uk

FRED+ERIC Belgium
32485628374

Freelance
United States
(505) 400 4474
nicholasangel.com

Frontline Technologies
United States
(610) 727 0382
www.FrontlineK12.com

FS Grafik Design
Germany
406027504

FullFill
Indonesia
www.fullfillisme.com

Funnel
United States
(317) 590 5355
www.funnel.tv

Fuszion
United States
fuszion.com

Fuzzco
United States
(843) 723 1665
www.fuzzco.com

Galambos + Associates
United States
(312) 291 9068

Gardner Design
United States
(316) 691 8808
www.gardnerdesign.com

Gearbox
United States
(541) 549 1478

Gizwiz Studio
Malaysia
www.logodesigncreation.com

GL Creative Design
United Arab Emirates
971507829509
www.gl-cd.com

Glad Head
Ukraine
632728988
www.gladhead.com

Glitschka Studios
United States
(971) 223 6143
www.vonglitschka.com

GOOD CANOE, INC

United States
(704) 617 3332
goodcanoe.com

Grafixd
Hungary
www.grafixd.com

Grain
United States
(314) 972 4790
grainforall.com

Grant Currie
Canada
(780) 908 8620
grantcurrie.ca

Graphic design studio by Yurko Gutsulyak
Ukraine
380674465560
www.gstudio.com.ua

Graphic D-Signs, Inc.
United States
(908) 835 9000
www.graphicd-signs.com

Graphics Factory CC
South Africa
27 44 690 4796
www.logoground.com

Grason Studio
United States
(407) 765 9509
www.zadok44.com

Green Ink Studio
United States
(281) 207 6170
www.greeninkstudio.com

Greg Valdez Design
United States
gregvaldezdesign.com

gresus.com
Russian Federation
79103849900
gresus.com

Greteman Group
United States
(316) 263 1004
gretemangroup.com

GreyBox Creative
United States
(646) 354 7770
www.greyboxcreative.com

Greyta
Lithuania
www.greytastudio.com

grifter design
United States
(773) 220 3117

grupo oxigeno
Chile
562 222444447
www.grupoxigeno.cl

Gustav Holtz Design
United States
(612) 965 7072
gustavholtz.com

Gyula Nemeth
Hungary
www.gynemeth.com

Haffelder Studios
United States
(512) 650 8821
www.haffelderstudios.com

Handsome
United Kingdom
44 20 3142 6289
www.handsomebrands.co.uk

HanleyCreative
United States
(214) 564 1576
www.hanleycreative.com

HASAN ALI AKHTAR
Pakistan
923008265547
www.hasanaliakhtar.com

Hayes Image
Australia
www.hayesimage.com.au

Headron Collider
United States
(907) 744 5165
www.headroncollider.com

Heffley Creative
Canada
(604) 578 8348
heffley.ca

Helikopter Brand Design
Sweden
46911221060
www.helikopter.nu

Helms Workshop
United States
(512) 775 6329

Hiebing
United States
(608) 256 6357
hiebing.com

Hornall Anderson
United States
(206) 826 2329
www.hornallanderson.com

Hubbell Design Works
United States
(714) 227 3457
www.hubbelldesignhub.com

Hürsu Öke
Turkey
905337119489
www.hursu.com

Husbandmen
United States
(512) 627 8730
www.husbandmen.com

IDEAS
United States
(407) 601 7878
IDEASorlando.com

Ideogram
United States
(205) 915 3255
www.ideogramstudio.com

idgroup
United States
(850) 438 7823
idgroupbranding.com

Independent graphic designer
Russian Federation
ivanbobrov.com

IndigoPark
United States
(443) 690 1694
www.indigopark.com

INNERPRIDE
Romania
40 0748 22 21 20
www.inner-pride.ro

Iris Design
United States
(310) 488 2978
www.qlidesign.com

Ishan Khosla Design
India
www.ishankhosladesign.com

J Fletcher Design
United States
(843) 364 1776
www.jfletcherdesign.com

J.Wick Design
United States
(717) 671 1720
www.jwickdesign.com

JACK
United States
jackmuldowney.com

Jack in the box
Australia
08 9751 1122
www.thebox.com.au

Jackson Spalding
United States
(404) 214 2198
www.jacksonspalding.com

Jakshop
United States
(970) 556 4473
www.jakshop.com

James Dean & Company
United States
(316) 409 0440
jamesdeancompany.com

James Michael Design
Canada
(403) 875 5957
be.net/James_Michael

Jarheadesign
Canada
(416) 780 0776
www.jarhead.com

Jarrett Johnston
United States
(806) 690 5261

Jason Durgin Design
United States
(510) 682 0478
www.jasondurgin.com

Jeff Ames Creative
United States
(303) 522 5134
www.jacreative.org

Jeff Phillips Design
Canada
www.jeffphillipsdesign.com

Jeffhalmos
Canada
(416) 850 9616
www.jeffhalmos.com

Jeremiah Britton Design Co.
United States
(517) 962 9002
blog.jeremiahswork.com

Jerron Ames
United States
(801) 636 7929
jerronames.com

Jess Glebe Design
United States
(215) 970 4964
www.jessicaglebe.com

Jesse Arneson
United States
www.jessearneson.com

Jibe
United States
(801) 920 7914
jibemedia.com

Joce Creative
Canada
(506) 855 4788

Jody Worthington Graphic Design
United States
(713) 591 3233
www.jodyworthington.com

Joe White
United Kingdom
yeoldestudio.co.uk

John Mills Ltd
United Kingdom
2076913800

johnshoward
United States
(704) 421 8152
johnshoward.com

Johnson & Sekin
United States
(972) 567 1301
johnsonandsekin.com

Jon Eslinger / Design
United States
(517) 974 3043
rdsq.com

Jon Kay Design
United States
jonkaydesign.com

Jonathan Schubert
United States
(214) 335 8562
dribbble.com/jonathanschubert

JonathanHowell.com
United States
(239) 734 8701
www.JonathanHowell.com

Jordahl Design
United States
(320) 226 4190

Josh Carnley
United States
(251) 463 5562
www.carnleydesign.com

Joy Rubin Creative
United States
(206) 940 6797
joyrubincreative.com

Juicebox Designs
United States
(615) 297 1682
www.juiceboxdesigns.com

Juicebox Interactive
United States
(515) 244 6633

Julian Peck Creative
United States
(415) 246 4897

Just Creative Design
Australia
justcreative.com

Justin Gammon | Design + Illustration
United States
(864) 420 9014
justingammon.com

Kairevicius
Lithuania
37066299933
www.kairevicius.com

kantorwassink
United States
(616) 233 3118

Karl Design Vienna
Austria
www.karl-design-logos.com

Karla Portocarrero
United States
(787) 413 9447
www.karlamportocarrero.com

Karlis Dovnorovics
Latvia

Kay Loves Candy
United States
(850) 341 1000
kaylovescandy.com

Keith Davis Young
United States
(979) 777 3135
livetomake.com

Keystone Resources
United States
(713) 874 0162
www.keystoneresources.com

Keyword Design
United States
(219) 384 7344
www.keyworddesign.com

Kneadle, Inc.
United States
(714) 441 1157
kneadle.com

KOSMA Design Studio
Poland
48 512 59 36 29
www.kosma.pro

Kovach Studio
Serbia
381642938614

Kreativbuero Jonas Soeder
Germany
4916094845499
www.jonassoeder.de

KW43 BRANDDESIGN
Germany
49 211 557783 10
WWW.KW43.DE

Larry Levine
United States
(412) 980 1426

Latinbrand
Ecuador

Launch
United States
(678) 907 1772
LetsLaunchIt.com

LETR & Co.
United States
(912) 655 0896

Letter Shoppe
United States
(954) 793 7432
lettershoppe.com

Levogrin
Russian Federation
levogrin.com

Linda Bourdeaux
United States
(615) 491 5650

Link Creative
United States
www.link-creative.com

Lippincott
United States
(212) 521 0054
lippincott.com

Liquid Agency
United States
www.liquidagency.com

Live Nation Labs
United States
(714) 609 6480
www.lisaviado.com

Logo Geek
United Kingdom
7846732895
www.logogeek.co.uk

Logo Planet Laboratory
United States
www.logoplanetlab.com

London Dewey
United States

Longo Designs
United States
(818) 585 4972
www.longodesigns.com

LONI DBS

Slovenia
38631419688
www.loni.si

Lucas Marc Design
United States
www.lucasmarc.com

Luka Balic
Croatia
385959032681
www.lukabalic.com

Luke Bott Design & Illustration
United States
(316) 371 7043
lukebott.com

Luke Despatie & The Design Firm
Canada
www.thedesignfirm.ca

Luke Lucas
Australia
lukelucas.com

Lukedesign
Netherlands
31 6 30 03 52 24
lukedesign.nl

lunabrand design group
United States
www.lunabrands.com

M@OH!
United States
(218) 409 5540
matthewolin.com

M3 Advertising Design
United States
www.m3ad.com

MAD CONSORT
Netherlands
31619421242
madconsort.com

Marakasdesign
Ukraine
380504450528

Mark Huffman Creative
United States
(309) 826 2260

Martín Azambuja
Uruguay
598 99 753 220
www.maz.com.uy

Maskon Brands
India
918447338668
www.maskonbrands.com

Maurizio Pagnozzi
Italy
3493832680
www.mauriziopagnozzi.com

Maximo Gavete
Spain
0034 615120798
www.omixamestudio.com

Maykel Nunes
Brazil
5511943882144
www.maykelnunes.com

McGuire Design
United States
(347) 635 4609
www.mcguiredesign.com

McMillianCo.
United States
(718) 636 2097
www.mcmillianco.com

MeatStudio
United Kingdom
7870226859
www.meatstudio.co.uk

Meir Billet Ltd.
Israel

Mendiola Design Associates
Indonesia
62 8161435928
www.mendioladesign.com

Michael Lashford Creative
United States
(415) 519 6627
www.michaellashford.com

midgar.eu
Poland
48 605 226 550
midgar.eu

Mikey Burton
United States
www.mikeyburton.com

Mikhail Polivanov
Ukraine
380661685805
polivanov.me

Miller Meiers Communication Arts Agency
United States
(785) 856 6622
www.millermeiers.com

Mindgruve
United States
www.mindgruve.com

Miriad
Hungary
36302683682
www.miriad.hu

Miro Kozel
Slovakia
421907319339
www.mikodesign.sk

Misign - Visual Communication
Italy
www.misign.it

MKJ Creative
United States
(215) 997 2355
www.mkjcreative.com

mmplus creative
Indonesia
www.mmadv.biz

More Branding+Communication
United States
(918) 519 1605

Musab
Saudi Arabia
966540474205

MVC Agency
United States
(818) 718 2005
www.mvcagency.com

MW Design Studio
United Kingdom
44 770 319 3733
www.mw-designstudio.com

Naughtyfish Garbett
Australia
02 92123474

Neuronalics Ltd.
United Kingdom
34652493755
www.neuronalic.com

Never North
United States
(713) 737 5651
www.nevernorthlabs.com

Niedermeier Design
United States
(206) 351 3927
www.kngraphicdesign.com

Ninet6 Ltd
United Kingdom
www.ninet6.com

NO-BAD

United Kingdom

Noe Araujo
Mexico
115281833008
www.noearaujo.com

Norfolk Southern Corp.
United States
(757) 629 2301
www.nscorp.com

Noriu Menulio
Lithuania
37067113180
www.noriumenulio.lt

Nosh Creative
United States
www.noshcreative.com

notamedia
Russian Federation
7 495 995 15 21
notamedia.ru

Nox Creative
United States
(512) 557 2966
noxcreative.com

O' Riordan Design
Ireland
353876568098
www.shaneor.com

o5 Design
Bosnia And Herzegovina
387 65 751 797
www.o5design.com

OCD | Original Champions of Design
United States
(212) 420 9270
originalchampionsofdesign.com

Odney
United States
www.odney.com

Oluzen
Dominican Republic
809 852 9907
www.oluzen.com

OneFish Creative
United States
(231) 218 0782

ONY
Russian Federation
7 495 4113561
www.ony.ru

Opacity Design Group
Canada
(604) 831 1453
www.opacitydesigngroup.com

OPEN
Israel
972 3 6244449
WWW.OPEN.CO.IL

Open Door Design Studio (ODDS)
United States
(352) 792 5100
www.opendoordesignstudio.com

Optimacad
Romania
40724055840
www.optimacad.com

Oronoz Brandesign
Mexico
www.alanoronoz.com

Ortega Graphics
Canada
ortegagraphics.com

Outdoor Cap
United States
(479) 464 5243
www.outdoorcap.com

Oven Design Workshop

Colombia
3006354721

Oxide Design Co.
United States
(402) 344 0168
www.oxidedesign.com

p11creative
United States
(714) 641 2090

Paradigm New Media Group
United States
(314) 621 7600
www.pnmg.com

Paradox Box
Russian Federation
7 347 276 84 14
www.paradoxbox.ru

Parallele gestion de marques
Canada
(418) 682 1436
www.parallele.ca

ParkerWhite
United States
(760) 783 2020
www.parkerwhite.com

Patrick Carter Design, Inc.
United States
(904) 626 4645
patrickcarterdesign.com

Paul Tynes Design
United States
(601) 520 5131
paultynes.com

Paul von Excite
Netherlands
31 0621264295
www.paulvonexcite.com

Paul Wronski Graphic Design, LLC
United States
(203) 506 0030
paulwro.com

Pavel Saksin
Russian Federation
79199948144
www.behance.net/paul_saksin

Pavlodar School of Design
Kazakhstan
77776104077
www.behance.net/xs-exes

Peppermill Projects
United States
(410) 934 1073
www.PeppermillProjects.com

petervasvari.com
Hungary
36 209 349 873
petervasvari.com

PhD-mtl
Canada
(524) 802 5169

Pix-I Graphx
United States
(201) 553 1200
www.pixlgraphx.com

Pixler Designs
United States
(303) 378 5481
pixlerdesigns.com

Pixonal
Egypt
www.pixonal.com

Plenum Brand Consultancy
Russian Federation
www.gbnd.ru

Plumb and Pixel
United States
(410) 530 6250

PM Design / Restaurant Identity

United States
www.pmdesign.com

Polypod
Lebanon

Prejean Creative
United States
www.prejeancreative.com

Principals Pty Ltd
Australia
61 2 9251 3833
www.principals.com.au

Projektor Brand Image
Canada
(416) 524 0115
www.projektor.ca

Proof Positive Brand Design
United States
(231) 357 2450
www.proofpositivedesign.com

PytchBlack
United States
(817) 570 0915

QUIQUE OLLERVIDES
Mexico
www.ollervides.com

Quiskal
Canada
(581) 990 9311
quiskal.com

R&R Partners
United States
(480) 317 6054
www.rrpartners.com

R&R Partners
United States
rrpartners.com

Raineri Design Srl
Italy
39030381740

Rainmaker Creative
United States
(509) 499 3399

Rainy Day Designs
United States
(970) 963 9748
rainydaydesigns.org

Rami Hoballah | Graphic Designer
Kuwait
www.behance.net/RamiHoballah

Rayat Brands
Saudi Arabia
966126101111
www.rayatbrands.com

Rebrander
Serbia
381641179800
www.logoaday.co

Red Studio Inc
United States
(503) 228 9493
www.redstudio.net

RedEffect
Greece
306945557736
www.redeffect.gr

RedSpark Creative Ltd
New Zealand
www.redspark.co.nz

reedesign studio
Croatia
www.reedesignstudio.com

Refinery 43
United States
(617) 797 1063
refinery43.com

Reghardt

South Africa
www.reghardt.com

re-robot
Uruguay
www.re-robot.com

Resource Branding & Design
United States
www.resourceatlanta.com

RetroMetro Designs
Canada
www.retrometrodesign.ca

Rhombus, Inc.
United States
(206) 441 1061
www.rhombusdesign.net

Rick Carlson Design & Illustration
United States
(919) 604 1912
rcarlsondesign.com

Rickabaugh Graphics
United States
rickabaughgraphics.com

Riddle Design Co.
United States
(864) 933 6613

Riggalicious Design, LLC
United States
(260) 402 9082
www.riggdesign.com

Right Angle
United States
(337) 235 2416
www.rightangleadv.com

RIJK Concept & Creation
Netherlands
0031 0 6 4304 7889

Riordon Design
Canada
(905) 339 0750
www.riordondesign.com

Rise Design Branding Inc.
China
www.clevay.com

Robert Finkel Design
United States
robertfinkel.com

Robot Agency Studios
United States
(832) 859 0650
www.robotagency.com

Rocksauce Studios
United States
(512) 623 7865
www.rocksaucestudios.com

Roger Strunk
United States
(316) 651 7111
rogerstrunk.com

RolandRekeczki
Hungary
36705815001

Roman Zolotorevich
Russian Federation
79851624957
www.zolotorevich.com

Romulo Moya Peralta / Trama
Ecuador
593 2 2246315
www.trama.ec

Roost Designs
United States
(336) 676 5763
www.roostdesigns.com

Roy Smith Design
United Kingdom
www.roysmithdesign.com

Rule29
United States
(630) 262 1009
www.rule29.com

Rural City Creative
United States
(206) 779 2243
ruralcitycreative.com

Ryan Bosse
United States
(913) 558 2868
dribbble.com/rdbosse

rylander design
United States
(415) 309 1998
www.rylanderdesign.com

Sabingrafik, Inc.
United States
(760) 431 0439
tracysabin.com

Sachs Media Group
United States
(850) 251 2732

Sakkal Design
United States
www.sakkal.com

Salih Kucukaga Design Studio
Turkey
salihkucukaga.com

SALT Branding
United States
(415) 616 1515
www.saltbranding.com

Salvador Anguiano
Mexico
4626263763
www.cargocollective.com/salvador

Sam Dallyn
United Kingdom
44 759 031 7293
www.samdallyn.co.uk

Samarskaya & Partners
United States
(646) 441 1213

saputo design
United States
(805) 494 1847
saputodesign.com

Sarah Rusin Design
United States
(305) 298 7914
www.sarahrusin.com

Saywells Design Co.
United States
(520) 302 4689
www.saywellsdesign.com

Scott McFadden Creative
United States
(214) 284 9626
scottmcfaddencreative.com

Scott Oeschger Design
United States
(610) 457 3188
www.scottoeschger.com

Sean Heisler Design
United States
(402) 917 6100
www.seanheislerdesign.com

Sebastiany Branding & Design
Brazil
55 11 3926 3937
www.sebastiany.com.br

Second Shift Design
United States
(404) 704 2445
www.secondshiftdesign.com

Second Street Creative
United States
(317) 426 9799
www.2ndcreative.com

Severance Digital Studio
United States
www.severanceds.com

Shadia Design
Australia
61 409 715 075
www.shadiadesign.com.au

Shierly Design Creative
Malaysia
601126446867
www.shierlydewi.com

Signals Design Group Inc
Canada
(604) 803 7577

sk designworks
United States
(215) 568 4432

Slagle Design
United States
(614) 804 6234
www.slagledesign.com

Sloane Design
United States

Small Dog Design
Australia
61 3 5333 7777
www.smalldog.com.au

smARTer
United States
(952) 994 7625
www.smARTerMpls.com

SMOKE SIGNAL DSGN
United States
smokesignaldsgn.com

sodesign
Belarus
375336264564
www.sodesign.by

Sophia Georgopoulou I Design
Greece

Sparkfly Creative
United States
www.sparkflycreative.com

SparrowDesign
Poland
48 607910785
www.sparrowdesign.pl

Splash:Design
Canada
(250) 868 1059
SplashDesign.biz

Square Feet Design
United States
(646) 237 2828

Squid Ink Creative
United States
(316) 260 3805
www.squidinkcreative.com

Stan Designworks
Malaysia
60125216098
www.stan-design.com

Stebbings Partners
United States
(508) 699 7899
www.stebbings.com

Stephan Smith
United States
(316) 993 6093

Stephen Lee Ogden Design Co.
United States
(270) 799 5237
StephenLeeOgden.com

Stevaker Design
United States
(423) 385 5989
stevaker.com

Stevan Rodic
Serbia
381637424332
stvdesign.com

Steve Bullock Design
United States
www.SteveBullockDesign.com

Steve DeCusatis Design
United States
(215) 840 0880
www.stevedecusatis.com

Steve Wolf Designs
United States
(214) 998 0281
www.stevewolf.com

Steven Schroeder
United States
(214) 551 6085

Stiles Design
United States
brettstilesdesign.com

Stitch Design Co.
United States
(843) 722 6296

Studio Absolute
United States
(541) 280 6836
www.studioabsolute.com

Studio Botes
South Africa
www.studiobotes.com

Studio Ink
Australia
61411899840
www.studioink.com.au

Studio Science
United States
(317) 713 7500
www.studioscience.com

studio sudar d.o.o.
Croatia
385 98 98 36579
www.iknowsudar.com

Sudduth Design Co.
United States
(512) 632 6150
sudduthdesign.com

SUMO
United Kingdom
0191 261 9894
www.sumodesign.co.uk

Sunday Lounge
United States
(719) 207 4616
www.sundaylounge.com

Swanson Russell
United States
(402) 818 1125
www.swansonrussell.com

Swin Huang Design
United States
(415) 218 3906

T&E Polydorou Design Ltd
Cyprus
www.polydoroudesign.com

Tactical Magic
United States
www.tacticalmagic.com

Tactix Creative
United States
(480) 688 8881
www.TactixCreative.com

Tamer Koseli
Turkey
90 532 5273431
tamerkoseli.com

Tangens
Brazil
5511982060131
www.tangens.com.br

Tarsha Rockowitz Design
United States
(206) 437 7327
www.theworldoft.com

Taylor Goad
United States
(405) 650 3112
taylorgoad.com

TerriLowry.com
United States
(917) 544 3499
www.terrilowry.com

Tether
United States
(206) 518 6300
tetherinc.com

The Blksmith Design Co.
United States
(909) 380 4247
theblksmith.com

The Brandit
United States
(910) 508 9938

The Design Office of Matt Stevens
United States
hellomattstevens.com

The Logoist
United States
(314) 954 2182
www.behance.net/iamthelogoist

The Quiet Society
United States
(949) 230 4850
thequietsociety.com

Think to Make
United States
(303) 250 1851
www.thinktomake.com

Think Topography
United States
(607) 229 1488
thinktopography.com

THINKMULE United States
(303) 718 2914
thinkmule.com

Thoburn Design & Illustration LLC
United States
www.thoburnillustrations.com

Thomas Cook Designs
United States
(919) 274 1131
www.thomascookdesigns.com

Tim Frame Design
United States
(614) 598 0113
www.timframe.com

Timber Design Company
United States
(317) 213 8509
www.timberdesignco.com

Tin Bacic
Croatia
www.tinbacicdesign.com

Todytod

Netherlands
076 641 33 90
www.todytod.com

Tokshok
Russian Federation
7 987 241 92 92
tokshok.ru, art-yakovlev.ru

Tom Hough Design
United States
(214) 679 3250

Torch Creative
United States
www.torchcreative.com

Tortoiseshell Black
United Kingdom

Tortugastudio
Belarus
375256476737

Traction Partners
United States
(517) 482 7919
ProjectTraction.com

Tran Creative
United States
(208) 664 4098
www.tran-creative.com

Trevor Rogers
United States
(714) 269 5060
trevorgrogers.com

Tribambuka
United Kingdom
www.tribambuka.co.uk

Tribe
United States
(304) 279 7034
www.tribecol.com

Tricia Hope Dugat :: Art Direction & Design
United States
(713) 502 4246
www.cargocollective.com/triciahope

TriLion Studios
United States
(785) 841 5500
www.trilionstudios.com

TrioSigns,Inc.
United States
(270) 707 7900
www.triosigns.com

Twist
United States
(314) 863 3033

TYPE AND SIGNS
Germany
www.typeandsigns.com

Type08
Croatia
38598694174
dribbble.com/type08

Ulyanov Denis
Russian Federation
www.caspa.ru

Unboxedesign
United States
(951) 553 5044
www.unboxedesign.com

Unipen
Macedonia
38978337734
www.unipen.co

UNIT partners
United States
(415) 409 0000

Univisual S.r.l.
Italy
39 02 66 84 268
www.univisual.com

Varick Rosete Studio
United States
(904) 874 2025
varickrosete.com

Visual Dialogue
United States
(617) 247 3658
www.visualdialogue.com

Visual Lure, LLC
United States
(618) 407 9231
www.visuallure.com

Vitamin Group
Russian Federation
7 342 210 31 47
vigroup.ru

Voov Ltd.
Hungary
www.voovstudio.com

Webster
United States
www.websterdesign.com

WeLoveNoise
United States
(415) 202 4831

WestmorelandFlint
United States
(218) 727 1552
www.flint-group.com

Wheelhouse Collective
United States
(402) 651 7165
www.wheelhousecollective.com

WIRON
Romania
www.wiron.ro

wray ward
United States
(704) 332 9071
wrayward.com

Xander
Australia
61 2 99775510
www.xandercreative.com.au

Xcluesiv Cloud Technology
Singapore
923452130920

Xplaye
Mexico
8119671577
www.xplaye.com

Yana Okoliyska
Bulgaria
359886969610
yana-okoliyska.com

Yatta Yatta Yatta
United States
(509) 996 2899

Ye Olde Studio
United Kingdom
7789287944
www.yeoldestudio.co.uk

YhankTou Creative
Mexico
5585405251
www.dribbble.com/YhankTou

Yondr Studio
United States
(918) 704 1809
yondrstudio.com

Your Just Lucky
United States
yourjustlucky.com

Yury Akulin I Logodiver
Russian Federation
www.logodiver.com

Z&G
Russian Federation
www.zg-brand.ru

ZEBRA design branding
Russian Federation
7 8482 538000
www.zebradesign.ru

Zenetic
Romania
40722719640
www.visualidentity.ro

zero11
United Arab Emirates
971551086192
www.zero11design.com

Zync
Canada
(416) 322 2865
www.zync.ca

MORE GREAT TITLES FROM HOW BOOKS

Building Better Brands

By Scott Lerman

Building Better Brands is a focused, comprehensive, and practical guide to building brands. It makes sophisticated branding development techniques accessible and actionable. This is the essential book for individuals and organizations that want to create and evolve brands.

The Strategic Designer

By David Holston

The Strategic Designer helps creatives become experts in strategy, not just design. By adopting a process that includes collaboration, context and accountability, you will learn how to think through business and design problems rationally, use your own standard process to solve problems and increase your project success rate.

Build Your Own Brand

By Robin Landa

Whether your goal is to land a new freelance job, in-house job or launch a design business, this guide is your pathway to success. *Build Your Own Brand* will help you explore, develop, distill and determine a distinctive brand essence, differentiate yourself, and create your visual identity and personal branding statement.

Find these books and many others at MyDesignShop.com or your local bookstore.

SPECIAL OFFER FROM HOW BOOKS!

You can get 15% off your entire order at MyDesignShop.com! All you have to do is go to www.howdesign.com/howbooks-offer and sign up for our free e-newsletter on graphic design. You'll also get a free digital download of HOW magazine.

For more news, tips and articles, follow us at **Twitter.com/HOWbrand**

For behind-the-scenes information and special offers, become a fan at **Facebook.com/HOWmagazine**

For visual inspiration, follow us at **Pinterest.com/HOWbrand**